Reviewed by Sister Joseph Damien Hanlon in the *American Historical Review*, 77 (June, 1972), 785-786.

Reviewed by Patrick McGrath in the *Journal of Ecclesiastical History*, XXIII (October, 1972), 360-361.

REMAINS

Historical and Literary

CONNECTED WITH THE PALATINE COUNTIES OF

Lancaster and Chester

VOLUME XIX—THIRD SERIES

MANCHESTER:

Printed for the Chetham Society

1971

for
ANDREA
PENNY and PHILIP

ELIZABETHAN RECUSANCY
in
CHESHIRE

by

K. R. WARK

MANCHESTER

Printed for the Chetham Society

1971

Published for the Society by
Manchester University Press
316–324 Oxford Road
Manchester M13 9NR

ISBN 0 7190 1154 X

Printed in Great Britain by Butler & Tanner Ltd., Frome and London

CONTENTS

PREFACE

Almost a quarter of a century ago the Chetham Society published a survey of recusancy in Lancashire in the reign of Elizabeth I, and it was Professor T. S. Willan who first suggested that I might attempt a study of Elizabethan recusancy in the other county whose history is the concern of the Society. Since J. S. Leather-barrow's study of Lancashire was written the student of Cheshire recusancy in the sixteenth century has been helped in two particularly important ways. A good deal of light has been thrown on the enforcement of the penal laws against recusancy, most notably by Dom Hugh Bowler's introduction to the second of the Recusant Rolls, whilst the vast amount of documentary evidence on Tudor Cheshire has been made much more accessible than ever before at both the city and county record offices.

As Joan Beck has recently pointed out in her bold outline of Tudor Cheshire, there is no lack of documentary evidence for its history, but little of it has been digested. Thus our knowledge of much of the religious and social background that would alone make it possible to understand fully the nature of Elizabethan Cheshire recusancy is slight. This provides an obvious limitation to this study, as does its restriction to recusancy rather than Catholicism. Little attempt is made to assess the extent to which Cheshire men and women of the late sixteenth century adjusted their ideas and feelings to the official Protestant Christianity of their day: it deals instead only with those who openly rejected it in favour of Catholicism. This is largely because only those who took up a publicly Catholic position by failing to attend worship at the parish church made any significant impression on the documents of their day. Those who shared their beliefs but not their defiance of the harsh penal law remain almost wholly unknown.

Needless to say, I owe a great deal to Professor T. S. Willan, who must often have assumed that this work would never be completed: without his patience, helpfulness, good humour and encouragement it is unlikely that it would. I am also most grateful to Geoffrey Chesters for unselfishly making available to me the results of his own researches into the subject, to Elizabeth Berry, archivist of Chester City, and to B. C. Redwood and the staff of the Cheshire Record Office for their helpfulness in facilitating my researches. Stephanie Bailhache, a former archivist of Chester City, was equally helpful some years ago when I first became interested in Cheshire recusancy. Finally, my wife has offered constant interest and encouragement, and, along with my children, has patiently endured more than she has ever said.

ABBREVIATIONS

Anstruther.—Anstruther, G., *Elizabethan Seminary Priests, 1558–1603*
A.P.—Assembly Petitions (Chester)
A.P.C.—*Acts of the Privy Council*
C.R.S.—Catholic Record Society
C.S.B.—Quarter Sessions' Books (Cheshire)
C.S.F.—Quarter Sessions' Files (Cheshire)
Cal. S.P. Ireland.—*Calendar of State Papers, Ireland*
Chester.—Assize Records, Cheshire, P.R.O.
D.N.B.—*Dictionary of National Biography*
E.D.A.—Proceedings of the Ecclesiastical Commission, Chester Diocese
E.D.B.—Bishop's Transcripts of Parish Registers, Chester Diocese
E.D.V.—Visitation Books for the Diocese of Chester
Ex. Dep.—Exchequer Depositions, E 134, 25, Trinity, No. 5, Lanc. & Dio.
    Chester
Harl. MSS.—Harleian Manuscripts
H.M.C., Salis. MSS.—Historical Manuscripts Commission, *Salisbury Papers*
Lansd. MSS.—Lansdowne Manuscripts
M.B.—Mayors' Books (Chester)
M.L.—Mayors' Letters (Chester)
Ormerod.—Ormerod, G., *History of the County Palatine and City of Chester*
Peck.—Peck, F., *Desiderata Curiosa*
Q.S.E.—Quarter Sessions: Depositions and Examinations (Chester)
Q.S.F.—Quarter Sessions: Files (Chester)
R.R.—Recusant Roll: Exchequer L.T.R., 22A, 377, Pipe Roll Series
S.P.—State Papers Domestic, Elizabeth I
S.P.D.—*Calendar of State Papers, Domestic*
Strype, *Annals*—Strype, J., *Annals of the Reformation*
V.C.H.—*Victoria County History*
W. N. & Q.—*Wirral Notes and Queries*
York, H.C.—Act Books of the Ecclesiastical Commission, York
York, R.VI.—Visitation Books, Metropolitan Visitations, Chester Diocese

CHAPTER I

LOST HORIZONS

1559–69

The things which so long experience of all ages hath confirmed and made profitable, let us not presume to condemn as follies and toys. . . .

R. Hooker, *Laws of Ecclesiastical Polity*

Cuthbert Scot, the Marian bishop of the diocese of Chester, was one of the leading opponents of the religious legislation of 1559 in the House of Lords. There, in a long polemical speech, arguing carefully from history, tradition and scripture, he stated that '. . . no temporal prince hathe any aucthoritie ecclesiasticall in or over the churche of Christe', whose true head was the Pope, without whom the unity of the church could not be preserved. He ended with an appeal to his fellow-peers to stand by 'our forefathers in the catholike church' against those adversaries whose doctrine 'is not yet fifty yeres old'.[1] He had noted at the beginning of his speech that the Queen was an interested party in the bill: in other words, to oppose the bill was to oppose the Queen; his deprivation quickly and not unexpectedly followed in June, 1559.[2]

Similar clearcut opposition to the religious settlement on a large scale would have made the new government's position impossible, and the deprivation of most of the Marian bishops was followed by the setting up of a special visitation to investigate the loyalty of the clergy. The visitors for the northern province of York reached Cheshire after dealing with the more northerly parts of the Chester diocese and did not stay long: after their opening session at Northwich on 20 October 1559, 'for certain reasonable causes, and especially on account of the plague raging both in the city of Chester and in the surrounding districts' from which 'manye fledd to escape', they subdelegated their powers to two local gentlemen, Sir Edward Fitton and William Norton, and a cleric, Edmund Scambler, later bishop of Peterborough.[3] These surrogates held sessions at Tarvin on 24 and at Chester Cathedral on 26 October, after which they recorded that all the clergy willingly subscribed to the requisite oath of loyalty.[4]

However, this picture of clerical conformity to the settlement of 1559

---

[1] Strype, *Annals*, I, Pt. 2, 408–23.

[2] Scot was imprisoned in the Fleet till he was released on bond 4 years later. He then escaped to the Spanish Netherlands, where he died in 1564. Cf. D.N.B., XVII, 953.

[3] S.P., 10, 52. S.P. 10 is the Visitation Book of 1559 for the Province of York.

[4] Accounts of the Visitation are in H. Gee, *The Elizabethan Clergy and the Settlement of Religion, 1558–1564*, 81–2, and H. N. Birt, *The Elizabethan Religious Settlement*, 157–65, each being based on S.P., 10.

needs modification. Thirty-one clergymen from Cheshire failed to appear before the commissioners and it has sometimes been assumed that such absentees from the visitation were, in fact, opponents of the religious settlement, some of whom might be regarded as the first recusants; as a sixth or seventh of the clergy of the county they could be seen as forming a substantial opposition.[1] But, of course, clerics could have been absent for many reasons that had nothing to do with hostility to the religious settlement, for example, sickness at a time of plague, and a comparison of the lists of absentees with the names of the clergy in the diocesan Visitation Books for 1554, 1563 and 1565 led W. Ferguson Irvine to conclude that 21 of the absentees took the oath of allegiance, two died at about this time, of six nothing definite can be said, and only two were clearly deprived.[2] For one particular group of the clergy, the Cathedral Chapter, R. V. H. Burne concluded that the settlement involved no change.[3] Thus, whether from conviction or indifference, the care of souls or the love of a living, almost all the clergy in Cheshire conformed to the religious settlement of 1559.[4]

The only stir that was created by the clerical opposition in the early years of the reign of Elizabeth was the work of the former chaplain to Bishop Bonner, John Morwen, who in 1562 'wandereth in Staffordshire and Lancashire very seditiously; it is the person who cast abroad the seditious libel in Chester'.[5] The 'libel' was an eloquent tract in confutation of a sermon preached by Bishop Pilkington of Durham after the fire caused by lightning at St. Paul's Cathedral, which took place on 4 June 1561. The tract was 'An Addicion, with an Apologie to the causes of the brinnynge of Paule's Church, the which causes were uttred at Paule's Cross by the Reverend Byshop of Duresme, the 8th. of June, 1561'. It argued that the fire was a judgement of God for the abandonment of the ancient faith and was considered weighty enough to merit a lengthy written reply by Pilkington.

Morwen's well-argued pamphlet, the work of a Greek scholar of some

---

[1] W. Ferguson Irvine, 'Clerical Changes in 1559', *Cheshire Sheaf*, Third Series, III, 39. Irvine suggests that there were between 200 and 220 clergy in the county.

[2] Ibid., 29–34, 38–9. The two who were deprived were T. Buckleye of Cheadle and W. Hill of Malpas, though the evidence for their deprivation seems inconclusive.

[3] R. V. H. Burne, *Chester Cathedral from its founding by Henry VIII to the accession of Queen Victoria*, 37–8. He points out that the inclusion of Robert Percival, Thomas Wilson and William Collingwood in the list of deprived clergymen drawn up by Nicholas Sanders in 1571 is quite misleading. Each appears in the Cathedral account books after 1559, while Percival's deprivation of his cure of Ripley, Yorkshire, may have been merely to allow the restitution of the married cleric deprived of the cure under Mary.

[4] It must be said, however, that Irvine opens up again the whole question of the changes in personnel in 1559 by pointing out the startling difference between the number of clergy appearing in the 1554 Visitation Book and the number appearing in the book of 1563. 1563 shows less than a quarter of the 1554 members in many cases, 'looking as if the changes were most severely felt in the ranks of the unbeneficed clergy' (loc. cit., 38).

[5] S.P., 15, 11, 45.

repute, perhaps reveals the attitudes that lay behind recusancy, even if in a more learned and sophisticated way than would usually be the case, and is therefore worth outlining.[1] It is mostly taken up with attacks on four particular aspects of the new Church, beginning with the argument that the Anglican faith was newfangled and schismatic.

First search, whether the faith and religion now used was taught with the blessed fathers of Christ's church in times past: ye shall prove by no record of authority or chronicle, that this manner of service now used in the church was ever heard tell of afore Luther's time, which is not forty years old. Therefore, it is to be rejected and put away, as a new fangled doctrine and schismatical: therefore come back again unto the old fathers' steps.

Next, Morwen stated that the new worship was schismatic, for the new preachers pollute

the temple with schismatical service, destroying and pulling down holy altars that were set up by good blessed men, and there the sacrifice of the blessed mass ministered according to the orders of Christ's catholic church. Yea, where the altar stood of the Holy Ghost, the new bishops have made a place to set their tails upon. . . .

Thirdly, he went on to state that the new church was disobedient to the universal church of Christ in four separate ways.

. . . where the universal church of Christ commands mass and seven sacraments . . . they call it abomination with their blasphemous mouths: where the church commands to fast, they command to eat: where the church commands continual prayer of the clergy, they call it superstition and blind ignorance: where the church commands the clergy to live in chastity, they command and exhort the clergy to marriage . . . obeying no law, but follow their own carnal lust.

Fourthly, Morwen attacked the irregular consecration of bishops and priests, for

. . . they have invented a new way to make bishops and priests, and a manner of service and ministration, that St. Augustine never knew . . . nor ever one bishop of Canterbury, saving only Cranmer . . . In Duresme have been many good fathers; but he that is now bishop can not find any one predecessor in that see that was of his religion, and made bishop after such sort as he was. . . .

With this jab at Pilkington Morwen concluded the first part of his pamphlet. He then put forward two more general ideas that are frequently used in the defence of conservative faiths and ideologies. The first of these was a contrast of the miserable present with the golden age of the past, in which the new faith was blamed for the misery.

. . . then was the commandment of God and virtue expressed in living: now all is in talk and nothing in living: then was prayer, now is prating: then was

---

[1] It is printed in the *Works of James Pilkington*, ed. J. Scholefield for the Parker Society, 480–6.

virtue, and now is vice: then was building up of churches, houses of religion and hospitals, where prayer was had night and day, hospitality kept and the poor relieved: now is pulling down and destroying such houses . . . then was plenty of all things, now is scarceness of all things. . . .

From Protestant dearth Morwen finally turned to Protestant immorality, for he saw the new heresy as the source of contemporary low moral standards.

. . . they have set the people in such case as no prayer is used, no fasting, little almsdeeds, 'all liberty used'; what disobedience children be in against their parents, how untrustworthy servants be, what swearing and blaspheming of God is used of all people; what theft, whoredom, craft, subtlety and deceit: these be fruits that come of the new-fangled doctrine.

Curiously enough, though the tract was circulated in Chester, news of it was sent to the Privy Council by the Council of Wales, not by the new bishop, William Downham, or any other Cheshire authority. This may be one of several examples of the slackness for which Downham was notorious, or it may be that the bishop was scarcely familiar with his new diocese when Morwen's work was distributed. Morwen had written in answer to Pilkington's sermon, which had been preached on 8 June 1561, and the Council of Wales forwarded the tract to the Privy Council in January 1562; Downham had been appointed on 4 May 1561.

William Downham was no extremist. At the beginning of his career he had been a monk of Bonhommes, Ashridge, Buckinghamshire, an independent order that followed the Augustinian rule. Later he had become a fellow of Magdalen College, Oxford, and private chaplain to Princess Elizabeth, remaining in England during the reign of Mary, so that his outlook was unaffected by life among the continental Protestant extremists. He was appointed Archdeacon of Brecknock in 1559 and Canon of Westminster in 1560. His promotion to the see of Chester 'for the good opinion we conceaved of you in your former service'[1] was thus the recognition by Elizabeth and Cecil of a fellow-conformist rather than the martyr's crown of a Protestant enthusiast newly returned from exile.

His diocese was, however, no ecclesiastical plum. It stretched northwards from Cheshire into Lancashire and even into the southern halves of Westmorland and Cumberland, finally bulging eastwards to take in the Yorkshire Dales. Attractive to twentieth-century city dwellers as the north and north-east of his diocese would be, a sixteenth-century bishop must have winced at the administrative difficulties that their inaccessibility involved. It was easy enough for Bishops Pilkington of Durham and Barnes of Carlisle to criticise Downham for his slackness in enforcing the law;[2] their dioceses were relatively compact: Downham's was one of the

[1] S.P., 12, 46, 33. For his life, cf. D.N.B., V, 1302.
[2] M. Parker, *Correspondence*, 222: H. N. Birt, op. cit., 314.

biggest in England, 'of length above six score miles', as he later wrote.[1] Downham rapidly adjusted himself to the difficulties, according to Bishop Pilkington, who concluded a letter to Archbishop Parker, in which he grumbled dismally about the evil state of the church in Lancashire, 'the bishop of Chester has compounded with my lord of York for his visitation, and gathers up the money by his servant; but never a word spoken of any visitation or reformation: and that, he says, he does of friendship, because he will not trouble the country, nor put them to charge in calling them together'.[2] However, all the northern bishops shared a handicap at the opening of the reign; their appointments were delayed until 1561.[3] Bishoprics left vacant for up to two years allowed slackness to develop, and Downham was not the man to stop the rot. He was as slack in enforcing the settlement of 1559 as his predecessor had been ardent in opposing it.

In 1559 the clergy of the county seem to have been as compliant as their future bishop, and their conformity seems to have been reflected by the laity. The visitation of 1559 revealed that in Chester city 'Mistres Dutton kepith secreatlye a Rode, too pictures and a masse boke' belonging to St. Peter's Church, to which Thomas Byldon the elder 'comethe seldom', and that Peter Fletcher 'hathe certin ymages whiche he kepithe secreatlye' belonging to St. Mary's.[4] The reasons for Byldon's absence from church are unknown and the examples of those who kept Catholic objects hidden for the day of their faith's return at a time when the new regime was not yet securely established are the only examples of their kind recorded by the visitors in the whole county.

Little more of this type of evidence appears in the other extant sources for the early years of the reign. Such visitation records as exist are fragmentary, so much so that conclusions about the county as a whole can scarcely be drawn from them.[5] Most of their brief and scanty entries deal with sexual offences or church buildings in disrepair. There is no pre-occupation with the repression of religious conservatism, revealed in the concealment of forbidden church ornaments, like those dealt with in 1559, or in the continual use of illegal practices which A. G. Dickens noted in the visitation of 1567–8 in Yorkshire,[6] and certainly no pre-occupation with recusancy. Between 1561 and 1565 21 men and women were presented for failure to attend their parish church; the charges follow the

---

[1] S.P., 12, 48, 36, dated 1 Nov. 1568.
[2] Parker, op. cit., 222, probably from 1564.
[3] The dates are given in P. Hughes, *The Reformation in England*, III, 45, n.1.
[4] S.P., 10, 134–5.
[5] E.D.V., 1, 2a, 1561–2, cases from Macclesfield Deanery; 2b, 1562, cases from Frodsham, Middlewich, Chester & Malpas Deaneries, and 1563 cases from Frodsham Deanery; 3, 1563, cases from Nantwich Deanery; 4, 1563, cases from Macclesfield Deanery; 5a, 1563, cases from Nantwich and Middlewich Deaneries; 5b, 1563–4, from Frodsham Deanery; 6, 1565, cases from Frodsham Deanery.
[6] The 'First Stages of Romanist Recusancy in Yorkshire, 1560–90', in *Yorkshire Archaeological Journal*, XXXV, 161–4.

formula normally used in presenting recusants in later years, but only one of those presented, Henry Bolton of St. Mary's, Chester, was probably a recusant, in later years at least.[1] Most of the offenders did not appear to answer their charges, as was usual, and of those who did John Chorlton and Elizabeth Browne of Cheadle were each fined 12d., while Thomas Dey of Macclesfield and Thomas Wetnall of Acton were warned to attend church under pain of the law.[2]

The records of the Ecclesiastical Commission, set up in July 1562[3] to deal with offences concerning religion in Chester Diocese, are equally unilluminating, for they suffer from a grave weakness as sources in that they frequently give no indication of the nature of the offences of those who were dealt with by the Commissioners, and only a handful of these unstated offences seem to have arisen from recusancy or allied offences. Again, of the stated offences most were fornication or adultery, so that even though the records of a large number of cases that were dealt with by the Commissioners between October 1562 and the end of 1565 survive[4] they throw little light on the development of recusancy.

Six men, Henry Bolton, Thomas Birkenhead and Robert Carter(?) of St. Mary's, Chester, and Richard Dandwall, Richard Coke and John Whitwell were presented for absence from church: all except Carter, who did not appear before the Commissioners, were ordered to comply with the law. Again, of these Henry Bolton was probably the only recusant. Fulk Aldersey of Chester, a recusant in later years, may have been dealt with for recusancy, though the charge against him was not stated. Margaret Aldersey of Chester, whom the Commissioners had already examined 'concerninge the concealinge of an image', about which she 'confessed that she had sold and convayed it away bie a Spaniard', was also 'enjoyned that she shall not use any Latin Primers hereafter'. She was dealt with in November 1562: almost a decade later, in April 1571, she was again brought before the Commissioners and ordered 'to bringe in a Latin Primer boke which she useth'. Twenty years later still, elderly and ailing, she was to suffer imprisonment as a recusant.[5]

John Eldershawe of Audlem was apparently more pliant when he appeared before the Commissioners on 15 May 1564.

Forasmuch as, beinge examined whether he, his two sons, wief and daughter received the communion at Easter last (he) hath denied the same, declaringe the cause therof to be for that he cold not get his adversary reconciled to hym,

---

[1] E.D.V. 1, 2b, f. 14. The test of recusancy that is adopted here is the appearance on a charge of absence from church of any given person in more than one source or in such circumstances as suggest recusancy. This is perhaps an over-cautious test at this stage in the development of recusancy, for until the 1590's records are so scanty that frequent references to one person's absence from church can scarcely be expected. Nevertheless, some such test seems to be the only safe way of eliminating those who were absent because of sickness or old age or even for some relatively frivolous reason.

[2] Ibid., 1, 4, f. 4: 1, 5, f. 2, f. 4.   [3] S.P., 12, 23, 56.

[4] E.D.A., 12, 2.   [5] Ibid., ff. 2, 81v, 82 & 132.

betwene whom ther was knowne displeasure. And that his wief and children, Richard and Mawde, were, as he thinketh, in like offence and displeasure, and for that cause onlie they staid from the receyvinge and not for that he hath any evill opinion of the sacrament, openlie protestinge that he thinketh the same godlie in all pointes and that he received the same at Easter last before this last Easter at Whitchurch whereat he then dwelled.[1]

There was probably more to all this than Eldershawe admitted, for he, his wife and his son, Richard, eventually emerged as recusants.

Nevertheless, none of the offenders mentioned so far could positively be called recusant at this time, the early 1560's, and such other offences as were dealt with by the Commissioners reveal only the small-scale survival of traditional practices. John Bastwell, formerly a friar of Chester, was told not to wear beads, and Edward Griffes, possibly the former porter of Chester Abbey, was 'enjoyned that he shall not use his beades hereafter under paine of the lawe'. The churchwardens of Church Lawton parish were bound in recognisance to the sum of £20 to 'take downe their roade lofte of Church Lawton to the lowest beame of the same and . . . also do cause all alters, images and all other monumentes of idolatry and super-sticion to be removed out of their church and leave destroid, and do also prepare and ordaine a decent table whereon the Communion shal be said'. Similarly, the removal and defacement of a rood loft was also ordered at Bromborough.[2]

The enactment of a minor Catholic practice by John Bolt and James and Richard Shawe of Sandbach, who 'did ring on All Saintes Daie at nyght' was suitably compounded for by the three men: 'amonge them bie order they have geven iiis. to the buyenge of a Paraphrases (of Erasmus) towardes, for the churche of Sonbage'. They appeared before the Commissioners in November 1564: 12 months later, in December 1565, a similar offence was penalised more severely. Thomas Starkey

did enter into his parish church and did toll the belles there upon All Saintes Daie at nyght last, wherbye he procured diverse evill disposed persons to repaire unto hym and to ringe the belles a gret parte of that nyght to the mainteynaunce of supersticion, etc. . . . for his said offence and for other causes . . . (he is to) be committed to the castell of Chester there to remaine in gaole without baile or mainprise till further order be taken for his enlargement.

What aggravated Starkey's action is not stated, but he was the only offender of this type who was dealt with at all harshly.[3]

In a handful of these cases dealt with by the Ecclesiastical Commission in the 1560's the later recusancy of the person concerned is at least fore-shadowed. The rest are more puzzling, like those of two clergymen in whom opposition to the established church was observed. Robert Kinsey, the parson of Barthomley, was 'suspected to be a favorer of the masse and of suche papisticall tradicons', and John Barlowe was 'an hinderer and

[1] Ibid., f. 72.   [2] Ibid., ff. 13, 26 & 82.   [3] Ibid., ff. 86v & 103v.

obstinate against the religion nowe most godlie set furth', but in each of these cases the main charge against the cleric was sexual immorality.[1] Clearly, the nature of the records of the Ecclesiastical Commission and the incompleteness of the Visitation records mean that only a partial account of the development of recusancy in Cheshire in the early 1560's emerges from them. However, quite apart from the nature of the surviving records the inherent weaknesses of the Tudor local administration, both lay and ecclesiastical, make it unlikely that they were dealing adequately with evasions of the newly established religion. In particular, the slackness and partiality of its personnel, in spite of attempts to weed out recusants and recusant sympathisers, is notorious. As early as 1564 a report on the loyalty to the state religion of the justices of the peace had been demanded and made on a nationwide basis. Downham drew up an outstandingly full and systematic report on the J.P.s of his diocese.[2]

In Chester city only six of the existing justices and five aldermen were declared to be favourable to the settlement of 1559, and eight justices and four aldermen unfavourable, while 11 others were named as 'meete to be Aldermen for their zeale and habilitie': in the county 12 justices were declared to be favourable, nine unfavourable and 18 other men were named as fit to be justices. As far as the City goes what is most striking about this carefully drawn up list is that its classifications correspond little to the religious loyalties of the local magnates in so far as they are ascertainable elsewhere. Only one of the unreliable justices in Chester city, William Aldersey, and possibly one unreliable alderman, Robert Johns, can be traced elsewhere as recusants, while two of the gentlemen commended as worthy of being aldermen, John Fisher and Christopher Morville, are non-church attenders of later years. No clear taint of recusancy touches any of the favourable justices of the county commission, and five of the nine unfavourable members certainly belonged to families to which suspicion of recusancy always clung, though none were themselves definitely recusant: two of the nine are later loyal supporters of the settlement. Further, six of the nine reported as hostile to the religious policy of the realm were not only still on the bench in 1569, but then signed the obsequious declaration of loyalty made necessary by the northern rebellion. 'Albeyt somewhat torne and ragged' it declared their allegiance to the Act of Uniformity as well as to the Queen, 'by whome is oppenyd to us the pleane pathe of virtue to oure eternall salvacion', as Sir John Savage wrote in sending the declaration to the Privy Council.[3] On the other hand only six of the 18 men recommended

---

[1] Ibid., ff. 20, 24, 85v & 102.

[2] Printed in 'A collection of Original Letters from the Bishops to the Privy Council, 1564', ed. M. Bateson, in *Camden Miscellany*, IX, 73–8. Nothing indicates that this was sent in by Young, Archbishop of York, as stated by W. R. Trimble, *The Catholic Laity in Elizabethan England*, 34: it appears to be Downham's work.

[3] S.P., 12, 60, 30. No trouble was experienced in Cheshire in 1569.

in 1564 as fit to be justices had been appointed by that time. One important negative point in favour of the accuracy of the report can, however, be made; no member of any family that was later to be stubbornly recusant was regarded as a reliable office-holder or recommended as fit for office.

It is, in fact, unlikely that an accurate report on religious loyalties could have been drawn up by 1564, as the divisions of later years had not yet emerged clearly.[1] The settlement of 1559 was sufficiently comprehensive to discourage clearcut opposition, and this uncertainty in religious loyalties is reflected in the attitude of Catholics to attendance at Anglican services, failure to attend which alone made them recusants. A recusant was someone who refused to attend the parish church on Sundays and holy days;[2] the demand for only outward conformity gave to the loyal Catholic wide scope for casuistry and compromise, so much so that this provided the early Catholic leaders with one of their chief problems, as is clear in the work of two of them in the north of England, William Allen and Laurence Vaux. Allen, 'anti-1559 incarnate', firmly resisted any compromise in this after his return to England in 1563–4: no-one could be a Catholic and attend the parish church, he said. Vaux felt it necessary to write a stern letter, probably intended for circulation, taking up the same position, in November 1566. Even the Douai priests, working from 1574 onwards, found the same insistence on the need for the Catholic to separate himself from Protestant church worship to be their first task.[3]

The decade after 1559 was thus a time in which those who adhered to the Catholic faith often avoided the pains of the law against recusancy by their outward conformity, which was all that the law demanded. Nevertheless, sufficient illegal acts took place within Downham's diocese for the Council to give him a sharp rap for his slackness in February 1568. It was the first of many, though it had been preceded by a mild purge of suspected recusants, all from Lancashire, from the diocesan Ecclesiastical Commission in 1567; Christopher Goodman and John Pierce, Dean of Chester, were the new Cheshire nominees to the commission.[4] The government had received

credible reportes of disorders and contemptes to the contrary (of uniformity in religion) in your diocese, and specially in the County of Lancaster (so that) we find great lack in you, being sorry to have our former expectation in this sort deceaved. In which matter of late we wrote unto you and others our Commissioners joyned with you to cause certen suspected persons to be apprehended, writing also at the same time to our . . . Cosin and Counsellor the Erle of Derby

---

[1] M. Bateson, loc. cit., preface iv, comments thus on the 1564 census of J.P.s, 'These lists … give a complete religious census of the leading men of each county.' The analysis of the Cheshire list given here shows that this is a rather misleading view as far as that county is concerned.

[2] 1 Eliz., c. 2.   [3] P. Hughes, op. cit., 249, 260, n. 1, 285–6.

[4] S.P., 15, 13, 123.

B

for the ayding of you in that behalf. Since which tyme and before the delivery of our said lettres to the Erle of Derby we be duly informed that the said Erle hath upon small motion made to him caused all such persons as have ben required to be apprehended and hath showed himself therin according to our assured expectation very faithfull and carefull for our service.

Now therefore considering the place you hold to be principall minister in these causes and such disorders found within your diocese as we here not of the like in any other partes of our realme, we will and charg you further to have other regard to your office, and specially to foreseing that all Churches and Cures be provided of honest and as well lerned Curates as ye can cause to be provided, using therin the ordinances and censures of the Church to the remedy of the defaultes, and suffer not for the lack of your own personall visitation of your diocese by repayring into the remoter partes and specially into Lancaster, that obstinate persons having ben justly deprived of offices of ministry be secretly mayntayned to pervert our good subjectes within any part of your diocese, as we understand they have now of long time ben . . .[1]

This letter finally stirred Downham into considerable activity. He stated in a letter written on the following 1 November that during the summer he had visited the whole of his diocese 'and had found the people very tractable', though 'my jorney was very payneful by reason of the extreme heate: and if I had not receyved great curtesie of the gentry, I must have left the most of my horses by the waye: such droughte was never sene in these parties'.[2] The main problem and the main drive had obviously been in Lancashire, where the Ecclesiastical Commissioners under the leadership of Downham and Edward, Earl of Derby, had dealt with several leading recusants whose activities had created a great stir.[3] Recusancy was plainly a lesser problem in Cheshire, though it was possibly as a result of Downham's drive that 11 men were assessed for 12d. fines for absence from their parish churches in Chester before the Quarter Sessions of the city on 2 September 1568.[4] Six of them were clearly recusants, as they were charged with the same offence in later years.[5]

It is difficult to avoid the conclusion that there was very little open opposition to the Elizabethan religious settlement and only the mildest signs of anything that might be called recusancy in Cheshire in the first decade of the reign of Elizabeth I, and this judgement is confirmed by the failure of the rising of 1569 to gain support there. In spite of the incomplete and enigmatic nature of the surviving sources, the inadequacies of the administrative system and the failure of William Downham to deal with

---

[1] S.P., 12, 46, 33, dated 21 February 1567/8.
[2] Ibid., 48, 36.
[3] Ibid., 34–6.
[4] M.B., 1567–8, 2 September, 10 Eliz. The men were Fulk Aldersey, Robert Amnyon, Henry Bolton, Richard Bunbury, William Cones (?), Laurence Dickenson, Robert Granwall, William Jewet, Peter Orrell, Roger Radford and Richard Smith.
[5] Aldersey, Bolton, Granwall, Orrell, Radford and Smith.

the problems of his diocese energetically, the existing evidence suggests that there was little of either religious conservatism or recusancy in the county. Downham's rebuke by the Privy Council and the activity of the Chester Quarter Sessions in 1568 indicate the development of clearer opposition to the religious settlement than had earlier been apparent and of an attempt to stamp it out.[1] But each was on a small scale.

[1] About a third of the City Quarter Sessions' Books (Mayors' Books) are extant from 1562–9 and this is the only entry relating to recusancy in them; there are no such entries in the County Sessions' Books, where entries begin in 1565. In his *Chester, a Diocesan History*, R. H. Morris stated that there are many presentments for recusancy in the Chester Mayors' Books, but, in fact, he treats some recognisances as being those of recusants where there is nothing to indicate that they are such, his dating is unreliable and the number of probable recusancy cases is not great when the time-span covered by them is borne in mind. Thus from 1562–1603, 43 presentments for absence from church were made, an average of only one a year (and for these years as a whole there are entries for about half the Sessions held). A handful of presentments can also be found in the Quarter Sessions' Files of the City.

CHAPTER II

EPISCOPAL SLACKNESS

1570–9

The end of the 1560's and the opening of the 1570's saw the political implications of recusancy grow clearer with the northern rising of 1569 and the excommunication of Elizabeth I in 1570. It became both more imperative and more dangerous for the loyal Catholic to break openly with the Anglican church. There is little enough evidence of the activities of Cheshire Catholics at this time to show just how they made their choices, but such as there is perhaps suggests a transition from partial conformity to the clear rejection of the worship of the established church by those who were to form the hard core of recusancy in Cheshire by the late 1570's. Some of these men and women faced the Ecclesiastical Commission, either its diocesan arm in Chester or its metropolitan arm in York, at the opening of this decade. Thus Margaret Aldersey of Chester appeared before the Diocesan Commissioners in April 1570. Seven and a half years earlier they had warned her to make no further use of a Latin primer: in 1570 she was ordered 'to bringe in a Latin Primer boke which she useth', and at the same time was charged as a non-communicant and ordered to receive the sacrament at Easter. She was not yet a recusant, but took that step in the years between 1570 and 1577, when she was listed as a recusant in a diocesan return. Similarly, Dr. John Eldershawe, who had been an apparently pliant non-communicant in 1564 and yet by 1575 could be listed as one of the handful of the county's obstinate recusants, appeared on an unstated charge before the Commissioners in York in 1571. Are these in fact illustrations of an attempt by the diocesan and metropolitan commissioners to prevent the step into recusancy that may have been contemplated by Margaret Aldersey and Richard Eldershawe and possibly by others like John Whitmore, later to be an unyielding recusant, who appeared twice before the Diocesan Commissioners in 1570 and twice before the Metropolitan, in 1571 and 1572, on all four occasions on a charge that remains unknown?[1]

It is unlikely that the initiative in this came from the diocesan bishop, William Downham; for him *plus ça change, plus c'est la même chose:* 1570 saw

---

[1] E.D.A., 12, 2, ff. 129, 132, 133v: York H.C., A.B., 16, ff. 78v, 80, 140v–141. Other Cheshire men who were later recusants and who appeared on unstated charges before the Commissioners in York were Henry Bolton of Chester and Thomas Maddocks of Thurstaston, while a Margery Grosvenor, possibly one of the Cheshire family of that surname, was imprisoned in York Castle by order of the Commissioners in 1571, and in her case recusancy was clearly the issue. (York, H.C., A.B., 16, ff. 45, 73–4, 80, 141 and 178v.)

him being reprimanded for slackness once more. 'Sundry disorders' over religion in his diocese led to a rebuke on 12 November by the Privy Council 'bycause her Majestie supposeth the same hath cume to passe through his (Downham's) remissnes in not looking so diligentlye to the charge committed unto him', and he was ordered to appear before the Council 'bringing with him such matters for declaracion of his procedinges towardes such as have refused to cume to Common Prayer as may best serve for his purgacion and for the answering of all other thinges committed to his charge'.[1] The Archbishop of Canterbury was further ordered to examine him on these matters: the letter arranging this makes clear that the disturbances had been in Lancashire and the Archdeaconry of Richmond, not Cheshire.[2] The final shame for Downham was the appointment by the Archbishop of York of Barnes, Bishop of Carlisle, to hold a visitation of Chester diocese.[3]

It seems likely that even these humiliations failed to make Downham more efficient, for he was singled out from his fellow-bishops by the Privy Council once more on 26 November 1575, for his failure in 'the redresse of suche as beinge of this Diocese of Chester have not of longe tyme come to any Church or publique place of praier and other godlie exercises of religion allowed and set furthe bie the Lawes of this realme'. Downham's reply of 1 February 1576 assured the Council that

we have made diligent inquisicion throughout the said diocese what such gentlemen and other persons there be that refuse to come to the church and therbie have bene enformed of diverse suche whom we have sent for, of which some have come before us and by good perswacons have shewed themselves conformable.

Not all had been so amenable, for

the other have not come but either remaine in their wilfullness still or els have shewed in the cuntries where they dwell some token of obedience as we have understandinge from those whom we judge worthie of credite.

A list, in which each person was noted 'in respect either of their obstinacye or conformitye', was enclosed.[4] In this the names of 73 Lancashire men and women were followed by only eight from Cheshire, a telling contrast as to the relative gravity of the recusant problem in these counties, even when the difference in their size and population is borne in mind. The eight names reveal the preoccupation of the authorities in these years with bringing the recusant leaders into conformity; there were two landed gentlemen, John Whitmore and William Hough, and their wives, the wives of two other gentlemen, namely Mary, the wife of William Tatton,

[1] A.P.C., 1558–70, 399.
[2] Ibid., 1571–6, 5, dated 13 January 1570. Burghley's 'Notes on the state of Lancashire and Cheshire', possibly drawn up for or shortly after these enquiries, emphasise Lancashire almost to the point of excluding Cheshire (H.M.C., Salis. MSS., 1, 575).
[3] A.P.C., 1571–5, 26, dated 12–14 May 1570.
[4] Harl. MSS., 286, 19, f. 27.

and Anne, the wife of Thomas Grosvenor, and an aged doctor, John Eldershawe, and his wife. Only Mrs. Grosvenor and Mrs. Tatton were described as conformable, the rest being obstinate. The obdurate six were, in fact, part of the hard core of recusant gentry in Cheshire, especially Whitmore and Hough, for along with ten Lancashire men these two received special mention:

Of all the rest theis xii are in our opinions of longest obstinacy against religion and if by your Lordships' good wisdomes these cold be reclaymed we think the other wold as well followe their good example in embrasinge the Quene's Majesties' most godly procedinges as they have followed their evill example in contempninge their dutie in that behalf.[1]

By this time the government were contemplating dealing with such implacable recusants by hitting harder at their purses than was done by the 12d. fine of the Act of 1559. Thus on 15 October 1577, the Council wrote to the diocesan bishops, demanding within a mere seven days returns of the names of all recusants with the value of their lands and goods.[2] Downham compiled the list for his diocese, but it was one of his last public acts, for he died in November 1577, before it could be forwarded to the Council. In its clarity, brevity and incompleteness the list forms a fitting epilogue to his episcopate. It ran as follows:[3]

A true copie of the certificate which the late Bushop of Chester, decessed, wolde have returned to the right honorable Lordes of her highnes' Previe Counsell (yf he had not bene prevented by deathe) concerning all suche persons within the Counties of Chester, Lancaster and the Cittie of Chester as refuse to comme to the churche to heare devine service.

Com. Cestr:

William Houghe of Leighton, Esquier. His landes be accompted of the olde ancient rent fiftie poundes by yere, whereof greate parte is in demayne. His goodes not valued, for that his father died of late and charged the said William with greate legacies.

John Whitmore of Thurstanton, Esquire. His landes are accompted of auncient rent three score poundes by yere, whereof greate parte is in demayne.

Richard Massie of Churcheon Heathe, gentleman, hath lyvinges worthe tenne poundes by yere.

John Birtles of Birtles, gentleman, hath landes of auncient rent xiij li. vis. viijd. by yere; a great part thereof is in demayne.

John Hocknell of Prenton, gentleman, hath landes worthe twentie poundes by yere, whereof a great parte is in demayne.

John Eldershaw of Aldelem practiseth Phisicke and hath lyvinges worth six poundes xiiis. iiiid. by yere.

[1] Harl. MSS., 360, 39, f. 68. This folio is quite separate from the letter of 1 February 1576, and is undated. Its method, however, is exactly as outlined in the letter, noting in each case whether the person named was obstinate or conformable, and is thus almost certainly the schedule originally attached to the letter.

[2] S.P., 12, 116, 15.

[3] Ibid., 118, 49, given verbatim in C.R.S., XXII, 68–9.

Anne Gravenor, weif to Thomas Gravenor of Eaton, Esquier.

Sir John Bushell, clerke, an olde preist, remayninge commonlie within the parishe of Bunburie, and a fugitive or latitant.

Civitas Cestr:

Ralph Worseley, a Counsellor at Lawe, valued by the said Bushop to be worthe fourtie poundes in goodes.

Mistress Langton, a widowe, esteemed by the said Bushop to have landes in joynture or dower worthe tenne poundes by yere.

Richard Sutton⎤ two olde preistes, verie wilfull and obstinate,
John Culpage ⎦remayninge in the Castell of Chester.[1]

William Aldersey, lynnen draper, and his weif. They are but pore, and he lieth bed rotten, as it is said.

Widowe Malpas, late weif to Thomas Malpas.

Thus, in Cheshire, 14 recusants are listed in all, eight in the county, and six in the city of Chester. Lesser gentry like Hocknell, Hough and Whitmore, and a lawyer, Ralph Worsley, buying his way into their ranks, are the wealthiest figures. Downham had obligingly allowed Hough, Whitmore and Birtles to be underassessed by accepting the traditional rent of assize instead of the current rental value of their lands.[2] With similar tolerance and as in his list of the previous year he had named only the more obvious recusants, and not all of them. The list claimed to be complete: it was nominally of 'all suche persons ... as refuse to come to the churche to heare devine service',[3] but in sending it to Walsingham, Sir Edward Fitton stated that 'relative to the recusants in the county of Cheshire; the chief of them are not touched who hear mass daily'.[4] Indeed, only a week had been given for the compilation of the list, and the bishops complained of this. Over the diocese as a whole Fitton asserted that 7,000 had been lost to the Church in seven years.

If Fitton's statements need not necessarily be taken at their face value it is equally obvious that Downham's lists are incomplete. Unaware of the latent strength and importance of the recusants, he had never got to grips with the problem they presented: his lists were selective, as is clear from the fact that some 30 recusants were dealt with during a visitation of the diocese that was authorised by the Archbishop of York during the two-year-long vacancy of the see that followed Downham's death.

As, unlike the earlier extant diocesan visitations, this visitation revealed significant evidence of recusancy, this is perhaps an appropriate point at which to examine some aspects of the hitherto unexamined background to recusancy that are also revealed in the visitation records. For a visitation dealt with many other matters besides recusancy: if few sermons were

---

[1] They were still imprisoned there two years later (Lansd. MSS., 28, 97, f. 213) and Sutton seems to have died in prison between 1579 and 1581 (cf. entry on Sutton in Appendix II).

[2] S.P., 12, 194, 73.   [3] Ibid., 118, 49.

[4] Ibid., 48. Fitton's son, Francis, became a priest (cf. Appendix II).

preached, if the service books were in disrepair, if the vicar was a pluralist, and if so whether or not he paid a curate to act for him, if the vicar preferred to meet his parishioners in the alehouse rather than the church, all these and other matters had to be reported to the visitors. In fact, in 1578 the blemishes were few. There was one pluralist[1] and four cases of non-residence.[2] There was suspicion of simony at Wistaston, where 'one of the sworne men doth say that the parson tolde him that his benefyse was bought and solde as an oxe or a cowe, and that if he had bene pryvy therof he would not have had yt for an hundreth poundes', and at Nether Peover was the inevitable curate who 'haunteth ale howses, hunteth, hawketh, and now and then daunceth and plaieth uncomelie for his callinge'.[3] Finally there was the parish of Weaverham, for listing whose iniquities almost a complete folio side was needed.

They want a Communion Booke, a Bible of the largest volume, the first tome of the Homilies. Ther is in the church an altare standing undefaced. There lacketh a lynnon clothe and a coveringe for the Communyon table, a chest for the poore and keping of the Register in. The parishoners refuse the perambulacion. The people will not be staied from ringinge the bells on All Saints' Daie. They frequent alehowses in service tyme. Great talkinge used in the churche. No levyinge for the poor of the absents from the churche. Morres Daunces and rishe bearinge used in the churche. Jane(?), an old noonne, is an evell women and teacheth false doctrine. They refuse to communicate with usuall breade. None come to the Communion iii tymes a yeare. They refuse to bring in ther yowth to be catechised. Crosses ar standinge in the churche yeard. The Vicar weareth not the surplesse . . . Ther is a pece of an altare standing in Mr. Ireland's quier.[4]

More to the point, at Alderley, Eccleston, Thurstaston, Wilmslow, Wistaston, and at St. Bridget's, St. John's, and Holy Trinity, Chester, as well as at Weaverham, the 12d. fine for absence from church was not levied by the churchwardens.[5] Only in the case of Alderley was this because 'they have no offenders'; at Thurstaston, on the contrary, it was 'because of ignoraunce of the statute'. Between them these parishes provided 33 of the 57 parishioners who were charged with absence from church (or a related offence), and even though some of them may have been neither Romanist nor recusant, this is the charge most closely allied to recusancy; of the 57 charged with it 30 can reasonably be regarded as recusants.[6] In turn, of the 30, 18 were from the handful of parishes in

[1] At Tilston (York, R.VI, A 7, f. 8).
[2] At Stockport (ibid., f. 5), Aldford (ibid., f. 8v), Bebington (ibid., f. 15v) and Astbury (ibid., f. 30v).　　　　　　　　　　　　　　　　　　[3] Ibid., ff. 12v & 29.
[4] Ibid., f. 29v. It did not improve with the passing of time; cf. infra, 95.
[5] Ibid., ff. 4v, 5v, 12v, 15v, 19v, 20v, 21, 22v.
[6] This judgement is based on their presentment elsewhere as recusants or absentees. The 30 were:
Gentry. Anne Grosvenor of Eaton, Eccleston; William Hough and Jane, his wife, of Leighton & Thornton; Richard Massey, junior, of Waverton; Mary Tatton of Northenden; John Whitmore and Elen, his wife, and one or more of their family, of Thurstaston.

which fines for absence were not enforced. Is it possible that it was in the parishes whose officials were slack in this that recusancy gained its earliest foothold in the first half of the reign of Elizabeth I? It is usual to emphasise the slackness and partiality of the justices as a crucial reason for the failure to stamp out recusancy, but it may well be that similar factors at a strictly parochial level were at least as important. The failure of the church-wardens in so high a proportion of the Chester churches may in fact explain the activity of the city justices in enforcing the 12d. fine at this time. In 1576 they fined four absentees 12d. each and a fifth 6s. 8d., in 1578 one absentee was fined 12d., and in 1579 12 suffered the 12d. fine, one of them twice.[1] Though the Quarter Sessions records of Chester city are fairly well-preserved for the 1570's, these are the only fines for absence from church that are recorded;[2] what is noteworthy is that most of them were levied on the very parishioners of St. Bridget's, St. John's and Holy Trinity who were dealt with by the Visitors in 1578, and these parishes were those whose churchwardens were presented for their failure to levy the fine for absence.

Such absentees as were presented before the Visitors in 1578 were never described as recusants; the word 'recusant' does not appear in their records, though Hugh Bromley, a gentleman of Hampton Post, was charged as 'a supposed papist', John Whitmore, his wife and family neither came to church nor communicated, 'being seduced with papystrye', and John Shaw, Nicholas White, Francis Bamvell and Alice Ball of Holy Trinity, Chester, were 'suspected of popery and mainteyne their errors openly in talke'.[3] 'Popish practises' were also not unusual at Holy Trinity, where Fulk Aldersey, Alice Ball, Francis Bamvell and his wife, Ralph Thornton and Nicholas White 'refuse to communicate oneles they

---

Professions and business. William Aldersey, linen-draper, and his wife, Margaret, of Chester; John Eldershawe, physician, and his wife, of Audlem; John Fisher, lawyer, of Chester; Christopher Morville, merchant, of Chester; Richard Smith, cutler, of Chester; John Whitehead, baker, of Chester; Ralph Worsley, lawyer, of Chester.
Priest. Thomas Houghton, an old priest, of Wrenbury.
Husbandmen. Robert Alger and Katherine, his wife of Barthomley.
Craftsmen. Richard Whitmore and Katherine, his wife, of Guilden Sutton.
Of unknown occupation or status. Fulk & Thomas Aldersey, Geoffrey Bickley, Robert Granwall, James Knowsley, Peter Orrell, Ralph & Roger Radford, all of Chester.
    [1] M.B., 1572–7, 3 May & 9 August, 18 Eliz. (Fulk Aldersey, John Fisher, Christopher Morville, Henry Pemberton & Ralph Radford); ibid., 28 November, 21 Eliz. (John Hallywell); ibid., 1578–81, 22 April, 21 Eliz. (Robert Granwall, James Knowsley & Peter Orrell); ibid., 22 September, 21 Eliz. (Fulk, Jane, John, Margaret & William Aldersey, Geoffrey Bickley, Henry Bolton, John Fisher, Robert Granwall & Ralph Worsley).
    [2] The county records from this decade contain only one case, that of Thomas Houghton, who was indicted at the Quarter Sessions of 7 Jan. 1578, for absence from his parish church of Wrenbury (C.S.B., Indictments, 1565–92, f. 112). He was a former priest, as is clear from his appearance before the Metropolitan Visitation in 1578 (York, R.VI, A 7, f. 10).
    [3] York, R.VI, A 7, ff. 8v, 15v & 20.

have singing breades or wafer breade, albeit the parson minister with usuall breade and singinge cakes'.[1] However, it was decided that Alice Ball 'is old and appointed to receave in wafer breade'. Even the parson, John Blaken, 'useth more circumstances at the bidding of fastinge daies and holidaies than nedith, after the popishe maner, consumying the tyme unprofitablie'.[2] Elsewhere, similar practices were reported, as at Tilston, Malpas, where 'Ralphe Leche useth praier for the deade and willeth the people to praie and saie a Pater Noster and de Profundis for the deade when the people do rest with the dead corps'.[3] At Grappenhall, Catholic vestments and ornaments had been retained:

Thomas Satton hath in his hands a cope of read velvet imbrodered with gold, a cope of white satten bridges,[4] blacke and grene, a vestment of counterfeyte clothe of golde, a vestment of sackclothe, another of sackclothe, a banner of grene sarcenet, iii cansticke and ii crosses latelie belonging to the churche, the which they presented to my Lord of Chester who appointed it to be sold to the churches use, but yet it is not.[5]

Nevertheless, such evidence of conservatism was not widespread, and some aspects of it were petty enough, as in the case of six parishes and a chapelry in which churchyards still contained standing crosses: at Warburton it was, in fact, only 'the stump of a cross ... the head being smitten off', while the one at Church Lawton was 'onlie to sitt upon'.[6]

How the Visitors dealt with the accused or whether most of the accused even appeared to answer their charges is not clear; excommunication would be the normal penalty for non-appearance. Certainly, several of the leading recusants whom even Downham had regarded as worth his attention were ordered to confer 'for ther better resolucion in matters of religion wherewith they ar intangled' with specified preachers, usually Christopher Goodman, the Archdeacon of Richmond, or John Lane, a prebendary of Chester Cathedral. This was to be once a fortnight for Richard Massey senior and junior of Waverton, and once a month for Mary, the wife of William Tatton of Northenden, and William Hough

[1] York, R.VI., f. 19v. The use of wafers rather than common bread was a delicate issue. The directions appended to the Injunctions of 1559 authorised the replacement of ordinary bread by wafer bread, but plain and somewhat thicker than in earlier days. In 1580, when dealing with difficulties encountered in Lancashire by Bishop Chadderton, the Privy Council advised 'that in such parishes as doe use common bread, and in others that embrase the wafer, they be severallie continued as they are at this present' in order to avoid open dispute. (Peck, I, 91, dated 26 July 1580.) Later, as the problem had not been resolved, the Council advised Chadderton 'charitabley to tollerate them (that esteem wafer bread), as children, with milke'. (Ibid., I, 94, dated 11 Aug. 1580.)
[2] Ibid., A 7, f. 19v. With nine absentees as well as all this, Holy Trinity seems to have sheltered plenty of Romanists at this time.
[3] Ibid., f. 8.
[4] Satin of Bruges.
[5] York, R.VI, A 7,f . 29.
[6] Ibid., ff. 29 & 31v. The other parishes were Grappenhall, St. John's and St. Michael's, Chester, and Weaverham, and the chapelry was Poynton (ibid., ff. 4v, 19, 20v, 29 & 29v).

and his wife, Jane, of Neston; conformity was to be shown by Easter, 1579; if not, further orders would be issued by the Archbishop or his associates.[1] No such time for reflection was allowed to John Whitmore of Thurstaston or John Eldershawe of Audlem, for a decree of attachment was issued to compel their attendance in York on 7 October before the High Commission, to appear before whom Robert Poole of Chester and Richard Fox of Manchester had also been cited because 'they harbor a popish priest or Busshop of Ireland, and Pole is accused to be an usurer'.[2]

William Whitmore of Neston was dealt with more leniently than his nephew, John. It was merely 'thought that he was not so dutifull in receaving (the communion) and frequenting the church as he ought to be', and he was therefore ordered to receive the communion before Easter, 1579. Meanwhile, Ralph Bostock promised to ensure the attendance at church and the reception of the communion by his daughter, Katherine Whitmore, the wife of a tailor of Guilden Sutton 'after her purificacon (if she tary with him)', and thereby gained her dismissal.[3]

As well as the 30 absentees who were probably recusants, Hugh Bromley, the 'supposed papist', was another, as was one of the 54 people who were presented as non-communicants,[4] namely Richard Massey, senior, of Waverton. Thus, some 32 recusants appeared before the Metropolitan Visitors in 1578, while in the 1570's as a whole 47 recusants are known to have been dealt with by the authorities, an insignificant total when compared with the vast numbers that might be expected on the basis of Fitton's comments on the 1577 diocesan return. And when the authorities took action it was directed against the recusants of substance; in the county they were largely the gentry. Their names, Birtles, Bromley, Grosvenor, Hocknell, Hough, Massey, Tatton and Whitmore are a roll-call of the prominent landed recusants of the next decade. Similarly, in so far as their statuses or occupations are known the recusants of the city of Chester were merchants, lawyers and tradesmen.[5] Whereas in later years these men and women of property, even though always disproportionately large in number, were usually outnumbered by those of lesser status, they were almost alone until 1580. The authorities were not yet concerned with those of little wealth. Similarly, whereas of the recusants dealt with by the authorities in later years, women frequently outnumber men, only a quarter of the recusants were women at this time. But even the recusants of some substance were dealt with lightly. More drastic

[1] York, R.VI, A 8, ff. 10–10v, 16v & 36.
[2] York, H.C., A.B., 6, ff. 172v, & 199v.
[3] York, R.VI, A 7, f. 19, & A 8, f. 15.
[4] Many of these were absentees as well and have been included in the 31 already listed. Figures given by J. S. Purvis in *Tudor Parish Documents in the Diocese of York*, 79, produce a different total of non-communicants, namely 65.
[5] This generalisation rests on knowledge of the statuses or occupations of only nine of the 21 involved.

punishments lay ahead; by the end of 1581 several Cheshire recusants were in prison.

One significant concentration of recusancy is apparent. Twenty of the 47 recusants dealt with by the authorities in these years were from the city of Chester; no other such concentration emerges. In itself the number is not large, but it is strange that recusancy should apparently be stronger in the city than in the rural areas of the county in the 1570's.[1] It is usually assumed that Chester was strongly Puritan at this time and it is thus possible that it was the very desire of the city council to eradicate the Romanists that makes the city seem to contain almost as many recusants as the whole of the rest of the county.

Strictly speaking, the 47 men and women dealt with by the authorities were potential recusants rather than recusants. Only those from Chester had clearly been convicted of absence from church, while the terminology employed by the Metropolitan Visitation is 'pre-recusant'. By the end of the 1570's, while the opposition of the Catholics to the established religion was becoming more open, the authorities were merely feeling their way in dealing with it. They had only just begun to measure up to the problem in any way at all. The hard and fast lines of later years were still not clearly drawn.

[1] Cp. A. G. Dickens' conclusions about Yorkshire at this time in 'The First Stages of Romanist Recusancy in Yorkshire, 1560–90', *Yorkshire Archaeological Journal*, XXXV, 179.

CHAPTER III

TURNING POINT

1580–1

Heretics they are, and they are our neighbours.
R. Hooker, *Laws of Ecclesiastical Polity*

When Robert Persons and Edmund Campion, the first Jesuit missionaries to England, returned to their native land in 1580, sterner measures for their future flock had already been drawn up by the government. These had been contemplated for some years and were finally carried out in 1580 and 1581. On 3 July 1580 a letter from the Privy Council to the authorities of Chester diocese and York province stated that since the former slight penalties had been ignored by the recusants heavier fines should be imposed upon them,[1] while Halton Castle was specially designated for the safe keeping of the most obstinate, since 'heretofore such as have bene comitted to your ordinarie prisons, have growne . . . to be more obstinate'. Sir John Savage of Clifton, the constable and seneschal of the castle, was appointed custodian. It was some three miles from the village of Runcorn, and an equal distance from the Mersey Estuary and the border of Lancashire. There

such as bee notorious recusantes within the counties of Lancaster, Chester and North Wales should bee comitted . . . there to remaine togither and bee kept from infecting of others that are well disposed subjectes and obedient unto her highness' lawes. . . .[2]

These policies awoke a ready response in William Chadderton, the new bishop of the diocese. His consecration in November 1579 had at last

[1] A judicial opinion on this procedure accompanied the letter (Peck, I, 88–9).
[2] Peck, I, 87: A.P.C., 1580–1, 77; Stowe MSS., 160, f. 105v, dated 26 July 1580. Halton Castle never seems to have been used as a recusant prison. W. Beamont, *History of the Castle of Halton and the Priory or Abbey of Norton*, 101–2, states that Sir John Southworth, a prominent Lancashire recusant, was imprisoned there from 1579 to 1581, but this is based on a misreading of Baines, *History of Lancaster*, I, 236–7 (Baines' account is based on the correspondence printed in Peck).
Chester Castle and the New Fleet, Manchester, along with Derby's house at Liverpool, served as the diocesan prisons, as a Privy Council letter of 7 December 1581 implies had been the intention from the start: in discussing the removal of recusant prisoners from Chester Castle, to which the Ecclesiastical Commission committed several gentlemen in 1581, the letter stated, 'at such times as we made choyce of Manchester for the bestowinge of the recusants of that diocese, we considered that the (said) place was more fitt and convenient for that purpose than the castle of Chester . . .' (Peck, I, 110.) Halton seems to have disappeared from view altogether by this time as a recusant prison.
All these prisons were intended to serve as diocesan prisons, not as county prisons, for Lancashire on the one hand or Cheshire on the other. All the correspondence about them is in terms of their use as diocesan prisons, never as county or purely local prisons.

ended the dangerously long vacancy that followed Downham's death. Born about 1540 at Nuthurst, near Moston, Manchester, Chadderton was returning to his home country. Ten years before he had opposed the Puritan teachings of Thomas Cartwright, his successor as Lady Margaret Professor of Divinity at Cambridge, and helped to bring about Cartwright's removal from the post: now his considerable abilities could be used in the struggle against Romish recusancy in the North.[1]

Chadderton had naturally been appointed to the Ecclesiastical Commission for the diocese of Chester when it had been renewed at the beginning of June 1580, and he and Henry, Earl of Derby, were soon commended for their zeal in forwarding its work.[2] The bishop was advised to work closely with Derby; Chadderton took up residence in Manchester, having been provided with a house when he was made Warden of the collegiate church there in June 1580,[3] and Derby in the outskirts, at Alport Park, as the most convenient centre for dealing with the recusants. The bishop reported on their joint drive against recusancy in a letter to the Council in October. He covered two closely-written sides with an enthusiastic account of their progress: indeed, the work was so time consuming that the bishop requested permission to absent himself from Parliament. With naïve optimism and self-congratulation he even assured the Council that an early end to recusancy in Lancashire could be expected.[4]

The Council was so impressed by the work of Derby and Chadderton that they began to share such comforting dreams, though they could not tolerate inaccurate returns about recusancy, and former returns from Chester diocese were 'very unperfect', they wrote in October. Such essential information as the full names of the recusants, their places of residence and the shire in which they lived was often omitted, while some were listed 'not to come to the church, which afterwards have made dew proof to the contrarye'. A list of eight questions to ask of recusants under examination was included. Chadderton quickly replied in his own defence, but Walsingham tartly responded,

touching the certificate required of the recusants: in case you cannot make the same in all points and circumstances so perfect as my lords prescribe, yet let yt be done in the best sort you can, which I doubte not but their lordships will take in good parte.[5]

Further thanks for the energetic work of Derby and Chadderton arrived just before Christmas, though with the letter bearing them came instructions that, for the recusants, were less seasonable. They were the general

[1] For detail of his life, cf. D.N.B., III, 1341–3, & J. S. Leatherbarrow, *The Lancashire Elizabethan Recusants*, 60–1.

[2] A.P.C., 1580–1, 53, & Peck, I, 85, 90–2.

[3] D.N.B., III, 1342.

[4] S.P., 12, 143, 11, dated 8 October 1580.

[5] Peck, I, 91, dated 26 July 1580: ibid., 98, dated 24 October 1580 (the questions are given in Leatherbarrow, op. cit., 65): ibid., 97, dated 12 November 1580.

regulations of the Council for imprisoned recusants.[1] On the same day, 16 December, the bishops throughout the country were instructed to take substantial bonds from parents whose children were being educated outside the realm: the money would be forfeited if the children had not returned home within three months. Chadderton was ordered to take bonds from nine Cheshire men who were listed curtly as 'Hollineberrie, Savage, Turbridge, Hurleston, Chumleye, Dutton, Brewreton, Manweringe, Roche'.[2] Though none of the men referred to can positively be identified as a recusant, John Dutton was probably a Catholic, and his son Peter was educated abroad, while a Jesuit named Brewerton was reported to be active in Scotland in 1582.[3]

Although 1580 was a year in which Chadderton was active against the recusants of his diocese, no clear picture of the situation in Cheshire emerges from the small amount of evidence of the dealings of the authorities with the recusants there that has survived. The considerable correspondence between the bishop and the Council concerned almost exclusively Lancashire and the more northerly parts of the diocese, and Cheshire hardly at all. The initial energies of the new Ecclesiastical Commission and the new bishop were expended in the parts of the diocese that lay outside Cheshire. It was not until the beginning of 1581 that the Cheshire recusants met their new bishop.

It is possible that at the very moment when Chadderton began the serious repression of recusancy in Cheshire Edmund Campion briefly succoured some of his victims. On 23 February, in its frantic search for Campion, the Privy Council instructed Sir George Calveley, the Sheriff of the county, to make inquiries at the home of Ralph Dutton of Hatton as to Campion's whereabouts.[4] Campion was active in Lancashire and Yorkshire at this time,[5] and Hatton, near Warrington, was only two or three miles south of the Lancashire border. The Council believed that Campion and George Gilbert, the lay leader of the Catholic Association, had been taken to Dutton's home at Hatton by Robert Townshend of Ludlow.[6] Townshend was Dutton's brother-in-law and Gilbert's uncle and former guardian. When the sheriff visited the house he found only Dutton and Townshend. Townshend denied all knowledge of the whereabouts of both Campion and Gilbert, though he did admit that he had

---

[1] A.P.C., 1580–1, 282.　　　　　　　　　　[2] Peck, I, 99–100.

[3] *Cal. Border Papers*, I, 85, quoted A. L. Rowse, *The Expansion of Elizabethan England*, 36.

[4] Dutton's wife, Ann, came from a recusant family, the Townshends. The Dutton's of Hatton and the Dutton's of Dutton came under constant suspicion of recusancy, especially Peter Dutton of Dutton and his wife, Elizabeth (cf. relevant entries in Appendix I). Ralph's daughter, Alice, married John Starkey of Olton: their third son, John, became a priest (Ormerod, II, 192 & 796).

[5] E. Waugh, *Edmund Campion*, 3rd edition, 132–3.

[6] For Gilbert's life, cf. D.N.B., VII, 1025–6. Townshend was a member of a Catholic family: his sister, Ann, was Ralph Dutton's wife, and another of his sisters was evidently the mother of George Gilbert (E. St. J. Brooks, *Sir Christopher Hatton*, 216–17).

seen his nephew (Gilbert) for three days in the previous summer. Then, 'presentlie, I the sherife delt with Mr. Dutton towching his knowledge of this Campion, who I was assured would tell me his knowledge. I found he never either knewe or heard of the man'.[1] The sheriff's trust in Dutton's word was evidently as great as his own ignorance of 'the man', Campion. Nothing was gained by the investigation, but suspicion of Catholic sympathies clung to Dutton's family.

As Chadderton journeyed from Lancashire to Chester at the beginning of 1581, he might possibly have travelled via Warrington and thus have passed unawares within a mile of Campion and Gilbert if they had indeed visited Hatton. However, the bishop had much to do: his initial purge of Lancashire was only just completed and Cheshire required his immediate attention. The importance of his task had been recognised by the Council, for his request to be excused from attending Parliament had been granted, providing his proxy attended.[2] While Parliament passed the Act to retain the Queen's Majesty's subjects in their due obedience,[3] by which the fine for recusancy was increased to £20 a lunar month, the bishop carried forward the equally vital administrative campaign against recusancy.

The Ecclesiastical Commission appears to have begun its work in Cheshire on 1 February 1581, at Middlewich.[4] Mrs. Elizabeth Oldfield of Middlewich parish, who was then fined 40s. for 'dyvers contemptuous speeches', may or may not have been a recusant: no other trace of her can be found in the documents of the period. Such difficulties in the identification of recusancy arise in dealing with many of these cases. The chief evidence of the activity of the Commissioners consists merely of lists of fines imposed by them, in most cases because the offenders had failed to appear to answer the original charge against them (then the original charge is not stated). Recusancy or near-recusancy can, however, be assumed when an offender has appeared earlier or does so subsequently upon a charge of or allied to recusancy. Thus, when the Commissioners next met in the Common Hall at Chester on 21 February, Fulk Aldersey was fined 20s. 'for dyverse contemptuous speeches uttered before her

---

[1] S.P., 12, 148, 11, dated 4 March 1580–1.

[2] Peck, I, 100, dated 13 January.

[3] 23 Eliz., c. 1.

[4] The account given here of the work of the Ecclesiastical Commission in 1581 is drawn from three sources, none of which provides a great deal:

(1) A list of fines imposed by it in the Chester diocese from 1581–3, in Exchequer Depositions, P.R.O., E 134, 25, Trinity, No. 5, Lanc. & Dio. Chester.

(2) Peck, for the case of James Apsden. After giving a good deal of the correspondence that arose during the drive of the Commission in Lancashire, Peck contains little written in the first third of 1581, when the Commission was active in Cheshire. Peck also provides hints, firstly, that many Cheshire recusants failed to appear before the Commissioners when cited, and secondly, that some recusants were imprisoned by the Commissioners.

(3) The records of the Cheshire Quarter Sessions also provide evidence that recusants were committed to prison by the Commissioners.

Detailed references are given in the text.

Majesties' Commissioners'. As he had appeared on three previous occasions before the Chester Quarter Sessions charged with absence from church, and also before the Archbishop's Visitation of 1578 on a similar charge, as well as one of popish practices, it may be assumed that he was appearing before the Commissioners as a recusant. His speeches doubtless made his position quite clear.[1]

On the following day, 22 February, in the Shire Hall, Chester, eleven men and women who are known to have been recusants were fined in and for their absence.[2] Richard ap Robert, alias Richard Thatcher, of Malpas, Philip Spurstowe and George Garnet of Bunbury, Thomas Maddocks of Thurstaston, William Dorington of Astbury, and William Granwall of Brindley, along with two women, Jane, the wife of Thomas Ball of Bickley, and Eve, the wife of Richard Woodward of Agden, were each fined 40s. The gentlemen involved were more heavily fined: John Whitmore of Thurstaston was fined £10 and Hugh and Sampson Erdeswick of Leighton 100s. and 66s. 8d. respectively.[3] The latter two actually came from Santon, Staffordshire, but they were descendants of a Cheshire family, originally seated at Erdeswicke Hall, Minshull Vernon, Cheshire, and still held lands in Leighton, where they were presumably resident at this time. Hugh was a staunch Catholic, while his son, Sampson, a notable antiquary, was 'the sorest and dangerousest papist, one of them in all England'.[4] Either their unshakeable persistence or their social standing would sufficiently explain the size of their fines, though the Commission may have punished them more heavily than the rest because of the evasion of the law implied by their presence in Cheshire. Many landed recusants owned estates in more than one county and evaded punishment by moving frequently from one county or diocese to another. Later in the year Chadderton informed the Council that two Cheshire women were seeking to evade the penalties of the law in this way. The Council ordered 'diligent search and enquiry' to be made for 'one Mrs. Davenport to Buxtons and Mrs. Lawton to Batterley or thereabout' in the neighbouring diocese of Coventry and Lichfield, where the two women were thought to have taken refuge.[5] The Commissioners dealing with the Erdeswicks may have wanted to show that traffic into Chester diocese would not pay.

One offender was reconciled to the church at the session of 22 February. He was John Ridley of Wistaston; after being fined £10 for having abused the parson of Wistaston 'at the time of Dyvine Service', he submitted

---

[1] Ex. Dep., m. 3.
[2] I.e. known to be recusants from earlier or later cases dealt with. Cf. the relevant entries in Appendix I.
[3] Ex. Dep., m. 4 & 12.
[4] Report of May 1582, of Overton, Bishop of Coventry & Lichfield, to the Privy Council, quoted D.N.B., VI, 806.
[5] A.P.C., 1581–2, 123, dated 4 July 1581.

c

himself to the Commissioners so convincingly that they halved his fine. He was not actually charged with recusancy or even a clearly allied offence, though in later years, 1588, 1590 and 1592, he appeared before the Queen's Visitors as a persistent non-communicant. In 1590 he was charged with failure to communicate 'these xii yeres', which was echoed in 1592 as failure to receive communion 'these xii or xiii yeres at his owne parish church'.[1] He was thus already a non-communicant when he appeared before the Commissioners in 1581. One who tried to reconcile his faith with attendance at service, but not at communion, emerges, a 'church-papist' (or, of course, a Puritan); limited conformity of this sort was, as has been seen, general in the 1560's, but in Ridley's case it persisted long afterwards, possibly producing such conflict of conscience that on one occasion he could not restrain himself from abusing the parson: he did not, however, risk abusing the Commissioners.

A tougher case was dealt with on 11 May. Then James Apsden, 'an obstinate papist and a person of verie lewde demeanor', was punished severely. 'Blasphemous speeches against God, as his notorious disobedience to her Majestie's laws' led the Commissioners to commit him to prison and then to consult the Council 'what further cause to take with him'. The Council advised the severest possible punishment 'to the end that other her Majestie's subjects be feared, by his example, to fall into soe notorious crimes'.[2] Apsden was evidently dealt with again on 14 June, to the approval of the Privy Council, who referred 'the qualifyinge of his punishement to youre discretion, to doe therein, as, upon his repentance and conformity, you shall see cause'.[3]

At the session at which Apsden first appeared, on 11 May, Richard ap Robert and Eve Woodward were each fined 10s. for their second non-appearance: their fines were only a quarter of their previous ones. Hugh Bromley, a gentleman of Hampton Post, Malpas, was treated quite differently at the next sessions. A fine of 20s. for his first failure to appear was increased to 100s. when, on 14 June, he defied the Commissioners for a second time. Also at the June sitting Eve Woodward at last appeared before the Commissioners to be fined 20s. 'for irreverent and prophane behaviour at the tyme of holye communion upon the sabaoth daie'. This was, presumably, the charge which she had already twice failed to answer. Finally, John Hocknell of Prenton, a leading recusant from the Wirral, was fined £10 for his failure to appear, and on 14 June George Hulton of Davenham was fined 10s. 'for keepinge in his house certain papisticall reliques'.[4]

---

[1] Ex. Dep., m. 4; E.D.V., 1, 7, f. 33v; York, R.VI, A. 12, f 109v: E.D.V., 1, 10, f. 90v. When charged as a non-communicant in 1598 he claimed to possess a certificate authorising him to receive at another church instead of at Wistaston (E.D.V., 1,12, f. 68).

[2] Peck, 1, 103: letter from the Council to Chadderton dated 18 May: it does not state that Apsden was from Cheshire.

[3] Ibid., 106, dated 4 July, in answer to letters of 16 June.   [4] Ex. Dep., m. 4–5.

If the culprits concerned conformed to the law the Commissioners promised to remit several of the fines, 'which our decree, upon their conformacion, we performed accordingly'. The Commissioners were a little apprehensive about this when they eventually forwarded the rest of the fines to the Exchequer: 'praying your honours that which wee have done (as we thincke) upon good discrecion may be confirmed by your lordships' good lyking and authorytie, for that yt greatelie concerneth our honor and credyt in the cuntrey'. Thomas Maddocks, Jane Ball and Eve Woodward all conformed to the satisfaction of the Commissioners and were discharged from their fines, while John Whitmore was discharged of half his fine; very little time would be necessary to show how easily the Commissioners had been deceived by them.[1]

Several of the recusants who came before the Commissioners were evidently too intractable to be dealt with merely by fines, or else they refused to pay them, and they were imprisoned in Chester Castle, as is clear from a letter written at the end of the year, on 6 December, by the Council. It was a reply to a letter from the diocesan leaders

of the xxviith. of September laste, certifying their whole proceedinges with the recusantes at their sundrie sessyons within the dyoces of Chester, whereby it appeareth they have committed certen gentlemen, whome they have found very obstinate and not willing to yield to conformetye, unto the Castle of Chester. . . .[2]

At least four of these, John Hocknell, William Hough, John Whitmore and Ralph Worseley, were Cheshire men, for they were already in prison when indicted for recusancy at the October Quarter Sessions, only a short time after the diocesan leaders had written to the Council. Their treatment in this way marks the adoption of imprisonment as a means of dealing with lay Cheshire recusants: previous recusant prisoners in Chester Castle had been priests.

Of course, other recusants who were presented before the Commissioners would have appeared and submitted: they would be omitted from the list of those on whom fines had been imposed and thus remain unknown. One, however, was probably John Probin, a husbandman of Malpas; he was indicted before the Quarter Sessions as an absentee a few months later, in October, 1581, but in April, 1582, the charge against him was denied by the clerk and curate at Malpas. They stated that Probin had conformed 'ever sithence he was presented to appear before my Lord and other her Majestie's Commissioners for absentinge himselfe from the churche . . .'[3]

Throughout their sittings the Commissioners had probably dealt largely with such recusants as were of some social standing. The original

[1] Peck, 1, m. 11–12, where John Whitmore's Christian name is given as William in the list of those whose fines were discharged.
[2] A.P.C., 1581–2, 279, dated 6 Dec. 1581, & Peck, I, 110, dated 7 Dec. 1581.
[3] Cf. infra, 32.

instructions for the Commission on its appointment in 1580 had emphasised that

it is thought meter that in the execution of the commission you begin first with the
best of the said recusants. For that we suppose that the inferior people will thereby
the soner be reclaymed and brought to obedience: which, in oure opinions, will
be not a little furthered yf you shall at the place of youre assemblies cause some
learned minister to preach and instruct the saide people during the time of your
staye in those parts.

Shortly afterwards the same social distinctions were drawn by Burghley
in a letter to Chadderton, though they were framed with a larger measure
of both piety and insight, as follows:

Good my lorde, now that you are once entered into the way of reformation,
remember S. Paul, 'tempestive, intempestive'. Somewhere you must be as a
father, somewheare as a lord. For so the diversitie of youre flocke will require.
With the meanest sort courtesie will serve more than argument; with the higher
sort, auctoritie is a match.[1]

Chadderton's methods of dealing with recusancy were not entirely
repressive. He made use of 'exercises' in order to improve the quality of
his clergy, but was discreetly rebuked for this by Sandys, the Archbishop
of York, in a letter of 2 May.

My Lord, you are noted to yield too much to general fastings, all the day preaching and praying. Verily a good exercise in time and upon just occasion, when it
cometh from good auctority. But . . . neither will her Majesty permit it.[2]

Chadderton must not arm the Puritan fiend to lay the ghost of popery.
    More orthodox methods were recommended by the Privy Council at
this time. On 7 May the Council wrote to the local authorities that imprisoned recusants should be released on bail and confined to their own
homes.[3] Later, on 28 May, they issued instructions to the bishops about
the new act under which the fine for absence from the Sunday service was
substantially increased to £20 per lunar month. Such large sums could
obviously not be levied at the discretion of the churchwardens: instead,
the justices of the peace and assize would levy them and thus play a more
regular part in coping with recusancy. The bishops were therefore instructed to inquire into the extent of recusancy and to send the names of
those who would not conform to the laws concerning religion to the
custos rotulorum and the justices, so that offenders might be indicted at
the next sessions.[4]

[1] Peck, I, 85 & 90 (the latter dated 23 July 1580).
[2] Ibid., 102.
[3] A.P.C., 1581-2, 41. Proceedings in Cheshire quite contradict this order.
[4] Ibid., 63, & Peck I, 103-4.

At this point Chadderton was called upon to deal with a more unusual case, the

fained visions of a younge mayde put into writinge and scattered abroad amongst the papists and ignorant people of your diocese; which appears to have bene the invention of some Jesuite or other devilishe seducer to abuse the vulgar and ignorant sort.

The visions of the maid, Elizabeth Orton, were treated by the Privy Council as spurious from the start, but a northern Maid of Kent could be dangerous. Chadderton was therefore instructed to seek out the authors of the writing

by the best meanes you maye . . . as well by due examininge of all such as shal be found seased of anie copies of the sayd visions, as of the yonge mayde (in case by feare meanes she shall not be induced to bewraye the same) to be secretlye whypped, and so brought to tell the truth of this imposture.

She should be sent up to the Council in London if the Bishop failed to get the truth from her. With or without the whipping, Elizabeth Orton evidently confessed her visions to be fraudulent before the ecclesiastical commissioners, only to retract the confession afterwards. Later, before the Council, she acknowledged her confessions to be true, after which Chadderton was asked to arrange

that (in some parishe church or open places . . . where the fame of her saide visions have bene most divulged) she be brought both to acknowledge her first confession to be trew and to declare by whom she was induced to retract the same.

Popular religion was too anarchic to be tolerated under the Tudors, though any kind of ammunition to use against the Jesuits was welcome.[1]

Chadderton and Derby could be relied upon to deal promptly with any threat to the unity and stability of the state. The capacity of the leaders of the anti-recusant drive in Cheshire was no longer open to question, as it had been when Downham was bishop. The Ecclesiastical Commission in the county was well led: its work obviously impressed the Council. By the middle of 1581 it was becoming clear that any failure in the anti-recusant drive could not be blamed upon particular individuals but was inherent in the administrative system. If an offender was cited to appear before the Ecclesiastical Commission or Quarter Sessions and failed to do so, the only certain punishment to be incurred was purely formal. The ease with which refuge might be found in an England still

---

[1] Peck I, 105–6, 113, dated 22 June & 4 July 1581, and 31 January 1582 respectively. Elizabeth Orton seems to have been born in Orton Madoc, Wales (*Lancashire Lieutenancy*, II, 123, Chetham Society, O.S., 50), and it is not clear from the correspondence contained in Peck as to the precise part of the diocese in which all this took place. An Elizabeth Orton of Orton appeared to face the Diocesan Chancellor on 29 April 1589, on a charge of absence from church (E.D.V., 1, 8, f. 9).

largely rural, the difficulties of communication with isolated rural areas and the lack of an effective police force all made the enforcement of the law extraordinarily difficult.

Many recusants had failed to appear before the Ecclesiastical Commissioners. The Council advised firmness in dealing with them, 'such as lurk in the countrie and refuse to make there appearance before yow'. They desired 'the precepts to be dulie served and executed, without any fraud or collusion' by the sheriffs and J.P.s, 'as they will, upon there perill, answere the contrary'.[1] The conclusion was probably an empty threat, for in the previous year Nicholas Annesley, to whom the fines levied by the Ecclesiastical Commission in Lancashire were farmed, had experienced great difficulty in getting distraints executed upon the lands and goods of recusants who would not pay their fines:[2] the sheriff was inactive in this, whilst the recusants were equally unco-operative, refusing 'reasonably to compound with the said Anesley' for a smaller sum, and 'doe rather chuse to be imprisoned, which their Lordships (of the Council) thincke no sufficient punishment'.[3] Imprisonment was the only alternative to letting fines go by default. The effectiveness of Tudor conciliar government petered out in the lesser runnels of the administration. This can be seen in the proceedings of the Cheshire Quarter Sessions in 1581.

It was, in fact, in October 1581 that the first large group of recusants appeared before the county Quarter Sessions, doubtless the result of the inquiry into recusancy ordered by the Council in the previous May and the Act to retain the Queen's Majesty's subjects in their due obedience that had been passed in January 1581. This group was prefaced by a handful who came before the July Sessions, on 4 July, at Chester. William Cocker, his wife, Margery, and Elizabeth Cocker, widow, were indicted for failing to attend their parish church at Great Budworth. The jury that presented them had noted, 'What is the cause? We knowe not', and a legal objection to the indictment was raised and the case seems to have gone no further.[4] Previously, in June, Dr. John Eldershawe of Audlem, near Nantwich, and his son, Richard, were presented for failure to attend their parish church, though the jury noted, 'whether he have Service in his owne house or not we knowe not'. Richard was bound in recognisance at the October Sessions, when his aged father, who had been in trouble with the authorities as a recusant for some time, was presented again, but was reported to be dead before the indictments were made out.[5]

As well as Eldershawe, 26 other Cheshire recusants were indicted at the October Sessions for absence from church during the six months from

---

[1] Peck I, 106, dated 4 July 1581.
[2] Ibid., I, 89, dated 15 July 1580, & A.P.C., 1580–1, 103–4.
[3] A.P.C., 1578–80, 446, dated 14 April 1580. Annesley's attempt to farm recusant fines is described more fully in Leatherbarrow, op. cit., 72.
[4] C.S.B., Indictments, 1565–92, f. 138: C.S.F., 1581, F 2, D 12.
[5] C.S.F., 1581, F 2, D 12: F 3, D 25; ibid., Estreats, 1576–99, m. 33.

18 March to 1 October 1581.[1] As has been seen, nine of them had been fined by the Ecclesiastical Commission earlier in the year; they were Hugh Bromley of Hampton Post, Malpas, William Dorrington of Astbury, John Hocknell of Prenton, William Granwall of Brindley, George Garnet of Barthomley, Philip Spurstowe of Bunbury, John Whitmore and Thomas Maddocks of Thurstaston, and Jane Ball of Bickley. The fines levied upon the last two by the Ecclesiastical Commissioners earlier in the year had been remitted upon their apparent conformity: even more paradoxically, their indictment was for breaking the law at the very time when their conformity to it had led to the remission of their fines.

Not only had nine of the 26 absentees indicted been fined earlier in the year, but six of them, John Hocknell, William Hough, John Whitmore, Ralph Worsley, John Culpage and Thomas Houghton, were already in prison (in Chester Castle).[2] Hocknell, Hough, Whitmore and Worsley had evidently been imprisoned in June by order of the Commissioners,[3] by whom Hocknell and Whitmore at least had also been fined. Culpage and Houghton were clerics: Culpage's imprisonment dated from 1577.

The rest of the 26 were, firstly, prominent recusants from the gentry like Lady Egerton of Ridley, Margaret, the wife of John Hocknell, Mary Lawton, the wife of William Lawton of Church Lawton, and Elen, wife of John Whitmore. Secondly, there were less familiar figures, Frances, the wife of Ralph Calveley of Saighton, John Fyncote of Barrow, Thomas Hatton of Stockton, Godfrey Manning of Wrenbury, Thomas Moulton of Faddiley, John Probin of Malpas and Ursula Thickness of Barthomley. Finally, there were the two Staffordshire recusants who frequently resided at Leighton, Hugh and Sampson Erdeswick.[4] Socially, the group was dominated by gentlemen or their wives, who together made up almost half their number. Eight gentlemen and four wives of gentlemen were indicted, along with the two clerics, one yeoman, one husbandman and ten others whose social status is unknown. Like the Ecclesiastical Commissioners earlier in the year, the justices aimed to subdue the socially more important recusants. In their geographical distribution they offer the first indication that recusancy in Cheshire was virtually confined to the western side of the county: three were from Chester, six from the Wirral and seven from the south-west, round Bunbury and Malpas: in miniature these figures point to the main concentrations of recusancy in later years.

The proceedings followed a predictable pattern. The indictments were all accepted by the Grand Jury. Apart from those already in custody only

[1] Ibid., 1581, F 3, D 3 & 10–38. Three Lancashire recusants were also indicted.
[2] Ibid., 1581, F 3, D 61–2.
[3] This is stated only in the case of Worsley, when he raised a legal objection to his indictment, but all four were probably among the recusants of whose imprisonment the Commissioners had notified the Council on 27 September.
[4] The Grand Jury for Staffordshire had evidently omitted them from their indictments, as the Privy Council complained in a letter of 4 December 1581 (A.P.C., 1581–2, 271).

Margaret Hocknell appeared to answer her indictment, though proceedings against Lady Egerton were stayed by order of the bishop. Mrs. Hocknell admitted to the charge brought against her and either then or later promised to conform to the law. Ralph Worsley, however, tried to evade the charge by raising a legal objection to his indictment. This was probably a test case for the group of imprisoned recusants as a whole: as a lawyer, Worsley was best placed to dispute in open court on legal matters. He argued that his imprisonment in Chester Castle since 15 June made the indictment invalid; it was at this point that he stated that his imprisonment had been ordered by the Ecclesiastical Commissioners. His plea was rejected and along with Hough, Hocknell, Houghton and Culpage he was sentenced to be fined £120—£20 for each of the six months they had been absent from church—and all five were evidently returned to prison.[1]

This meeting of the Sessions was in fact only the beginning of a lengthy legal skirmish for most of those who did not appear to answer the charges against them. John Fyncote and John Probin followed Margaret Hocknell along the road to submission in the following May, when their apparent reformation was accepted.[2] Then, the clerk and curate of Malpas certified that Probin had attended the parish church and communion ever since he had been presented before the High Commission for his failure to do so,

soe that there is not any contumacie or disobedience to be founde in him, for the which he ought to be blamed, so far forthe as we cane understand or perceave, but that he seemeth greatlie to repent that he ever gave eare to there persuasions which moved him to absent himselffe from Gode's devine Service used in the Church: but nowe he doth, and sayth he will frequent the Churche ever duringe his naturall lyffe, God willinge.

The clerk and the curate stated that they had previously sent notice of Probin's conformity, but the justices had evidently been informed otherwise: 'he is wrongfullye troubled by the informacion of some envious person, as maye appeare; whome he knoweth not . . .'.[3] The offer of a third of the fine awarded for recusancy to those who informed on the recusant must have attracted many unscrupulous informers, or enemies eager to pay off old scores, though the difficulty of collecting the fines must often have led to their disappointment.

Between this session of May 1582 and the next sitting in July, Thomas Maddocks and Elen Whitmore were apprehended and were examined at the July Sessions. Maddocks was then referred to the next Assizes, by the order of which he was probably imprisoned, for he spent most of the

---

[1] C.S.F., 1581, F 3, D 61–2. What happened to John Whitmore is not clear. He was not returned to prison, for writs for his seizure were issued in 1582 and 1583. He was clearly still at liberty in 1582 (cf. infra, 37). However, writs for the seizure of John Eldershawe, who died in 1581, were also issued.

[2] Noted on the rear of their indictments.   [3] C.S.F., 1582, F 1, D 52.

remaining years of the 1580's in Chester Castle. Elen Whitmore was bound in recognisance of £240 to appear at the next sessions, and the July Sessions also received a report of the conformity of Thomas Moulton from the vicar, churchwardens and swornmen of Acton parish. Further proceedings against him were therefore stopped, and he was examined and formally reconciled to the law at the October Sessions.[1]

Meanwhile, Lady Egerton had been removed from the hands of the justices, having been bound in recognisance to appear before the Ecclesiastical Commissioners. Now, a succession of prominent figures wrote to Derby and Chadderton on her behalf. First, Sir George Bromley, Chief Justice of Chester and uncle of the Lord Chancellor, wrote on 7 May, asking Derby and Chadderton to delay her appearance before the Commissioners for three months.

I have lately conferred with the said Lady Egerton touching her backwardness in religion heretofore shewed, and now doe finde good hope of conformitie in her, in that she can be content to conferre with some suche as I knowe to be well affected in religion and (for their sufficient knowledge and good opinion she hath of them) were able to perswade her, of whom also she herself hath made choyce.

Sir George concluded by balancing his sympathetic optimism with the wish that if she failed to conform after tolerant treatment the law should take its course.[2]

His plea for delay apparently failed, for when Sir Thomas Bromley, the Lord Chancellor himself, took up his pen on Lady Egerton's behalf on 1 July she had already appeared before the Ecclesiastical Commissioners and was to appear again on 7 August. Sir Thomas wrote to Derby and Chadderton,

I have been acquainted with her longe and have alwaies known her in other respects to be very well given and in regard thereof do pittie her the more. I would be glad that, by gentle means and by conference with some grave and learned men, she maie be perswaded and wonne (yf it maie be) whereof I have some good hope.

He thus repeated his nephew's plea for winning Lady Egerton's conformity by persuasion rather than constraint, but with a little less confidence in the outcome. At the same time he wrote to the lady herself, 'exhortinge her to frame herself to such conformitie . . . as becometh her. Wherein I trust my advice will work some good effect'.[3]

Lady Egerton was unmoved, so that by the beginning of 1583 an even more influential figure was needed to intercede for her. On 10 January 1583, Sir Christopher Hatton wrote to Chadderton and Derby; his

[1] Ibid., 1581, F 3, D 10 & 30: 1582, F 2, D 18, 29 & 48; C.S.B., 1576–92, Recognisances f. 204v–5.
[2] Peck, I, 117.   [3] Ibid., I, 122.

formal authority was less than that of a Lord Chancellor, but as the Queen's 'mutton' his influence was considerable. In asking for 'a time of tolleration' before Lady Egerton should appear before the Commissioners, he still held out a little hope of persuading her to conform, for

albeit she hath not hitherto conformed herself to her Majesties' proceedings upon a certain preciseness of conscience incident to diverse of her sexe, without reason or measure oftentimes; yet, in other respects she hath alwaies shewed herself very dutifull and of good behaviour, so farre forth as she continuallie entertaineth a chaplaine in her house, who usuallie saies the service both for her household and neighbours.

But, if this would do little to soften the commissioners, pity might:

. . . the gentlewoman is verie aged and in verie weake disposition of health, troubled oftentimes with sundrie infirmities, the which of late are much encreased upon her; in consideration whereof I thinke her case rather to be pitied. . . .

This frail old lady lived for another 16 years, and at this point Hatton disarmingly admitted what had been implicit in the preceding letters. 'I am earnestlie pressed by speciall frends.'[1] The Solicitor-General, Sir Thomas Egerton, was the natural son of Lady Egerton's husband:[2] what can only be thought of as filial affection or duty had led him to protect the lady by enlisting the prayers of several prominent men whilst he remained discreetly out of sight. This must have been clear to Chadderton and Derby from the start. Lady Egerton's treatment was infinitely milder than that of the other refractory recusants on whom the authorities laid hands.

The others had either conformed or been imprisoned. Death—as in the case of John Eldershawe—or conformity were the only ways to escape imprisonment at this juncture if one did not have age, femininity or powerful friends on one's side—unless apprehension by the authorities was evaded altogether, and, in fact, by the beginning of 1583, when Hatton was trying to help Lady Egerton, the succession of writs issued from October 1581 onwards had failed to bring to heel 12 of the 26 recusants originally indicted. They were eventually outlawed on 25 February 1583, though the ferocity of this threat was matched only by its fatuity: by mid-1583 only Jane Ball had appeared before the justices, to be bound in recognisance to the sum of £300.[3]

The final result of an attempt lasting over two years to bring 26 of the leading Cheshire recusants into conformity can now be seen. Seven men were in prison, two women were bound in heavy recognisances, and one aged and privileged woman was under the supervision of the Ecclesiastical

---

[1] Peck, I, 139.
[2] D.N.B., VI, 579.
[3] C.S.F., 1582, F 2, D 18: F 3, D 46; 1583, F 1, D 48: F 2, D 47: F 3, D 2. Further writs were issued in July 1583 and January 1584, for the apprehension of those still at liberty (ibid., 1583, F 3, D 5–6; 1584, F 1, D 7).

Commission instead of receiving the imprisonment that would normally have been the fate of one so stubborn. Eight men and three women were still at liberty, and one man had probably died.[1] Only four, two men and two women, had conformed. Both the determination of the recusants to retain their faith and the inability of the administration to subdue such intractable people are clear. These factors severely limited the success of Chadderton's first vigorous attempt to eliminate recusancy in Cheshire.

[1] Hugh Bromley was omitted from the final writ for the apprehension of those still at liberty, and though he was evidently a prominent recusant no mention of him has been discovered after this time.

CHAPTER IV

ADMINISTRATIVE WEAKNESS

1582

Sundry of them that be popish are eager in maintenance of ceremonies.

R. Hooker, *Laws of Ecclesiastical Polity*

Between 7 December 1581 and 31 January 1582 the recusants who had been imprisoned in Chester Castle were transferred to the New Fleet Prison, Manchester.[1] On 7 December 1581 the Council had directed the removal from Chester Castle of the obstinate gentlemen imprisoned there by the Ecclesiastical Commissioners earlier in the year. The prison at Manchester was 'more fit and convenient' than Chester Castle, 'for that the inhabitants of Manchester were found to be generally well affected in religion; and that the Castle of Chester stood too near unto the sea coast', a reason that might equally have been held against the use of Halton Castle, which had been the first prison in the diocese to be specially designated for the custody of recusants. Further, the Council argued, the concentration of recusant prisoners in Manchester would be more economical: 'one keeper, one diet, one chaplain and one guard would suffice'.[2] Manchester would therefore replace Chester as the diocesan recusant prison. The Council concluded by instructing Derby and Chadderton to arrange for the cost of the poorer prisoners' diet and the salary of a preacher from the recusant fines of the diocese; these were to prove extraordinarily difficult to carry out. The arrangements had one further advantage. In Manchester the recusants would be more closely watched by the Bishop, for the New Fleet Prison was, in fact, only a stone's throw from the collegiate buildings where Chadderton resided as Warden of the Collegiate Church.[3]

By 31 January 1582 the removal of the prisoners had been carried out. On that date the Council expressed their satisfaction with this and thanked Chadderton and Derby for their 'great paines' in dealing with the Lancashire recusants. The two leaders were not, however, wholeheartedly supported by the local justices, for of the recusants indicted in Lancashire at the October Quarter Sessions, 'in your opinion the one half have not bene

---

[1] The prison was probably the House of Correction on Hunt's Bank at the junction of the Irk and the Irwell, as shown on '*Plan of the Towns of Manchester and Salford*' (1741), by R. Casson and I. Berry. As such it was in Manchester, though the New Fleet had originally been on Salford Bridge. The new prison is usually called the Salford New Fleet, in spite of being sited in Manchester.

[2] Leatherbarrow, op. cit., 73.

[3] A.P.C., 1581–2, 279; Peck, I, 110; Baines, op. cit., I, 234.

presented, by reason of some slackness and partiallitye used by some of the justices', wrote the Council.[1] This was possibly true of Cheshire, to judge by a small entry in the Parish Register of Thurstaston, which, for 1581, lists five recusants and a non-communicant of the parish.[2] Of the five recusants only three, Thomas Maddocks, John Whitmore and his wife, Elen, were indicted in 1581, and at the beginning of 1582 these three and the other two, Joan, wife of Thomas Maddocks, and Alice, wife of William Whitmore, were still at liberty. John Whitmore's continued freedom astonished the Privy Council; as late as 15 June 1582,

. . . their Lordships are geven to understande that there is one John Whitmo(r), esquiour, a verie daungerous practising Papist, who notwithstanding that the . . . Sheriffe hath proces remayning in his handes for his apprehension is either by favour or negligence (wherat their Lordships do not a little marvaile) suffred to be at libertie, wandring and lurking within the . . . countie, where (as their Lordships are enfourmed) he hathe don and dailie dothe great harme.[3]

He was clearly entertaining priests about this time, for Humphrey Cartwright, who was arrested in 1582 or 1583 as a recusant, later told the Lord Keeper that he saw 'one Baret, a priest, at Mr. Whitmore's house in Cheshire'.[4] The sheriff was sternly admonished to do his duty and apprehend Whitmore. While a handful of unyielding recusants suffered the penalty of imprisonment others were either indicted but not apprehended or not even indicted.

Sterner treatment was also demanded for two other prominent recusants. On 21 February 1582 the Council wrote to the sheriff and justices of the county that

whereas their Lordships are enformed that among suche Recusantes as were lately endicted within that countye of Chester upon the last Statute, they have forborne to procede against one William Houghe and one (John) Hocknell, personnes, as their Lordships are enformed, notoriously knowen to be obstinately disobedient unto her Majestie's Lawes, by whose example many are continewed in lyke disobedience, so as if they shall be suffered to contynewe therein and not delt withal accordinglie maie animate the rest; wherefore they are required at their next Assises holden within that countye (to) procede against the said Houghe and Hocknell, as well with their indictement (if they stand not already indicted) as to their jugement and execucion according to the Statute; in the meane tyme to certifie their Lordships wherefore they have staid proceding against them.[5]

At this time Hough and Hocknell were in fact settling into the New Fleet Prison, Manchester, whither they had recently been transferred from

[1] Peck, I, 112, dated 31 January 1582.   [2] E.D.B., Thurstaston, 1581.
[3] A.P.C., 1581–2, 447.
[4] Strype, *Annals*, IV, 261. A note of the evidence gained by the Lord Keeper Puckering from recusant prisoners in 1593. Cartwright, a scholar of Warrington, had then been in prison in Manchester for about nine years and in the Counter for about a year, so that his arrest had evidently taken place c. 1582–3.
[5] A.P.C., 1581–2, 329–30.

Chester. Seven days after the despatch of the Privy Council's letter, Hough and Hocknell were mentioned by name in a letter to their Lordships from Sir Edward Trafford, the Sheriff of Lancashire, and Robert Worsley, the Keeper of the New Fleet. They related that Hough and Hocknell, along with other Cheshire prisoners, Ralph Worsley, John Culpage and Thomas Houghton, and several Lancashire prisoners,

do yet continue in their obstinate opynyons, neyther doe wee perceyve any liklyhode of conformitie in any of them, by reason of the wante of a precher for that purpose, whome wee do verelye thinke woulde doe very moche good in that cause, wherof wee are most humbly to beseche your Lordships to consider. And as towching the said Mr. Howghe he is tollerated and licensed by the Earle of Derby and my Lord Bisshopp and others, for a few daies to be and remayne at his owne howse and then to retorne againe to us, which thing was done to this end that therby (as they hope) some conformytie might in him afterward be found, which not only in him but also in the rest wee for our partes do greatly wish to be.[1]

This was the first of many letters to the Council about Worsley's affairs. At first they show an apparent concern both with the reformation and the welfare of the prisoners, but are increasingly taken up with ambitious schemes to increase Worsley's powers and to line his purse. His next letter, written on 13 April, stated again that the recusants in prison

do still contynue in their obstinate opynions, neyther do wee see anye likelyhoode of conformytie in any of them by reason of the wante of a preacher for that purpose whereof in our last certificathe to your honoures wee then did and yet doe most humbly crave to consider of.

A reader at meal times had been appointed, but Arrowsmith and Finch, two Lancashire recusants, continually disturbed him.

and further towching William Houghe, esquier . . . he is this daye tollerated by the . . . Earle of Derby, my Lord Bisshopp and others of hir Majestie's Commissioners and at the request of the said Earle to departe to his owne house, and for the acknowledging of a fyne by him to the said Earle at the next Assizes to be holden at Chester, and further assurance of landes betwene them, and is sufficiently bounden with suerties for the yeldinge and delivery of his bodie to hir Majesties' said gaole in Salford at or before the vth. daye of May next insuinge.[2]

On 13 May Worsley was able to report a minor success in his dealings with the prisoners. If his first attempts to persuade them to accept readings from the Bible had been ruined,

Since which tyme for the better drawing of them to heare the Worde (hoping thereby happily to wynne them) I Robert Worsley moved one of the said recusantes, Raphe Worsley, gentleman, by name, to read the said Chapters, whoe with some intrety agreed therunto and willingly satisfied my desire, and ther-

[1] S.P., 12, 152, 48, dated 28 February 1582.   [2] Ibid., 153, 6.

upon dothe now dayly use the said good exercise publickly in the howse afore the said meale tymes wherunto the whole number of the recusantes do repaire and heare dilligently.

Worsley the jailer and Worsley the lawyer and prisoner jointly produced an apparent reformation. The scheme was submitted to the Council for approval, but for 'the better hope to wynne them further' the need for a preacher was again emphasised.[1]

The prisoners evidently knew how to humour their keeper, co-operating in his schemes up to a point. Thus, when he wrote to the Council again on 13 October that they 'doe still continue in their former obstinate opinions, neyther doe wee see any likelyhoode of conformytie in any of them, by reason of the want of a preacher', he was nevertheless able to strengthen his pressing desire for the preacher's appointment, 'the rather for that some of the gentlemen themselves doe earnestlie crave the like which wee for our parte wolde as wee thinke moche prevaile'.[2] There would be no harm in a little tactful support of Worsley's desire. What could one Protestant minister do to win over the recusants when several priests were among them? The priests, in fact, seem to have formed themselves into a community by 1583, to judge by Laurence Vaux's invocation in a letter to John Culpage at that time.[3] The straitened circumstances of imprisonment would be turned to strengthen the prisoners in their recusant convictions.

Though the Council wrote to Chadderton on 3 December to remind him of the need for a preacher at the New Fleet,[4] this problem was by now overshadowed by more urgent requests from Worsley. Sixteenth-century prison keepers were not salaried officials, but made their livings from a variety of fines and charges whose payment would render prison life less intolerable for such prisoners as could afford to pay them. Thus, in return for payment, the more prosperous recusants in the New Fleet would doubtless have enjoyed extra and better food and drink than was otherwise possible, private quarters, beds with flock or feather mattresses, bedding, a fire and books; Hough's temporary liberty would have been allowed only after payment to the keeper. Such comforts and liberties were enjoyed by those who could afford to pay for them, but Worsley's prisoners included 'massing priests and others of very poore qualitie . . .';[5] these were unable to pay for extras. As a prison keeper had to keep his prisoners alive for gaol delivery their upkeep presented him with a financial problem. A statute of 1572 had attempted to meet this by authorising the justices to levy a sum not exceeding eightpence a week on each parish in the county, in order to provide food for poor prisoners.[6]

[1] Ibid., 153, 45.
[3] Cf. entry on Culpage in Appendix II.
[5] Ibid., 118, dated 24 June 1582.
[6] 14 Eliz., c. 5.

[2] Ibid., 155, 73.
[4] Peck, I, 125.

But Worsley was receiving no contributions from this when he informed
the Privy Council about the middle of 1582 that the past costs of the diets
of his poor prisoners totalled £252 17s. od. and he therefore requested
help in their upkeep.

The Council responded on 24 June by ordering the county authorities
of both Lancashire and Cheshire to pay Worsley from two sources. Firstly,
they were to use one-third of the monthly fines of the principal recusants;
as these, however, might be remitted on conformity, payment usually
hung fire for some months after conviction, and a second source was
therefore necessary for the maintenance of the poor prisoners. This was
to be the weekly rate of eightpence per parish authorised by the statute
of 1572, whose collection was henceforth to be arranged. When the Council
informed the bishop of all this they made it clear that the parish rate was
necessary in this case 'for that the first may seeme somewhat uncertaine'.[1]
The fines were, in fact, the source which Chadderton had originally been
instructed to draw upon to pay for both the food of poor prisoners and a
preacher's salary, and the uncertainty in collecting them was to be made
plain when trouble arose about the process of forwarding them to the
Exchequer in the following year.[2]

A third way of coping with the problem presented by the upkeep of
poor prisoners was, at the same time, recommended to Derby, who was
ordered to assist Worsley by freeing the poorest, most inoffensive recusants
on bonds when they were next answerable before the law: '. . . there are
many simple persons and women remaininge under Mr. Worsley's charge,
which will rather increase the expenses than otherwise doe anie hurt by
beinge abroad . . .' Women as well as men should be released on bond,
'there husbands undertakinge for them: foreseeing that nether anie priest
or notorious practicers be soe enlarged'.[3]

Worsley's problem was not to be so easily solved, for the proposal to
use the parish rate for the upkeep of his poor prisoners produced 'great
murmurings and opposition'.[4] Undeterred, Worsley went on to offer an
additional incentive for their collection, promising to erect a House of
Correction if he were given a year's payment of them.[5] But the opposition
to his schemes remained, producing further correspondence in 1583, and
even while these difficulties in the maintenance of imprisoned recusants
were being experienced steps were being taken which were bound to add
to their number. On 1 April 1582 the Council ordered the bishops to submit lists of all convicted recusants who had not conformed by coming to
church since the end of the last session of Parliament so that they might
be dealt with by the Court of King's Bench,[6] whilst in the following month

[1] Peck, I, 118–19.   [2] Cf. infra, 47.
[3] Peck, I, 120, dated 30 June 1582.   [4] Strype, *Annals*, III, Pt. I, 244.
[5] Peck, I, 126–8.
[6] Ibid., 116, & A.P.C., 1581–2, 376.

a larger number of recusants was indicted before the Quarter Sessions than on any previous occasion, and for the first time the indictment of a group accused of hearing a mass took place.

Forty-one recusants were indicted for absence from church for periods varying from two to 14 months before the county Quarter Sessions on 15 May;[1] but whereas gentlemen and their wives had made up almost half of the recusants who had been indicted the previous October, they numbered only seven on this occasion. The seven included five who had been indicted in October 1581, namely Hugh Bromley, Mary Lawton, Philip Spurstowe, and John Whitmore and his wife, Elen, along with Whitmore's aunt, Alice Whitmore, and John Birtles of Birtles, Prestbury. There was, secondly, a large group of yeomen and husbandmen or their wives;[2] those of yeomen rank were Margery, the wife of George Booth of Mottram, Richard Cawley and Roger Higginson of Woodchurch, Thomas Maddocks and his wife, Joan, of Thurstaston, and Thomas Sparrow of Bickley, Malpas, six in all; those ranked as husbandmen were Katherine, wife of Robert Alger of Barthomley, John Cane and his wife, Elizabeth, of Wigland, Malpas, Richard Cawley of Bebington, Thomas Maddocks and his wife, Elen, of Malpas, John Maddocks and his wife, Matilda, of Agden, Malpas, Alice, wife of John Nevet of Tushingham, Malpas, Richard ap Robert (alias Thatcher) of Malpas, Edward Probin and Joan, his wife, of Wichaugh, Malpas, Elen, wife of Randle Wooley of Bunbury, and Roger Yardley and his wife, Margaret, of Agden, Malpas, 15 in all. Thirdly, there was a miscellaneous group with relatively lowly occupations; Thomas Benyon of Malpas, a drover, George Litherland of Woodchurch, a weaver, Hugh Wilbraham of Malpas, a blacksmith, and two tailors, Richard Cheswis of Bunbury, and Richard Whitmore of Guilden Sutton and his wife, Katherine, six in all. Lastly, there were two labourers, George Garnet of Spurstow, Bunbury, and Thomas Jugram of Wybunbury, and five whose status is unknown: Roger Haye of Prestbury, Margery Mason, widow, of Malpas, and three spinsters, namely Elizabeth Andrew of Woodchurch, Margaret Bowker of Malpas, and Elen Robinson of Bunbury.

As with those indicted in 1581 the legal process against these 41 recusants was long and relatively ineffective. Only five appeared to answer their indictments, and three of them, the aged Roger and Margaret Yardley and their daughter, Alice Nevet, immediately promised conformity to the law and were then each bound in a recognisance of £200 to appear at the next Quarter Sessions; the other two, Elizabeth Cane and Margery Mason, speedily conformed after being committed to

---

[1] C.S.F., 1582, F 1, D 5–26.

[2] These classifications are not rigid; 12 of these recusants were indicted on the same day for attendance at a mass and only two of them were given the same status in both indictments.

prison.[1] Writ followed writ for the apprehension of the rest,[2] the final outcome being that 27 of the 41 originally indicted, almost three-quarters of them, remained at liberty. Of the 14 who were apprehended 12 conformed; several of these tasted prison life at some point, while the two who refused to conform, Thomas Maddocks of Thurstaston and Richard Cheswis, remained in prison.[3] As a whole, the proceedings of 1582 were more ineffective than those of 1581, for an even larger proportion of those indicted in 1582 kept clean out of the hands of the authorities.

Once more, these legal proceedings throw more light on the weaknesses of the Tudor administration than on the nature of recusancy. Much more is revealed about the latter in the examinations that preceded the indictment of 17 recusants for hearing a mass, on 15 May 1582, the same day as the indictment of the 41 recusants whose fortunes have just been examined and 12 of whom were, in fact, in the mass party. From the examinations of nine of them the following picture of the mass emerges.[4]

On Tuesday of Passion Week,[5] 1582, around dawn, a 'lewd Company', 22 in all, assembled in the loft of the house of Roger Yardley, a yeoman of Agden, near Malpas. All came from within two or three miles of Agden. A priest had been brought there during the previous night by Thomas Trine of Whitchurch; these two had been seen together on the previous Friday by one of those who attended the mass. The priest was a stranger to the company. Although he brought with him 'the challise and prestes clothes . . . and . . . caryed the said stofe in a boodget', yet he was, 'in aparrell not like a prest, but more lyke a playne whomely man abowt XXX yeres of age'. In his relative youthfulness he was in evident contrast to John Maddocks, another priest, no stranger to the company, who also appeared at Yardley's house, 'before Sonne rysing'. Four years later Maddocks was described as 'an old poore fellow and malicious, but no seminarye'.[6] The authorities were much less interested in an elderly priest like Maddocks than in the well-trained Jesuits and Seminaries; the younger priest was clearly one of these. He and a third priest, Benet, a Welshman, were the key figures at the mass, for Maddocks left before it was celebrated.

After the company had assembled the unknown priest was evidently roused from his bed. They were then shriven 'after the old maner' by Benet, except for Owen and Christiana Griffiths; 'he no more wolde have to do with' them when they 'confessed unto they preste they had byn at churche', and they acted as little more than spectators of the rest of the

[1] C.S.F., 1582, F 1, D 13, 17, 18, 30; C.S.B., 1576–92, Recognisances, f. 206–7v.
[2] C.S.F., 1582, F 2, D 21: F 3, D 11: F 4, D 27; 1583, F 1, D 10 & 49: F 2, D 6: F 3, D 3; 1584, F 1, D 9.
[3] Cf. the relevant entries in Appendix I.
[4] C.S.F., 1582, F 1, D 1–4. These four folios form the basis of the account and analysis that follows, and detailed references are not given.
[5] 12 April.
[6] S.P., 12, 195, 72.

proceedings. Their rejection by the priest emphasises the clearcut nature of the recusancy of the rest of the company;[1] if Alice Nevet also missed the confession it was only because 'being hindered with some busynes in the morning (she) came not to the said house untill about ix of the clock, at which tyme the priest had done shriftes and was at the aulter ready to say Masse'. She stated that 'she lyked very well of' the chance to hear mass, as did two of the others. Thus Nicholas Blundell, servant to John Colly of Wigland, averred that he had been notified of the celebration of the mass upon his own 'earnest request'; similarly, Margery Mason insisted that although 'she had warning geven her of the day and place by Hughe Wilbram' she was 'very desirous therunto herself'. Whilst the six others who were examined did not care to insist on their own complicity only Anne Brereton claimed that her attendance was not entirely voluntary: under examination

they said Anne saythe that uppon Monday in Passyon Wycke Margaret Madock[2] come to thys examinante's father's howse to Barrell, beying thys examinante's Godmother, and thyr got thys examinant leave to come play her or make mery (?) they next day at Agden at Roger Yardeley's howsse. And so, uppon Tuysday mornyng this examinant went to Roger Yardeley's howsse in Agden in company with Thomas Lloid, servant to William Brereton, her father, and came to Yardeley's howsse beffore sonne rysing . . . and when she came she saythe that her sayd Godmother tolde her that thyr was a preste wolde say an olde masse and so sayth that she thys examinant dyd (not?) know beffore anythyng of the matter and that her sayd Godmother dyd not make her privey upon Monday anythyng of the matter untyll Tuysday mornyng that she came thyr unto her Godmother.

The shriving took some time, for not until about 9 a.m. were matins and mass celebrated. They were said in Latin by the unknown priest. 'The old Sacrament' was received by the shriven company,[3] the 'singing bread' having been brought from Whitchurch by Yardley and the wine provided by John Maddocks, who also assisted at the mass (not the priest of that name, but the yeoman of Agden who was indicted for recusancy at this time as well as for attending the mass). Then,

after Masse was done the said priest sate him downe in a chair with his surplesse upon and there preached and used unto the audience certen speaches of exhortacion both in Englishe and Latin perswading them to forsake this service and the Churche and to come home and cleave unto the Masse and the auncyent catholike Churche.

Thus, by 'gretly dyscomendying the serves of commen prayer and comendying hys servesse ther sayd unto them' the priest emphasised the demand

---

[1] Nevertheless, Margery Carison, Jane and Randle Lawton, and Thomas Lloyd were never dealt with as absentees by the authorities, and thus cannot be regarded as recusants.

[2] i.e., Matilda Maddocks.

[3] Just what was 'received' by the participants is not clear: 'the old Sacrament' is the phrase most commonly used to describe it, though Elizabeth Cane stated that she 'recyved her rightes and had holy water and holy bread'.

for unmistakable recusancy already made by Benet in the shriving. Afterwards the priest left for Oswestry.

Of the 22 lay men and women who were present at the mass several, including Roger and Margaret Yardley, in whose home the mass was celebrated, were firm recusants. Nevertheless Margaret Yardley declared in her examination by the justices that no other mass had ever been performed in her husband's house. Further, apart from one attended by two of the women who were also examined, her husband had knowledge of only one other; he had attended this about two years before at the house of Randle Probin, a Malpas husbandman whose son was present in Yardley's house. Thus the judicial examination of several of the mass party revealed the celebration of only three masses in the Malpas area in the two years preceding April 1582, and the examinations were thorough enough; considerable pressure to tell all they knew of priests and masses was obviously put upon the examinants.

The mass was clearly a rare event for these recusants[1] and had been all the more carefully arranged in consequence. When asked 'whoo gave warning to all this lewd company to mete and come together' Yardley stated that John Cane 'gave knoledge to this examinant and warnyd most of the rest to come and mete at this examinante's howse the daye and tyme aforsaid'. Cane, a labourer from Wigland, thus appears to have played an important role in arranging the gathering, though, in fact, four of the other seven examinants were apparently told of the mass by someone else. A more important layman may have been Thomas Trine who, of course, brought the priest to Yardley's house, but did not stay for the mass. He came from Whitchurch, just over the Shropshire border. At all events, he was a convinced, and shortly afterwards a convicted recusant; from at least 1584 he was to be a prisoner for recusancy in Chester Castle, where he remained for several years. It would be interesting to know his precise status and role among the recusants.[2]

Within little more than a month of the celebration of the mass 17 of the participants were presented and indicted before the Quarter Sessions and eight appeared to answer the charge, conformed,[3] and were bound in heavy recognisances.[4] A series of fruitless writs for the apprehension of

[1] It is important to set this conclusion beside the statement of a loyal official like Fitton in 1577 that 'the chief of them . . . hear mass daily' (cf. supra, 15).

[2] He may have been a priest. When a visitor to Chester Castle gave evidence, admittedly of an unconvincing kind, about a mass that had been celebrated when Thomas Holford, a seminary, was imprisoned there in 1585, he described Trine as 'havinge uppon him a longe whyte surples, standinge by a table covered with a . . . cloth . . . havinge in his hande a challice or common cupp gylte, lyftinge and exaltinge the said cupp above his head and utteringe manie wordes in Latine verrie lewde . . .', and he was indicted, as a priest, for saying mass, at the September Assizes, 1585 (Chester, 24, 100, examination dated 31 July, 27 Eliz.: 21, 1, f. 121v).

[3] After brief imprisonment in the cases of Elizabeth Cane and Margery Mason.

[4] Of the 17 the eight who conformed were Nicholas Blundell of Wigland, labourer, Elizabeth, wife of John Cane (who was indicted but did not conform), Margery, wife of

those who failed to appear was duly issued.[1] Half the mass party had avoided apprehension while the other half conformed, though none paid the penalty of a fine of 100 marks and a year's imprisonment that had been laid down in 1581 for willingly hearing mass.[2]

In the same month that the county Quarter Sessions had been unusually active in dealing with recusancy, May 1582, a handful of recusants, four in all, were indicted for 13 months' absence from their parish churches before the city Quarter Sessions.[3] Two of them, William Aldersey and his wife, Margaret, had been dealt with by the authorities on several previous occasions; the other two, Alice Worsley and William Whitehead, were the wife and the servant of Ralph Worsley, the recusant in the New Fleet, Salford, on whose co-operativeness in reading from the Bible to his fellow-prisoners at meal-times his keeper was at that very time congratulating himself.

Thus, as in the previous year, a few recusants were dealt with by the city authorities, while 46 were indicted before the county Quarter Sessions as absentees or for hearing a mass. Of these exactly half were from Malpas and its neighbourhood alone; admittedly, the mass party, 17 in number, was from this area, but along with five others from Bunbury this large group reinforces the impression derived from the even smaller number dealt with in 1581 that it was in the south-west of the county that recusancy was strongest. They had formed the object of a greater effort to deal with recusancy in Cheshire than had ever been made before, an effort centred on the Quarter Sessions of Autumn, 1581, and Spring, 1582. It was part of a nation-wide drive, as were its somewhat disappointing results in terms of effective action. In 1582 some 22 counties certified a total of 1,939 recusants to the Council; the 41 from Cheshire were a relatively small number, especially when compared to the 428 from the neighbouring county of Lancashire.[4] A perusal of these returns thus led the Council to write to all sheriffs and justices in June 1582, with three complaints. Firstly, 'some are presented and not indicted', while, secondly, 'but a few (are) indicted, and convicted according to the late statute'. Finally, many had refused to appear to answer their indictments.

William Carison, yeoman, of Wichaugh, Margery Mason of Malpas, widow, Randle Lawton of Agden, yeoman, Alice, the wife of John Nevet of Tushingham, yeoman, Roger Yardley of Agden, yeoman, and his wife, Margaret. The other nine were Thomas Benyon of Malpas, husbandman, Anne Brereton of Tushingham, spinster, John Cane of Wigland, labourer, Thomas Lloyd of Tushingham, labourer, John Maddocks of Agden, yeoman, and his wife, Matilda, Edward Probin of Wichaugh, yeoman, and Joan, his wife, & Hugh Wilbraham of Malpas, smith. Five others attended the mass but were not indicted, namely, Margaret Bowker, servant to Matilda Maddocks, Owen Griffiths of Bickley, and his sister-in-law, Christiana, the wife of John Griffiths of Bickley, Jane, the daughter of Bartholomew Lawton, and Elen, the wife of Thomas Maddocks of Malpas.

[1] C.S.F., 1582, F 2, D 22: F 3, D 13: F 4, D 28; 1583, F 1, D 9.
[2] 23 Eliz., c. 1.
[3] S.P., 12, 153, 65, a certificate of those indicted, 25 May 1582, in Chester.
[4] Ibid., 156, 42.

These weaknesses were to be remedied at once. The principal recusants, gentlemen, ladies and widows, should be dealt with first; those not yet indicted should be indicted, and bonds should be taken of them all at the next Quarter Sessions for their appearance before the next Assizes, where the assize justices would convict them according to the late statute. Any who did not appear before the Quarter Sessions should be outlawed. Action against the 'meaner sort' might be forborne until the principal recusants, whose example the former follow, had been dealt with.[1]

This left little enough time to act before the next assizes, so that when the justices on circuit in the north notified the Privy Council of the recusants convicted at their various assizes held in 1582 only two Cheshire men were included, namely William Hough and John Hocknell, and they had evidently been indicted in accordance with special orders contained in a letter from the Council in February[2] and were listed along with two Lancashire fellow-prisoners in the New Fleet.[3] The assize justices explained that the small number of indictments, only 15 for the north as a whole, was because 'the resydue of the recusantes which have not reformed themselves neither were brought before us by reason they could not be taken althoughe dylygence had therein byn used, as we were informed'.[4]

However, even though the problem of the non-appearance of those indicted was repeatedly made clear the action to deal with it that the Council recommended was not carried out until February 1583, when the first outlawries were issued by the county Quarter Sessions of those who failed to answer their indictments of October 1581. The gap between the policies recommended by the Privy Council and their local execution was wide.

[1] A.P.C., 1581–2, 451, and Peck, I, 117.
[2] Cf. supra, 37.
[3] Hough was stated to be worth £40 and Hocknell £20 in lands and goods: the amounts were not fines, as is stated in his discussion of Hocknell by J. Gillow, *Biographical Dictionary of the English Catholics*, II, 314.
[4] S.P., 12, 155, 35 and 35 I.

CHAPTER V

SUSPICION AND EVASION

1583-5

William Mutton, sheriff of Chester in 1583, and 'a godly, zealous person . . . by commission from the Archbishop's Visitation, pulled down certayne crosses, one at the Barrs, another at the Norgate, a third neare unto Dickers howse on this side Spittle Boughton'. Mutton died shortly afterwards while still sheriff; he had 'soe offended the papistles that they ascribed it to the cause of his deathe'.[1] But, while the symbols of the ancient faith might be quickly cast down action against the recusants themselves was far less effective. Thus, in 1583, the ineffectiveness of the major attempt to deal with recusancy in the two preceding years was made even clearer.

In May, Burghley informed Chadderton that some of the Ecclesiastical Commissioners of the diocese had reported the receipt of £3,000 in ready money by the bishop as fines for recusancy. He ordered him to remit this sum to the Council along with all money received for bonds and recognisances as High Commissioner. The implication that he and possibly Derby as well had quietly pocketed a huge sum that should have been forwarded to the Council stung Chadderton to write in the margin of the letter, 'A most slanderous and shamefull lye, made by Randall Hurlestone, a malycyous varlet'.[2]

Chadderton's reply to Burghley is unfortunately not preserved, but the Council eventually apologised for doubting the honesty and enthusiasm of Chadderton and Derby, who had shown to their satisfaction that the total sum of all fines imposed had been only £757 3s. 4d, of which only £40 13s. od. had been received.[3] In other words, in the whole diocese the equivalent of less than 40 monthly recusant fines had been imposed and only the equivalent of two had actually been paid. Admittedly, this covers an unspecified period, possibly the previous two years during which the first forceful anti-recusant drive had taken place in the diocese. The Council went on to state that further order for the levying of the uncollected fines

---

[1] 'Annals of Chester, 1583', in *Cheshire Sheaf*, 3rd Series, XXX, 32.

[2] Peck, I, 134; Strype, *Annals*, III, Pt. I, 246; *Lancs. Lieutenancy*, II, 133. Hurleston appeared before the Star Chamber in 1584, accused of financial malpractice himself when feodary of Chester. 'He concealed wardships instead of discovering them, and collected appropriate sums from the grateful wards or their relatives' (J. Hurstfield, *The Queen's Wards: Wardship and Marriage under Elizabeth I*, 209). He was an extreme Puritan, losing office as J.P. under Mary, and later raising funds to bring pious preachers into the county. (Cf. Strype, *Annals*, III, Pt. I, 396-9.) A Ranulf Hurleston was a Puritan in the Parliament of 1586-7 (P. Collinson, *The Elizabethan Puritan Movement*, 307).

[3] Peck, I, 139, dated 2 December 1583.

should be taken, while in a letter written three weeks later they stated that the Exchequer processes for levying the fines would begin.[1]

The Council assured Derby that his reputation had not suffered by the dishonesty imputed to him:

her Majesty is soe farre from conceiving an evil opinion of youre lordship's doings that her Highness (having bene, by us, from time to time, made acquainted with the same) doth soe accept of your lordship's service in that country that, next unto God's goodness, she thinketh youre lordship to have beene the principall cause of stayinge of the country from falling to poperye, by the good assistance of the bishoppe, and (the) great paines taken in the execution of the commission directed unto you.[2]

Still later, on 14 March 1584, Walsingham wrote to Chadderton to express his trust in the bishop's integrity. All accusations from Hurleston and others also had been countered and Walsingham tried to explain away the sharpness of the original letter that had been written to call Chadderton to account.

. . . as in all like cases (especiallie when men of youre place are touched) I have, by good and long experience, learned not to geve hartie credit, but to reserve an eare for the partie accused, and therefore writ as I did to you[3] the more earnestlie to stirre your Lordship up to answere the same . . . I knowe, men of your callinge are moste subject to ill reportes from others. And so God, for the best, will have it.

And so would Walsingham, as he added a hint to 'direct all youre doings with greater Circumspection'.[4]

A record exists of the fines levied by the High Commission between 28 June 1580 and 1 July 1583,[5] so that some further estimate can be made of the financial burdens borne by the leading Cheshire recusants at this time. In the diocese as a whole £200 4s. od. was levied; of this £107 17s. 2d. was levied on Cheshire men and women and an additional £29 10s. od. was levied on them but later remitted on their conformity. Where these sums were levied on recusants they were in addition to the normal recusancy fines, though the totals include fines for many other offences quite unrelated to recusancy; most of the fines were for contempt of court, for recusants and others treated citation before the High Commission with no less indifference than they did the secular courts. Most of the people called before the High Commission from mid 1580 to mid 1583 do not appear to have been recusants: they cannot be traced elsewhere as such.

In general, extant records for 1583 are slight. A letter was sent out on

[1] Peck, I, 143, dated 22 December 1583; the sums differ slightly from those given elsewhere.
[2] Ibid., 141, dated 2 December 1583.
[3] Burghley had actually signed the original letter.
[4] Peck I, 146.
[5] Exchequer Depositions, P.R.O., E. 134, 25 Trinity, No. 5, Lanc. & Dio. Chester.

13 February 1583, by Sandys, the Archbishop of York, urging all the bishops in his province to enforce the ecclesiastical law against all evil-doers, but especially the recusants, 'the papal stragglers, those brands of sedition and pests of the church . . . who, by too much license, are made worse; and now becoming fierce by impunity, wax bolder, to the very great danger of all good men'.[1] Nevertheless, no recusancy entries appear in the Sessions' records, while only one person who was possibly a recusant appeared before the High Commissioners.[2]

One piece of evidence does, however, give a fascinating picture of the kind of activities that a Puritan informer would expect to find in recusant families.[3] It begins with a list of 'The names of the gentlemen whose houses are greatlie infected with popery and not loked unto'. These were:

Sir Randulph Brereton, knight, hymself, his house and famyly never come at the churche, and yet, notwithstanding, (he appears) at the assises tyme with the Justices and at Sermons.

George Massy, a Justice of the Peace, his wief, children and famyly are grevously infected, and neither he nor they doe at any tyme communycate.

. . . Manley of Poulton, esquier, himself and his household are vehemently infected, and his house is a common receptacle for Jesuits, Seminaries, Masse preistes and others like, that hide themselves for popery.

John Massy of Coddington, esquier, hath not communycated all this Quene's tyme and he hymself and his household are greatly infected with popery.

Richard Massy of Andford, gentleman, and his household, greatlie corrupted. His eldest sonne is very latelie retorned from Rome and his common speeches greatly advaunceth the state and government of Rome.

(Hugh) Bromley of Hampton Post, gentleman, with his famylie, are very vehementlie infected, and is a common enterteynor of Semynaryes, Masse Priestes and suche others.

The Ladie Egerton of Ridley, widowe, hirselfe, hir gentlewomen and divers others of her retynue resorte not to Churche, and hath for the mooste parte of hir Majestie's reigne harbored divers Chapleins late Bushop Boners[4] and suche like.

Sir Piers Legh, a Justice, never communycateth, his famylie greatlie corrupted, come not at Churche, and is a cherisher of Masse prestes and suche others.

John Dutton of Dutton, esquier, himself, children and famyly (savinge his wief) are very grevously infected, and is a common interteynor of Semynaries, Masse priestes and suche like. They come not at Churche. His eldest sonne is latelie arryved from Rome, and wandereth up and downe the country commending Rome, as doth the said Massy.

William Davenport of Bramhall, esquire, (and) his wief never cometh at Churche, and his famyly are greatly infected. He, his wief and famyly are

---

[1] Strype, *Annals*, III, Pt. I, 242–3, with Latin original, Pt. II, 257–9.

[2] Judging by the list of fines imposed between June 1580 and July 1583, Christopher Davenport of Woodford is the possible recusant.

[3] S.P., 15, 27, 94, undated but assigned to 1579; cf. infra, 50, n. 1, for note on dating. For details of the various gentlemen and women listed here: cf. Appendix III.

[4] i.e., John Morwen.

withdrawen by him to Casterton in Westmorland in Chester Diocesse, where he lieth without comptrollment, to the great hurte of that countrey.

William Tatton, esquier, his wief and mother, with many of his houshold never come at Churche.

. . . Massy of Sale, gentleman, his house greatlie infected, and (is) a common enterteynor of recusantes and others and shuld very latelie have marryed one of Mrs. Allen's daughters of Rosshall in Lancashire.

Roland Dutton of Hatton, esquier, his mother, wief and famylie vehemently infected, doe not resorte to the churche and doe entertein Semynaries, Masse priestes and others that hide themselves for Popery.

The Bushopp entertyneth greatlie many of those gentlemen whose houses are vehemently infected with Popery, and he likewise very muche resorteth unto those gentlemen's houses and pretendeth that he doth so for theire reformacon, but yet never reformed any.

This sly thrust at the bishop would seem appropriate if it referred to Chadderton's predecessor, but the document was clearly drawn up some years after Downham's death, probably late in 1583;[1] thus the implication that Chadderton was well-disposed to the recusants merely casts doubt on the value of the list as a whole.[2] Of the 13 suspects listed three were definitely recusants—Hugh Bromley, Lady Egerton and Richard Massey— but apart from these three, whom the authorities had not yet 'loked unto' (by comparison with William Hough, John Hocknell, John Whitmore and Ralph Worsley, already imprisoned), the gentlemen listed were those who hovered on the edge of recusancy in the early 1580's. The accusations most commonly made against them in the list are of harbouring priests or of various degrees of 'popish infection', either 'grievous', 'vehement' or 'great', which were a shade removed from open recusancy and infinitely more difficult to turn into a proven indictment. Few of them are accused of the crucial action—failure to attend their parish church. Some of them might have been influenced by the increased activity of the priests they were said to be harbouring; still others might have been influenced by a recusant wife or children—four of them, Sir Randle Brereton, John Dutton, William Davenport and William Tatton, had a wife or children who were recusant; but at the same time, since 1581, the penalties for recusancy had been such as to daunt all but the heroic or the fanatic, and some attempt at least had been made since then to enforce the law. Even if most of these men were sympathetic to the Catholic position at this time it is not surprising that they waded no further into such dangerous waters in later

---

[1] The earliest possible date of compilation is March 1581, when Ralph Dutton of Hatton was still alive, while his son, Roland, had succeeded him by the time of composition. On the other hand 1585 is the latest possible date, for William Davenport died in that year. Late 1583 fits exactly the statement that Richard Massey's son 'is very latelie returned from Rome', for Walsingham ordered his apprehension for that very reason on 17 January 1584 (cf. infra, 54); this list may have been the cause of his action. Before the year was out the elder Massey was probably in prison (cf. infra, 55).

[2] May the document be the work of Randall Hurleston, already an enemy of the bishop?

years. However, they were obviously not Anglican zealots, which would be evidence enough of their popish tendencies to some who were. Indeed, the second half of the document begins with such logic of intolerance:

The names of suche Justices of Peace not knowen to be of any religion, and therefore suspected to be Papistes.

Thomas Leigh of Highleigh, esquire.
Thomas Leigh of Adlington, armiger.
Sir Richard Buckley, knight.
William Glaseour, esquire.
. . . Vernon of Haslington, esquire.
John Poole, the elder, of Poole, esquire.
Sir Rowland Stanley, knight.
The names of four other gentlemen suitable to be placed in their room, viz,
Thomas Smyth,
Thomas Bunbury,
Richard Hurleston,
Thomas Venables.
The names of three personages fit for learned men, to which the now Bishop of Chester has admitted unworthy persons; and there are many more such personages. The curates in the diocese are mostly unlearned.
Andford, Bowden, Preston.

Taken as a whole the list shows the increasing attention being paid by the authorities to the county leaders, the gentry, and may be compared with a 'Note of the disposition of the gentlemen of Cheshire, how they are affected in religion', which was compiled about three years earlier, in 1579–80.[1] It is a list of names, 83 in all, grouped in the local Hundred divisions; beside each name is a cryptic remark, mainly one of five—'well-affected', 'neutral', 'weak', 'cold' and 'recusant'—though Thomas Leigh of Highleigh and Ralph Calveley are written off as 'worldlings', and Sir Hugh Cholmondeley's name carries beside it the enigmatic tag, 'No man knoweth, but obedient'; he could examine with the utmost care nine men and women who had attended a secret mass, but he evidently kept his own counsel.[2] In three cases no remark is given, and 'ignoramus' or 'no accompt' stands beside three others, while there are also slight variants to the five chief grades of loyalty and disloyalty. The list was probably intended as a guide to the government in the appointment of local officials.

Three of those listed were labelled as recusants, the familiar figures of John Hocknell, William Hough and John Whitmore. As many as 18 were listed as 'cold', which, as a rough equivalent of being 'infected with popery', provides a check upon and means of comparison with the pre-

---

[1] S.P., 12, 165, 23. It is in an undated volume of papers at the end of those for 1583 and is assigned to 1579–80 in *Cheshire Sheaf*, Third Series, V, 113, where it is printed.
[2] He was in charge of the examination of the men and women who attended the mass at Agden described in the previous chapter. M.P., 1584–5, he was knighted in 1588 and died in 1601, aged 49. (*Local Gleanings*, I, 380 & 407.)

vious document. Of the 12 men listed there, only five are actually included; three of them—George Massey, John Massey and Willian Tatton—are dubbed 'cold', while Sir Piers Leigh is 'neutral' and Sir Randle Brereton is 'an obedient subject'. Then, of the seven justices previously listed as 'not knowen to be of any religion, and therefore suspected to be Papistes', five are listed here in such a variety of classifications as to make clear the danger of the blunt suspicions exercised by the writer of the other document. They range from 'cold' in the case of Sir Rowland Stanley, through 'neutral' in that of Thomas Leigh of Adlington, 'worldlinge' for Thomas Leigh of Highleigh, 'simple' for John Poole, to no remark of any kind beside Thomas Vernon's name. Even if no single remark need be wholly accepted this variety bears more of the mark of truth than the rigidity of the other list. Once the field of legally defined recusancy is left, it is impossible to determine precisely the sympathies of the men and women who were neither recusant nor zealously Anglican or Separatist.

So far, of the 18 gentlemen listed as 'cold' in the 'Note of the disposition', four who appeared in the list of suspected papists have been dealt with. No further information has been found about eight of the 14 others.[1] Of the final six, Thomas Starkey of Stretton may well have verged on recusancy, for a Mr. Starkey of Stretton was later presented as a non-communicant.[2] John Bruen was the father of the remarkable future Puritan, another John Bruen, but Thomas Stanley of Alderley[3] barely emerges from the complete obscurity in which most of his fellows are clothed, and Thomas Venables of Kinderton may or may not have been the gentleman of the same name regarded as a papist in the list of 1583; his father died about 1580 and he may be the suspect of this list. But the inclusion of William Brereton of Brereton[4] and Sir John Savage of Clifton[5] is particularly surprising, as both were leading local administrators who played an active part in the suppression of recusancy. They were the leading Ecclesiastical Commissioners at the time of an inquiry into Jesuits and Seminary priests in the city and county of Chester in 1592,[6] while at about the same time as this list was drawn up Halton Castle, of which Sir John Savage was the seneschal and constable, was designated as a diocesan recusant prison and Sir John was appointed as custodian of the prisoners.[7] He was three times Mayor of Chester and seven times Sheriff of the county.[8] Brereton

---

[1] Roger Downes of Shrigley, Peter Bould of Upton, Jeffrey Shakerley of Hulme, Randle Rode of Odd Rode, Richard Brereton of Tatton, George Brereton of Ashley, Thomas Tuchett of Nether Whitley and Thomas Wilbram of Woodhey.

[2] E.D.V., 10 f. 62v (1592). A Thomas Starkey had been in trouble with the High Commission in 1565 (cf. supra, 7).

[3] He signed the 1569 declaration of loyalty and was county sheriff, 1572–3.

[4] Eldest son of Sir William Brereton; married Margaret, daughter of Sir John Savage; built Brereton Hall, 1586; knighted, 1588, & Muster Master for Cheshire, 1595. Died 1630. He was listed as a supporter of Mary Stuart in the unreliable list of 1574 (Ormerod III, 89; C.R.S., *Misc.*, VIII, 102).

[5] Builder of Rock Savage; died 1597, aged 73.

[6] A.P.C., 1591–2, 324.   [7] Cf. supra, 21.   [8] Ormerod, I, 716.

was his son-in-law, so that their interests were doubtless close-knit, though Brereton's career reached loftier heights than Savage's. He entered the House of Commons in 1614 and was created Baron Brereton of Leighlin, County Carlowe, in the Irish peerage ten years later.[1] It is thus highly unlikely that either of them dallied with recusancy in these years, though the compiler of the list may possibly have confused William Brereton with his recusant namesake from Shocklach. Suspicion had fallen equally upon two other prominent local public figures, Sir Randle Brereton and Sir Piers Leigh, in the list of 1583.

Suspicion and rumour were rife at a time of political and religious tension, and baseless as much of it would be, it is not difficult to believe some information that was in the hands of the government early in 1584. It gives substance to the statements of the Puritan informer of 1583 about Lady Egerton and Hugh Bromley. It is contained in a list of 'The names of the Jesuytes, Seminarye priestes and others, gentlemen, who are fled out of the countye of Lancashire since the last serche there, and of the places where they are now supposed to bee'.[2] The search of 17 January had led to some arrests, including that of a Cheshire-born priest, Richard Hatton, who had been committed to Salford gaol, but others had presumably fled into the surrounding counties. Thus, 'Maddockes, a priest, and others', were 'supposed to be at one Mr. Bramley's of Hampton Poste'; 12 months earlier an old priest named John Maddocks seems to have been a not unfamiliar figure to the recusants who attended a secret mass at Agden, which was only four miles away from Hampton, so that Bromley may have known him well. Lady Egerton was supposed to be sheltering 'Mr. Latham of Mossborrowe, Mr. Worthington of Blanchcombe and others'; there was little else about her recusancy that this stubborn old lady would conceal.

Another rumour pointed to Mr. Cotton of Pell Avenches (sic) and to Lady Warburton of Congleton.[3]

The Ladye Warberton at Congleton doth kepe ane old priest who calles hymselfe Watkenes, but his name is Wyllyam Worthyngton. He is her butler when he is thereat. Sometym(es) he goythe abrode for a monthe or syxe weekes and he hathe be(n) twyse at Rome. Mr. Cotton of Pell Avenches is verie greate resorte.

The writer of these 'Secret advertisementes touching massing priestes'[4] concluded with an assurance of his own accuracy.

Ryght honourables, the moste of these places I have bene at synce I was last with your honour(s), and for the rest, I am most assuryd to be most certayneof . . .

However, no further light can be cast on Mr. Cotton, and Lady Warburton does not seem to have been another Lady Egerton; when she was certified

---

[1] Ibid., III, 89.   [2] S.P., 12, 169, 27.
[3] Probably Mary, widow of Sir John Warburton of Warburton and Arley; Sir Peter Warburton was their heir (Ormerod, I, 574).
[4] S.P., 12, 175, 110, undated; possibly 1584.

to the Chester High Commission in 1592 as unable to attend church, the churchwardens listed her as 'impotente', quite separate from suspected recusants.[1]

Whatever their precise religious sympathies might be the gentlemen of Cheshire rallied to the support of the Queen in the autumn of 1584. A series of conspiracies against her and the assassination of William of Orange in July 1584 led to the threat of lynch law against Elizabeth's Catholic rival, Mary Stuart, in the form of the Bond of Association. This pledged its signatories to kill any claimant to the throne on whose behalf plots against the Queen might be organised. Derby was able to write a joyful letter to Leicester describing the zeal with which the gentlemen of both Lancashire and Cheshire joined it. Even before it was complete 66 Lancashire and 84 Cheshire gentlemen had already signed it, those from Cheshire 'with the same zeal and cheerfulness' as the smaller number from Lancashire. All, 'as being dutefull and good subjectes', readily took the oath, except those 'beinge aged and sicklie or in other countries'.[2] 'Lancashire and Cheshire were not a whit behind other counties in their adoption of it.'[3]

Meanwhile, action had followed the return from Rome of Richard Massey, the younger, about which Walsingham had obviously made careful inquiry. He wrote to Derby and Chadderton on 17 January,

Understandinge that there ys a gentleman named Richard Massye (sonne to one Massie dwellinge in the parishe of Aldford within the countie of Chester, nere unto the citie of Chester), who is of late come from beyond the seas from Rome, and remayneth with his father at the place afforesaid, having recourse to suspected places and familiaritye with ill-affected persons since his arrivall, and, as I heare, intendeth to make another jorney to the place from whence he came, verie shortlie, as may be gathered, to some evill purpose not meet for a good subject.

Derby and Chadderton were ordered to apprehend him and to search his father's house: as he was a neighbour and tenant of Sir Edward Fitton, Fitton's assistance should be gained.[4]

These instructions were quickly carried out. Massey was taken and examined, and in just over a month the Council were able to thank Chadderton and Derby for their work. Massey was to be examined further and they were to deal with him as they thought best. His father had evidently been bound in recognisance and this led Sir Christopher Hatton to intervene on his behalf. On 23 June he wrote to Derby and Chadderton asking them to delay taking further action against the elder Massey. Hatton had been informed that Massey had been bound to appear at the Feast of St. Bartholomew, 24 August.

[1] Cf. infra, 94.
[2] S.P., 12, 175, 4, dated 6 November 1584.
[3] W. H. Frere, History of the English Church in the Reigns of Elizabeth and James I, 242.
[4] Peck, I, 143.

I ame moved to intreat your Lordships to be pleased once againe to extend your favor towards hime; as namely, upon the removinge of his bands to forbear his appearance before you untill Candlemas next, by which tyme, I am perswaded, youre Lordships shall fynd such token of reformation in hime

as would justify such lenient treatment. Massey had been treated leniently in the past, but Hatton's plea that this should continue failed, for by the end of 1584 Massey was in prison, where he remained for about ten years until old age and infirmity brought about his release.[1]

This was not the first time that Hatton had intervened on behalf of a local recusant; he was, of course, descended from the Hattons of Hatton, Daresbury, and had bought large estates in Cheshire, so that he had obvious local interests. He had offered his patronage at court to another young man from Cheshire whom the Puritan informer of 1583 stated had 'latelie arryved from Rome'. This was Peter, the eldest son of John Dutton of Dutton;[2] Hatton described Peter Dutton's journey as 'his long and daungerous travell abroad' and commended him to his father on his return for his 'vertuous disposition . . . judgment and staydnes of behaviour' when he wrote on 16 December 1583. He went on to write that

Her Majestie doth verie graciouslye accept of the gentleman's travell . . . with assuraunce that he will prove a man meete to be hereafter employed in service, to the benefitt of his countrye . . . encourage him to houlde in that good course which he hath alreadie begunne.

The young man had been placed in Hatton's service and Hatton promised his continued patronage, in particular

in case I maie perceive anie desire in him to folowe the leif of a courtiar, yet, for a time, he shall have my best furtheraunce for his preferment.

Hatton concluded by stating his willingness 'to pleasure you in what I may'.[3]

Hatton's patronage in these cases seems especially generous,[4] not to say indiscreet, for even before the delay for Massey had been requested, Chadderton had received a letter from Leicester which ended enigmatically,

Your Lordship shall do well also to let him (Mr. Secretarie) knowe the braggs of the Papists; and by what means (they think) to obteyne frendship at L(ondon, at) the courte. I pray you do yt effectually, for I must tell it.[5]

Was Leicester seeking to make mischief for a rival?

Intervention by an influential court figure like Hatton could, of its very

---

[1] Ibid., 144 & 150. For Massey's later treatment cf. Appendix I.

[2] Peter Dutton and Richard Massey might well have been abroad together. Peter Dutton later married Massey's sister, Elizabeth, and Richard Massey married a Dutton.

[3] Peck, I, 142.

[4] He showed a good deal of sympathy to persecuted Catholics (cf. Brooke, op. cit., chs. xix–xx).

[5] Peck, I, 150, dated 5 June 1584.

nature, protect only a tiny minority of the recusants from the routine enforcement of the law. This indeed went on throughout 1584 and 1585, though from the available evidence it appears to have been irregular and capricious. In Chester city the only surviving cases to have been dealt with by the Quarter Sessions were those of William Aldersey and his wife, Margaret, and Alice, the wife of the imprisoned lawyer, Worsley. All three appeared on 21 January, but Alice Worsley alone on 6 November 1584; they were charged with absence from church and fined 12d.[1]

These three were well known to the justices as recusants and this is also true of 17 of the 18 indicted at the County Sessions in May 1584. All except Randle Probin, a husbandman of Malpas, had faced a similar charge of absence from church at the May Sessions two years before, and by September 1583 had been either imprisoned, or outlawed for failing to answer the charge. They were now indicted for absence from their respective parish churches from 20 May 1583 to 18 April 1584, and so faced a fine of £240 if found guilty. But first they had to appear before the justices; Thomas Trine and Thomas Maddocks had no choice in this as they were already prisoners in Chester Castle, but the only other to do so was John Whitmore, who joined Trine and Maddocks in prison; Whitmore's wife, Elen, was also indicted, but had recently died. A writ was immediately issued for the seizure of the 14 who had failed to appear. They were Richard Thatcher, Margery Mason, Edward Probin and his wife, Joan, Randle Probin, Hugh Wilbraham, John Maddocks and his wife, Matilda, and their daughter, Eleanor, and Hugh Bromley, the gentleman who was drawing so much suspicion upon himself at this time, all of Malpas. Then there were Richard Whitmore and his wife, Katherine, of Guilden Sutton, and lastly, Elen Wooley and Elen Robinson of Bunbury, the only two who eventually conformed. In the train of the first writ ordering their seizure went a second, third and fourth, culminating in their outlawry on 20 July 1585. Elen Wooley's name was scratched off this last writ, an action explained by her conformity at the October Sessions, 1585, at which Elen Robinson also expressed her willingness to abide by the law. Two out of the 14 had been brought to heel; the legal ritual whose enactment in 1581 and 1582 has already been seen was again largely barren.[2]

In fact, the only recusants who could, with any confidence, be expected to answer their indictment were those already in custody. Thus, in September 1584, Whitmore, Trine and Maddocks were brought before the Assizes to be fined £100 for their failure to attend the parish church of St. Mary on the Hill, Chester, during the five months that had passed since their last appearance. On this occasion they were joined by Chris-

[1] M.B., 1582–4, 21 January, 26 Eliz.: 1585–9, 6 November, 26 Eliz.
[2] C.S.F., 1584, F 1 D 19–23: F 2, D 1: F 3, D 9; 1585, F 1, D 5: F 2, D 1; C.S.B., 1576–92, Recognisances, f. 209v.

topher Isherwood and the brothers Richard and William Cheswis, who were each fined £260 for their absence during the previous thirteen lunar months.[1] This is the first reference that arises to both Isherwood and William Cheswis, though each was to spend several years in prison: the fact that such firm recusants could leave no earlier mark on the extant records is clear evidence of the latter's incompleteness.

Similarly, when they were next brought up to be fined, this time for seven months' absence, in April 1585, they were joined by Richard Massey and Alice Cheswis, who must have been imprisoned in the previous autumn in order to be charged with seven months' absence as prisoners, but no record of this survives. Richard Massey, senior, was the gentleman whose house had been searched at the beginning of 1584 after the alleged return of his son, Richard, from Rome. Alice Cheswis was the mother of her fellow-prisoners, Richard and William Cheswis. When all these recusants were indicted again in the following September Massey was, at least temporarily, out of prison and was indicted as from his home parish of Aldford.[2]

John Whitmore was rather out of place in all this, for he was one of those leading recusants of the county against whom punitive action had been taken as early as mid-1581. Then the High Commission had imprisoned Whitmore along with John Hocknell, Willian Hough and Ralph Worsley, but though the other three remained in Chester Castle after their indictment for recusancy in October 1581, Whitmore evidently regained his liberty. Now that he too was in prison he was still apart from these other gentlemen, as they had been transferred from Chester Castle to the New Fleet, Salford, at the end of 1581 and they continued to be indicted and fined for their refusal to attend church there. Along with the priests, John Morwen and John Culpage, they were arraigned before the Quarter Sessions in Manchester in January 1584, and assessed for a fine of £240 for 12 months' absence. In forwarding the 'kalendar' containing this information to the Privy Council Chadderton concluded,

There were also many recusantes of dyvers counties within the diocesse of Chester presented at the Lord Byshop of Chester his visitacion this last Sommer, but they cold not be indicted by reason the churchwardens and swornemen did not set down any certayne tyme of their absence.

Slackness, ignorance or connivance with the recusants wrecked the anti-recusant work of both Visitation and Quarter Sessions alike.[3]

The zeal of one minor official, at least, was beyond question, even though his zeal was for his own gain. This was Robert Worsley, the keeper of the New Fleet, Salford: by the middle of 1583 he had raised the bill for

[1] Chester, 21, 1, f. 114v: 29, 319, m. 18.
[2] Ibid., 21, 1, ff. 117v & 121v: 29, 320, m. 13.
[3] S.P., 12, 167, 40.

the diets of his poorer prisoners from the £253 of 12 months previous to £650, though Chadderton and Derby eventually succeeded in reducing Worsley's demands to a more suitable sum.[1] He was offered little more than sympathy by the government, who were unlikely to give him anything else, for other financial problems were more pressing, though, as with Worsley, recusancy was always a potential source of profit. Thus, as in the autumn of 1585, preparations were begun for Leicester's expedition to the Netherlands, a levy that was normally made upon the faithful clergy was extended to the unfaithful recusants to help pay for it. Lists of likely, that is, prosperous recusants were drawn up on the basis of the episcopal returns; in Chester diocese only two Cheshire names were included, those of John Whitmore and William Hough, each being assessed as able to bear the cost of one lance. Lady Egerton and John Hocknell were also dealt with, however, as the Cheshire reply to letters that were sent out by the Council makes clear. Thomas Wilbram, the sheriff, wrote on 22 October:

My dutie most humbly to your honours remembered: I received your Lordships' lettres of the xiith. of this October and according to the same I have repaired to such recusantes as by the same letters and scedule enclosed I was appointed. My Lady Egerton being my nere neighbour I first acquaynted with your Lordships' pleasure, who being weke and diseased hath dispossessed herself of suche lyving (as) she had to her two sonnes, and therefore not being (upon this sodayne) so well provyded of such horses and other furniture for her Majestie's service as she wold wisshe hath most willingely yelded to make undelayed payment of suche money as by your Lordships' said lettres is appointed in lieu of the same two horses, when and to whom it may stand with your honours pleasures.

I have also delt with John Hocknell, likewise named in the saide scedule, who is a prisoner of the Fleete at London and standeth bounden for his personall apparance there the last daye of this October. And albeit he was lately disarmed by my Lord Straunge and other Commissioners by your Lordships' aucthorisd of suche armour and furniture as the last yere he had provyded for her Majestie's service, yet is he most redy and willinge to accomplishe her highnes' pleasure with a serviceable man and a geldinge furnished, as any other thinge he hath for her grace's service, and hymself withall at all tymes most willing and redye to the same, if so it shall please her Majestie to appoynt hym who humbly besechethe your honours (for that convenient armour is not to be had in this countrey for money), if so it may attend with your Lordships' pleasures that he may by your honours discrettion receave from my Lord Straunge so moche of his said armour and furniture as may now suffice for her Majestie's present service.

And William Hough, one other named in the said scedule, dyed in the New Fleete at Manchester about the begynnynge of February last past, and Mr. William Whitmore hath maried his doughter and heire and hath his landes (at this present) in lease from her Majestie.[2]

---

[1] A good deal of correspondence between the Council and various local figures about Worsley's financial problems and demands took place at this time: cf. Peck, I, 133-48.
[2] S.P., 12, 183, 13 & 43.

The fact that Hough was dead penetrated to the highest authority very slowly: two years after his death Burghley could include him in a list of recusants to be restrained. The official mind was equally closed to Hocknell's protestations of loyalty even if, in 1585, he was enjoying relative freedom, being out of prison on recognisance. Having been transferred from the Salford to the London Fleet he was released on bond in March, when the following report was made on his inability to make any regular payment in lieu of his recusancy fines.

John Hocknell, gentleman, sayeth that he hathe ben prysoner in seven severall prisons these five yeres or thereaboutes for not comyng to churche and that there have ben dyvers fynes streated unto thexchequer agaynst hym for the same and all his land extended for 220 li. and letters out for x li. a yere for the terme of xxij yeres for the payment of thextent. He hathe nothing to lyve upon but that his freindes do give unto hym . . . he can offer nothing nowe then is alredy extended and if he had anything he wold gladly offer it.

Nevertheless, he was assessed to pay £25, and Lady Egerton £50 to the military levy in November. John Whitmore was again omitted. The stated sums were eventually paid.[1]

By this time a method of gaining religious uniformity that had earlier been frowned on was receiving official backing. Having been rebuked for his use of 'exercises' by Archbishop Sandys in 1581, in April 1584 Chadderton was reproved by the Council for failing to make more frequent use of them; 'onely thrice in the whole year' was not enough.[2] Chadderton made amends in the following year by issuing careful and full instructions for them to be held in his diocese. Meetings took place at four places in Lancashire in 1585 and in Cheshire also, though nothing is known of the latter. Thus an essentially Puritan means, the corporate clerical study and exposition of chosen Biblical passages, was used to strengthen the church against the papists.[3]

Meanwhile, in these years, 1583–5, the strength of the recusants themselves was drained by the apprehension of several of their priests. The most familiar of the dispossessed priests who continued to work in Cheshire, John Morwen, seems to have been arrested and imprisoned in the New Fleet, Salford, at the opening of 1583. Advancing age must have made it increasingly difficult for men like Morwen to lead the life of a fugitive priest; it is indeed remarkable that he had evaded arrest for so long. Another, John Maddocks, seems to have been apprehended some two years after Morwen, and imprisoned in the Counter, Wood Street,

[1] Ibid., 184, 61: 187, 48 II & XII: 198, 18: 200, 59 & 61: 206, 8. The clergy and recusants from the whole diocese together contributed £325 out of the national total of over £7,400 (ibid., 190, 74).
[2] Peck, I, 149, dated 2 April 1584.
[3] Strype, *Annals*, II, Pt. 2, 544–9.

where by comparison with some of his fellow prisoners who were 'to be hanged' or 'to be banished' he was merely 'an old poore fellow and malicious, but no seminarye'.[1]

Both Morwen and Maddocks may have ended their days in prison, but an even harsher fate awaited the more important figure who was arrested in Nantwich in the spring of 1585. He was Thomas Holford, a 44-year-old seminary priest.

a tall, blacke, fatte, stronge man, the crowne of his head balde, his beard marquezated.[2] His apparrell was a blacke cloake with murrey lace, open at the sholders, a strawe couloured fustion dublet laide on with red lace, the buttons red, cut and lade under with redd tafeta, ash coloured hose laid on with byllmit lace,[3] cut and laid under with blacke tafeta. A little blacke hatte lyned with velvet in the brymms, a falling band and yealow knitte stockes.[4]

This vivid portrait was penned by Chadderton, revealing in the bishop either an accurate appraisal of contemporary fashion or an equally remarkable power of exact observation and description.

Holford's dandified appearance was an effective disguise and when arrested he evidently refused to cast it off. When the sheriff, Thomas Wilbraham, and his predecessor in office, William Liversage, 'beinge at Nantwyche, apprehended one Holforde . . . and examyned hym . . . he wolde not confesse any mattere of importaunce'. Chadderton was thus able to gain the credit for unmasking him, for

because he was suspycyous, they sent hym to Chester, where I examyned hym, with the assystance of all the Justices of the Peace present at this last Quarter Sessyons . . . and he confessed hymselfe to have bene made priest in Fraunce and to have come over purposely to perswade her Majestie's subjectes to the Catholyque faythe of the Churche of Rome.

Having clearly incriminated himself as a traitor Holford aspired to martyrdom in equally uncompromising terms by declaring that he would not

departe the realme, but that ether Tyburne or Boughton shall have his carcase, nether will he be perswaded by any meanes to the contrarye.

He declared that he had ministered in England

the space of two yeares last past, for so long it ys since his last coming into Englande. Last of all being demanded whether he would conforme himselfe to her Majestie's lawes and come to the Churche, etc, he answeareth that he will not, for that yt is against his conscience.[5]

---

[1] S.P., 12, 190, 32: 195, 72. Cf. entries on Morwen and Maddocks in Appendix II.
[2] Shaven, except for the mustachios (P. Caraman, ed., *The Other Face*, 129).
[3] 'Byllmit' is an abbreviation for 'habilement', i.e., worn on the clothes, trimming (ibid., 130).
[4] S.P., 12, 178, 67 I.
[5] Ibid., 67 & 67 I.

He was committed to Chester Castle as a traitor. In relating these matters to Derby by letter Chadderton concluded with a comment on Holford's refusal to say more:

If your honour thinke good, you may advertise my Lords (of the Council) of him, for he knowethe muche, but will nether take othe nor utter any thynge.[1]

Such knowledge as Holford possessed, for example of the whereabouts of other seminaries or the recusants to whom he had ministered, might have been especially valuable, for he was possibly born within easy walking distance of his place of arrest and was therefore probably familiar with the locality and able to give topographically precise information. He was born, the son of a minister, at Aston in the parish of Acton, some four and a half miles north-west of Nantwich. Before he left England for Rheims he was tutor to the Scudamore family of Hereford.[2] He returned to England in mid–1583. But Chadderton was in a weak legal position in trying to penetrate Holford's obstinate reticence, for, as he wrote, 'I durst not deale by Commissyon'. Holford was only examined before the Quarter Sessions because the former Ecclesiastical Commission of the diocese, granted in 1580, had run out. Chadderton pleaded with Derby to expedite its renewal. 'The Commission was never more needfull, for the contrey is full of semynaryes and the people are bolde and contemptuous.' The authority of the High Commission would have enabled Chadderton to put much greater pressure upon Holford to make him reveal information whose value would be slight if not learned immediately.[3]

In Chester Castle Holford resumed his role of priest, saying mass on at least three occasions for a group of some 15 Catholics who included not only his recusant fellow-prisoners but several Catholics who visited the prison for two of the celebrations,[4] and even Joan and Anne Browne, the wife and daughter of his gaoler. Holford evidently struck up a warm and influential friendship with the Brownes. John Browne, the keeper, was reported to have delivered letters for him; at a mass said in Rogation Week Holford had heard the confessions of Joan and Anne Browne, laying his hands on their heads and talking secretly with them, 'at which tyme they twayne kneeled uppon theire knees'; and finally, when Holford left Chester Castle he and the other recusant prisoners, and Robert Browne, the gaoler's son, 'druncke towe or three pottles of wyne (and) the said Holford did embrace the said gaoler's sonne called Roberte Browne and bade him

[1] S.P., 67. He was indicted and assessed for a fine of £260 for absence from church at the same sessions of May 1585 at which he was examined to discover whether or not he was a priest (C.S.F., 1585, F 1, D 6, and ibid., Estreats, 1576–99, m. 36).
[2] Gillow, op. cit., III, 343. H.C.F. Beales, *Education under Penalty*, 73, lists him as a Catholic schoolmaster.
[3] S.P., 12, 178, 67.
[4] They included Mr. Litherland and Richard Bird, both tanners, Bird's wife, and the wife of a tailor named Thornley, according to the evidence of a non-recusant fellow-prisoner of Holford.

tell his father that he would keepe promises by the helpe of Jhesus'. Similar celebrations, described by another prisoner as a 'banquet', by the gaoler and his recusant charges took place when they heard some days later that Holford had escaped from captivity.[1]

Holford was clearly a resourceful priest. But if he was brave enough to face a grisly death upon the scaffold he did not, on the other hand, welcome it with otherworldly eagerness, for when he was shortly afterwards taken to London by two pursuivants he escaped, so grotesque in appearance (with white hose on one leg and yellow stocking on the other) that a fellow Catholic mistook him for a madman. He was re-arrested in London, ironically enough on a visit to a tailor, and brought to the scaffold in the year of the Armada.[2]

His arrest was a minor success for the Cheshire authorities in their conflict with recusancy, the most striking event in a relatively quiet period after the anti-recusant campaign at the beginning of the decade. This campaign had cut off some of the natural leaders of the recusants, the gentry, from the rest; Hough, Hocknell, Worsley the lawyer, and later, Whitmore and Massey were all imprisoned. Failure to pay the absurdly high fine of £20 a month for absence from church could bring imprisonment, while the wide powers of the High Commission enabled it to imprison any obstinate recusant regardless of any such technicality. This danger hung over those who, like Lady Egerton, for one reason or another, remained at liberty. But the leadership of this type of man or woman, based on social status, was being buttressed by the presence of Jesuit and Seminary, with their steely training and the backing of the forces of the Counter-Reformation on the continent. This vigorous Catholicism would not be rooted out easily.

[1] Chester, 21, 1, f. 121v: 24, 100, unnumbered examinations of William Bickley and William Poole dated 31 July, 27 Eliz. Robert Browne was a lasting convert (cf. Appendix I).

[2] Gillow, op. cit., III, 344–5, gives the fullest available account of Holford's escape, re-arrest and execution, based mainly on Challoner's *Memoirs of Missionary Priests and other Catholics*, 121–2.

CHAPTER VI

THE ARMADA CRISIS AND BEYOND:

THE LATE 1580's

> Bring hurdle nowe, knit knott on rope,
> whett kniffe, with speed fetche fyer.
> In Christ his cause to end my liffe
> it is my whole desyer.
>
> From a ballad in honour of Robert Anderton, priest[1]

By 1586 two relatively novel assumptions about recusancy were appearing in the correspondence of the Privy Council. Firstly, it was being thought of as a permanent feature of English life instead of as a pestilence that must be eradicated. Reformation and conformity were no longer the first consideration. Secondly, if it was impossible to collect the £20 fine laid down in the Act of 1581, nevertheless some sort of regular levy could be borne by recusants. An ineradicable religious minority could be a permanent source of revenue: if recusancy could not be tolerated at least it appeared to offer one way out of the abyss of near bankruptcy in which the government found itself.

These attitudes are clear in two letters written early in 1586. On 20 February letters appointing special commissioners in several counties, one of which was Cheshire, were sent out in order to ensure that certain named recusants should feel the rigour of the law. The commissioners were

to deale with the said recusantes, to delyver the trew rate of theyr lyvinges, revenues and lyvelyhooddes, that therby a proporcion might be made to allowe them that which might be thought convenyent for theyr maintenance, and the rest to be awnswered for the penaltyes they incurre by breache and offence agaynst the lawes. . . .[2]

Five days later a letter on an allied topic was sent by the Council to the sheriffs and justices in all the shires expressing the Queen's pleasure at the response of the recusants to the light horse levies. She was so impressed, the letter disarmingly continued, that she offered to 'grant them an immunity from the pains and penalties inflicted by law, on condition of their offering some reasonable compensation to be annually paid . . .'[3]

By October 1586, the replies to these letters were being considered, though a handful of counties had made no return of the work carried out by their commissioners; Cheshire was one of these. 'Observations in the

[1] Ed. T. B. Trappes Lomax, *Biographical Studies, 1534–1829*, I, 237.
[2] A.P.C., 1586–7, 8.   [3] S.P., 12, 186, 81–2.

63

offers of the recusantes (to be exempted of the penalty of the Statute)'
were noted. The conclusions drawn from the offers of the recusants as
well as from the work of the special commissioners included some familiar
complaints:

> There are many recusantes in divers counties which have not bin delte with,
> and (this) procedeth by reason that there hath not hitherto bin any perfect
> certificates sent out of the counties.
>
> In divers counties the gentlemen apointed to deale with them have not pressed
> them to deliver their livelihoodes, neither hitherto hathe there bin made anie
> true certificat thereof by such as were thereto appointed by reason that many
> which were resident in a countie are taxed onlie according to their proportion of
> living in that countie, though they are seased of far greater possesions in other
> shires. Others are favored in rating their livings and some (are) of so great
> alliance and partie in the countrie that they dare not well certifie the juste values.
>
> Manie have rated their livings according to the auncient rent of assize and
> by that proportion frame their offers and so every little semeth much.
>
> They certifie no other then those whose names are contained in the cedule sent
> from hence, though there are divers others not named in the same countie. And
> if anie named in the chedule were not at that time in the countie they are often-
> times certified 'non inventi', which bredeth a doubt that by mistaking the names
> (as it falleth owt) there are no such men, and yet they know that those men
> have land in the countie.
>
> Manie papistes in diverse counties which come to church but receve not and
> so escape the penaltie of the statute.[1]

The writer of these observations was concerned mainly with financial
aspects of recusancy and therefore concentrated on discussing how the
wealthier recusants escaped the penalties of the law. There were few
such recusants in Cheshire, and during the previous decade it had been
largely the same people who had been penalised again and again. This
suggests that the Cheshire authorities were content to penalise only such
landed recusants as had long been known to the government, that is,
'those whose names are contained in the cedule sent from hence'. Equally,
when Downham had sent in his first report of the lands and goods of the
recusants in his diocese in 1577, the lands of three of them were 'accompted
of the olde ancient rent', the abuse complained of in the third paragraph
of the 'Observations'. There had, of course, been ample time since then
to remedy this, but when William Hough was indicted before the assizes
in summer, 1582, he was stated to be worth £40 in lands and goods,[2]
which was actually £10 less than the valuation placed on his lands alone
'of the olde ancient rent' in Downham's return. These are only minor
blemishes in the work of the administration in Cheshire, but when added
to the far-reaching weakness that the dealings of the Quarter Sessions with

---

[1] S.P., 194, 73-4.
[2] Cf. supra, 46, n. 3. He does not appear to have parted with any land because of
his recusancy by that date.

the recusants in 1581–2 had shown, give one little confidence in the adequacy of its actions.[1]

All this is bound to remain speculative, for the 'Observations' on which it is based took little account of events in Cheshire, as the special commissioners for Cheshire had not yet sent in their report when the 'Observations' were drawn up, and the 'offers of the recusants to be dismissed of the penalties of the statute' were few. Only three are recorded from Cheshire. Lady Egerton offered £30, John Whitmore £10 and Richard Massey nil. Whitmore then owed £200 in fines, a comparatively small debt; John Hocknell and William Hough each owed £600, though death had just released Hough (if not his heirs) from this obligation.[2]

In its dealings with the recusants the government took for granted the importance of priests and of gentry like these. In fact, however, many humbler laymen and women seem to have occupied key positions in the organisation of recusancy. Thus in the late 1580's the Cheshire gentlemen who were in prison were accompanied by recusants of lower social rank. Three of them, Christopher Isherwood, Thomas Maddocks and Thomas Trine are styled indiscriminately as either labourer or yeoman, while three others, Alice, Richard and William Cheswis, mother and sons, bear a bewildering variety of labels indicative of their social position. Richard is labourer, yeoman and tailor, William a husbandman, yeoman or labourer, and their mother either a labourer or a spinster, the latter being used frequently in the Plea Rolls as the description of married women. However loosely these tags may have been used these six were socially undistinguished compared to their gentlemen fellow-prisoners. Alice Cheswis seems to have been the only Cheshire woman to undergo prolonged imprisonment for recusancy at this time.

Only in the case of Trine does it seem clear that he was important in the organisation of recusancy: perhaps he was a priest. But, unless a deliberate example was made of a handful of stubborn recusants of the lower orders in order to deter the rest, it seems likely that the others were of some importance. They all spent several years in prison. On the other hand, other individuals and families seem to have played vital parts in recusant affairs without incurring prolonged imprisonment. Thus, at Easter, 1586, a mass was celebrated in the house of Edward Probin of

---

[1] This is all the more interesting when the composition of the bench of justices at this time is borne in mind. An examination of the qualifications for office, both religious and otherwise, of the J.P.s of the various counties was made in 1587 (Lansd. MSS., 53, No. 86, f. 180 for Cheshire) and those from Cheshire seem quite free from recusancy, even though the commission was due for renewal. Of the 47 county J.P.s at that time (ibid., No. 91, f. 194), 38 were listed and of these 28 were regarded as wholly reliable in religion by the compiler. Nothing more than suspicion of the kind shown by the writer of the document discussed in Ch. 5 (supra, 49–51) can be held against any of the justices listed. By this date at least one justice, Sir Randle Brereton, had been left out of the commission because of the recusancy of his wife.

[2] S.P., 12, 189, 54, dated May 1586: 190, 43, dated 8 June 1586.

Wichaugh, Malpas. Four years earlier Probin had himself attended a mass at the house of Roger Yardley of Agden, Malpas; when Yardley was then examined by the justices about this event he stated that 'abowte two yeres past he was with others at a masse in . . . Rondle ap Robye's howse'.[1] Randle Probin was the father of Edward, so that the Probin family seem to have had a central role in the Malpas area.

The mass held at Easter, 1586, was a relatively small affair, according to Randle Probin, who was examined about it by Henry Towneshend, one of the Justices, on 22 April.

The said Randull confesseth and sayth that true yt is that he was at a hering of a masse at his sonnes house (named Edward ap Randell) the Tuesday after Polme Sonday last in the forenone in the company of Jone Madockes and one Maswen's doughter, with thre or four more whose names he this deponent knoweth not. Being examined whoe he was that sayed the said masse, sayth he was one Hughes, nere Bangor: his proper name he knoweth not. And beinge further examined whether he this deponent was at any more masses within this twelf moneth last past, sayth therunto that he is not advised to be at any more masses than the masse aforesaid.[2]

At this stage Probin's evidence stood alone, unsubstantiated. An inquiry was therefore ordered to discover if Edward Hughes, a yeoman of Bangor, Flintshire,[3] said the mass and if Probin and his son, Edward, and Joan Maddocks of Agden were present. All four were indicted at the May sessions, and within a year Edward and Randle Probin were in prison, as was Margery Mason, who may have been the 'Maswen's doughter' who was present at the mass but was not indicted.[4]

Meanwhile, the prisoners in Chester Castle were brought before the Assizes in April and October 1586: nine of them were those who were to spend the whole of the second half of the 1580's in prison, namely Alice, Richard and William Cheswis, Christopher Isherwood, Thomas Maddocks, Richard Massey, Thomas Trine, John Whitmore and Ralph Worsley, and these nine were joined in October by John Whitby of Aldford.[5] Ralph Worsley's presence meant that Robert Worsley, the Keeper of the Salford Fleet, had at last ended his dealings with Cheshire recusants; after William Hough had died in the New Fleet and Hocknell gone on to the London Fleet early in 1585, Ralph Worsley, as the only

[1] Cf. supra, 44.

[2] C.S.F., 1586, F 1, D 9. Hughes was Edward Hughes, a priest who was active in the nearby parishes of south-east Flintshire (cf. E. Gwynne-Jones, 'Catholic Recusancy in the Counties of Denbigh, Flint and Montgomery, 1581 1625', in *Transactions of the Society of Cymmrodorion* (1945), 116).

[3] Bangor is-y-coed, south-west of Wrexham and only a few miles from Wichaugh.

[4] C.S.F., 1586, F 1, D 10: F 2, D 3; 1587, F 1, D 3: F 2, D 7; 1588, F 1, D 6; F 2, D 6. C.S.B, 1576–92, Recognisances, f. 209v.

[5] Chester, 29, 323, m. 11: Chester, 21, 1, f. 123v & 127v. Sir John Southworth, the Lancashire recusant, was also still imprisoned in Chester Castle.

Cheshire recusant left in the Salford prison,[1] was presumably returned to Chester Castle.

The year 1587 opened with an event that made a Cheshire Roman Catholic notorious, the surrender of Deventer to Spain by the adventurer, Sir William Stanley. He had campaigned long and brilliantly in Ireland before accompanying Leicester to the Netherlands at the end of 1585 and had returned to Ireland to raise troops in the following year. When he finally left Ireland his wife, Lady Elizabeth, and their children remained, and their future was in question after Sir William had thrown in his lot with Catholic Spain. The Council decided that they 'shoulde remaine here in this Realme', entrusting the children to their grandfather, Sir Rowland Stanley, and allowing Lady Stanley 'to be deliverid into the handes of suche of her frendes as she shall choose to remaine with': she chose to join her father-in-law and her children. The generosity of the option open to her was tempered by the command that the custodians should be placed in bond for the safeguarding and delivery of mother and children,[2] but was in keeping with the somewhat courtly attitude to wealthy recusant women that, for others, was already being abandoned.

For not only was Alice Cheswis indicted before the Assizes in April and September with the usual group of her fellow recusant prisoners from Chester Castle,[3] but they were joined in April by 14 other recusant prisoners, of whom eight, including two from the gentry, were women,[4] while, in September, 20 other recusants were indicted,[5] though men were in the majority on this occasion. Once more, it was from the south-west of the county, especially from Malpas, that a large proportion of these recusants came. Thus, at one point in 1587 some 23 recusants were held

---

[1] It seems likely that the priests, Culpage and Houghton, who had been sent from Chester Castle along with Hough, Hocknell and Worsley, were no longer there: cf. the relevant entries in Appendix II.

[2] A.P.C., 1587-8, 4 & 5.

[3] Chester, 21, 1, f. 131v & 134Av.

[4] Ibid., 133v: it is dated as from April, 30 Eliz., but judging by its position between other entries it would seem in fact to be from April, 29 Eliz., i.e. 1587. The gentlewomen were Margaret Massey & Jane Whitmore, the wives of two of the existing prisoners. The other prisoners were John & Matilda Maddocks, and their daughter, Elenour, of Agden, Malpas, Margery Mason of Malpas, Randle Probin of Malpas, his son, Edward, and Edward's wife, Joan, Elen Robinson of Bunbury, Richard Thatcher of Malpas, Richard and Katherine Whitmore of Guilden Sutton, and Hugh Wilbraham of Malpas.

[5] Chester, 29, 325, m. 16d-17. Those indicted were, from the gentry, Hugh Bromley of Hampton Post, Sampson Erdeswick of Leighton, John Hocknell of Prenton, Mary, wife of William Lawton of Church Lawton, and Alice, wife of William Whitmore of Neston; the others were William Cooke of Bunbury, Richard Eldershawe of Audlem, Robert Foster of Newhouse, West Kirby, Thomas Huxley of Bunbury, John Maddocks of Agden, Malpas, Thomas Maddocks of Malpas, Anne Mallam of Grange, West Kirby, Margery Mason of Malpas, John Price of Cholmondeley, Edward Probin of Malpas, Gwen Probin of Wichaugh, William Ravenscroft of Newhall in Over, Hugh Wilbraham of Malpas, Thomas Williamson of Edge, Malpas, and Thomas Woodward of Bunbury. One of them, Richard Eldershawe of Audlem was indicted for absence from church at the Quarter Sessions in July (C.S.B., Indictments, 1565-92, f. 169: C.S.F., 1589, F 2, D 6).

as prisoners in Chester Castle, and such relatively large groups may have been imprisoned on the one hand or indicted on the other because of the current danger from Spain; though this activity may well have been related instead to the Act for the more speedy execution of certain branches of 23 Elizabeth, c. 1, which had been passed earlier in the year.[1] Because it was so difficult to collect the fine of £20 a month the crown was empowered by this Act to seize all the goods and two-thirds of the lands of any defaulter. At the same time it was declared illegal for recusants to make over any or all of their property to other members of their family in order to avoid the penalties of the law,[2] while a new and speedier method of gaining a conviction for recusancy was introduced: a suspected recusant who failed to attend the assizes when summoned could be proclaimed to attend the next assize and if he did not do so he was declared to be a convicted recusant without trial. The relatively large number indicted at the assizes may have been the obvious way of making clear the greater ease of gaining a conviction or of enforcing the new penalties for failure to pay fines, or it may be that the authorities were making use of the new legislation to deal with recusants who had formerly proved recalcitrant; most of those who were indicted in September 1587 had been indicted before the Quarter Sessions on previous occasions, and several of them eventually suffered the sequestration of lands or goods.

Sequestration of their property was one penalty that would be irrelevant to the recusant priests and it is clear that they continued to minister to their flocks in Cheshire, if only from the vaguest of references. In the autumn of 1586 the Council had information that 'Sir Richard Bannister, an old priest, is receipted at the house of one . . . Carter, nere Runcorn Boat'.[3] He may have continued his work until he died,[4] for he does not appear to have been captured or imprisoned, but, probably in the first half of 1587, three priests were apprehended in Cheshire. They were Christopher Thules, alias Ashton, a Lancashire man who had become a priest at Christmas, 1584, and entered England a year or two later, and two others known only as surnames, Jones and Salisbury. At some time between Easter and August 1586,[5] the three had been arrested together in Cheshire.[6] At the command of the Council Thules was speedily lodged in the Gatehouse. At the same time two Cheshire born priests who had

---

[1] 28 & 29 Eliz., c. 6.

[2] Lady Egerton, doubtless on the best legal advice, appears to have done this when she 'dispossessed herself of suche lyving (as) she had to her two sonnes' (cf. supra, 58).

[3] Quoted Baines, op. cit., I, 241, without reference to any source and I have been unable to trace it.

[4] Another old priest, who died about this time, was Roger Hough, priest of Chorley, who died at Wilmslow in May 1587; cf. R. Peel, in *Transactions of the Lancashire and Cheshire Antiquarian Society*, LVII, 184. Peel comments that he was probably the last priest to serve at Ryle's chantry chapel at Wilmslow.

[5] Cf. entry re. Thules in Anstruther.

[6] According to a note made at a later date by Lord Keeper Puckering (Harl. MSS., 6998, f. 235v).

been arrested in the south of England, Ralph Crocket and Robert Wilcocks, were in the Marshalsea.[1] Before leaving England in the mid-1580's to train as a priest Crocket had been a schoolmaster for seven or eight years, spending two of them in Cheshire. He and Wilcocks were executed in 1588, whilst Thules remained in prison for many years.[2]

At this time the authorities were being led by Ferdinando, Lord Strange, who was carrying out his father's local duties during Derby's absence in the Netherlands. The relative successes of the Cheshire authorities in 1587 may have owed something to Strange, who evidently blamed his father for the failure to stamp out recusancy in Lancashire.[3] At all events he was sent a letter by the Council on 7 February in the following year, 1588, 'commending his dilligent and carefull endevour used for the apprehension of the recusantes lurking and resyding in those partes'. He was at the same time asked to 'proceed to the apprehension and commytting of those sortes of recusantes' mentioned in former letters, and 'especiallie of such as should be deemed daungerous to her Majestie and her estate'. Further, as if to deal with Strange's critical attitude to his father, tribute was paid to Derby's influence in an aside in which it was said that 'uppon his Lordship's father's coming downe (the recusants) left their homes and usuall places of abode'. Strange was therefore 'to cause the recusantes . . . by all good meanes to be apprehended and fourth-coming in this daungerous time . . .'[4]

This 'daungerous time' was, of course, the year of the Armada, for whose onslaught Strange had obviously been preparing. Last minute instructions were sent to him in July after the Spanish Fleet had been sighted.

For that those partes have manie not soundlie affected in relligion, who in such a time maie take some courage to grow troublesome to this state . . . if anie such person or persones ill-affected do attempt or any waie make shew to stirre or be troublesom, that they be forthwith repressed in such sort as is most necessarie in this tyme . . .[5]

Rhetorical defences were in fact all that was necessary at this stage. The landed recusants contributed to the military defence of the realm along with their conforming fellows. Lady Egerton contributed £50 and Lady Warburton £25, and if two other leading recusants, John Whitmore and John Hocknell, failed to contribute, it is hardly surprising: they both owed huge accumulated fines and Whitmore was in prison for his failure to pay them.[6]

[1] S.P., 12, 202, 61. Two women called Crocket, Anne (or Katherine) of Tilston, Malpas, and Katherine of Tilstone Fearnall, Bunbury, were recusants in the 1590's; may Ralph Crocket have been related to either?
[2] Cf. the relevant entries in Anstruther.
[3] A. L. Rowse, *The England of Elizabeth*, 449, based on Peck, I, 147.
[4] A.P.C., 1587–8, 361.   [5] Ibid., 1588, 170, dated 23 July.
[6] *Cheshire Sheaf*, First Series, III, 157–8.

However, despite the advice given to Strange, the extant records reveal
little anti-recusant activity in the year of the Armada. At the opening of
the year William and Margaret Aldersey, William Bostock, an innkeeper,
Henry Primrose, a tailor, and Elen Wilden, all of whom were well known
as Catholics in Chester, were presented before the city Quarter Sessions
for absence from church for periods varying from two to 12 months;[1] in
August William Liverpool and his wife, Jane, of Chester, were presented
for absenting themselves from church and communion during the preceding two years;[2] the nine long-standing prisoners in Chester Castle were
indicted at the Assizes in April and August;[3] and the year closed with a
handful of non-communicants from the Middlewich Deanery being
presented before the diocesan chancellor.[4]

The year 1588 was thus one of routine rather than extraordinary anti-
recusant activity in Cheshire, and one pursuivant seems to have been hard
put to it to provoke even treasonable words from a Chester Catholic,
Ralph Langton, whose imprudent tongue was a frequent source of trouble
for him. On 29 July Langton set out for Chester Castle to visit the recusant
prisoner, Ralph Worsley, 'for his counsell in a matter of (Langton's) to be
hard in the Exchequer the nexte Assizes'. But he never saw Worsley, for
at the Castle gate he was met by John Milner, a pursuivant, who asked
'what newes he hard?' Langton's version of the Pinteresque conversation
that followed is worth quoting for what it reveals of the style of popular
argument on religious questions between Protestant and Catholic.

This examinant (i.e., Langton) answered and saied, none that he beloved to
be true. Whereupon the saide Milner sayd . . . What thinke you, Rauffe, concerninge this matter? Trulie, sayd this examinant, I knowe not what I shuld
think, but God send all well. Yea, sayd. . . . Mylner, thou knowest, for yt is most
about religion. I sayth . . . I am not to entermeddle in such matters. Why?
sayth . . . Mylner: wee serve God a ryght. Yea, said this examinant, who doubteth
that? But, sayd this examinant to the sayd Mylner, I pray you, let me ask you
one question. Where dost you think that the sole of thy grandfather is, and the
sole of thy great grandfather? (Milner) answered, he hoped with God. And, sayd
this examinant, whether thinkest thou we have bene in the right way, beinge a
thousand fyve hundred and fortie yeres together, or else but in the waye for these
xl yeres? (Milner) answered, I knowe not, but God turne all to the best. Then
sayd . . . Myllner to this examinant, Why, but do not these fellowes in the castle

---

[1] Q.S.F., 37, 41, 47, 53.   [2] M.B., 1585–9, 16 Aug., 30 Eliz.
[3] Chester 21, 1, f. 137 & 140.
[4] E.D.V., 1, 7, ff. 33–33v. One of those charged with failure to receive communion,
Thomas Laplove of Barthomley, 'confessed that he knowes manie recusantes and will not
name them', but lamely went on to say only that 'he mente Robert Anger and Robert
Fullyhurste, whoe appeared this day' (ibid., f. 32). Each of these two men had in fact
been presented as absentees at the Metropolitan Visitation in 1578, but never afterwards
appear as more than non-communicants. Alger's wife was a recusant, while Fullyhurst
had a dubious reputation sexually. May they have been two unpopular men, possibly
Catholic, rather than recusants?

and such like thinck that they shall taste of the enemyes handes as well as others. No dowbte of that, said this examinant, if yt be King Phillip's quarell. . . .[1]

Milner insisted that there was more to the conversation than this,[2] and when Langton was therefore examined before the Chester justices as to whether he had made any 'further speeche' to the pursuivant he said that

he had red boothe sides of the leafe where others had but read the one side, as some in these partes have, but saithe that he this examinant did not saie unto . . . Milner that if he . . . knewe soe muche as this examinant he would be of an other mynd.[3]

But the justices had not yet finished with Langton, for on 3 August they examined Thomas Watson, a London merchant, about more of Langton's indiscretions, uttered 'about chrispenmas laste.' Watson averred that Langton said that

he wold never goe to church for any man's pleasure in Chester, and toke therupon bred into his handes and sware by that bred that he wold not goe to church for any man, and therupon did eat the same bred . . . by which he soe sware . . . and . . . this examinant did therby remember that the said Langton wold not be compelled to goe to churche.[4]

Whether Langton was penalised in any way for this is not recorded, though four years later his loose tongue was to lead to his imprisonment in the Northgate.[5]

But if, in 1588, Langton had failed to penetrate into Chester Castle to speak to Ralph Worsley, a priest evidently did so and celebrated mass in John Whitmore's room. Worsley, Whitmore, Alice Cheswis and her sons, Thomas Maddocks, Richard Massey and Thomas Trine were all present when a Welsh priest, aged about 30, dressed 'in a white surples, did say service' and three or four of the prisoners 'did receve, and the service was in Lattin and ther bred was such as was used in the papish time. And . . . Mr. Whitmore's yonge sonne did help that preste to masse and did put the wine into the cup and . . . the preste lift(ed) it up over his head and . . . the preste was in white frece.' Ralph Worsley evidently used his lawyer's Latin to say the service on occasion, for when the evidence about the mass was given by Anne Dewsbury, niece of Alice Cheswis, she contrasted the 'diverse times' she attended service said by Worsley with the one occasion when she heard a mass said by a priest during one of her visits to her aunt in the Castle. She 'sometimes went into the castle to her awnt, Alis Cheswis, who is a recusant and a prisoner there, and used to buy victualles for her and Madock and Trine'.[6]

[1] Q.S.F., 37, 23, f. 1.   [2] Ibid., f. 2.   [3] Ibid., f. iv.
[4] Ibid., f. 24.   [5] Cf. infra, 105.
[6] Q.S.E., 4, f. 22. This is the record of an examination of Anne Dewsbury made in February, 1592. She then described this mass as having taken place 'about four yeres paste', dating it thereby c. 1588.

Anne Dewsbury gave evidence about the mass some four years after it took place; she stated that the underkeeper of the Castle was then John Taylor, but by the time the authorities knew of his slackness it was unnecessary to bring him to book. He had by then been condemned to death for a much more serious offence, the murder of John Hocknell, who came under Taylor's care when he was sentenced at the Assizes in September 1589, for the dissemination of false prophecies. It was then alleged that on 1 September 1589, at Hooton, Hocknell had said to Sir Rowland Stanley

that he had redd a prophesie wherein he found the letter G, whereof he cold make noe construction except it shold be that Queene Marie had a son called George. Whereof the prophesie made mencion as though he shold goe to Constantinople and theire fyght and lose his lief against the Sarizens.[1]

The injudicious suggestion that Mary Tudor had given birth to a male heir, even one who had cleared the way for Elizabeth by dying a Crusader's death, was construed as an attempt to stir up some rebellion and brought Hocknell a sentence of one year's imprisonment;[2] the authorities may have been glad to shut up so obstinate and eccentric a recusant on a charge that was clearly political. He joined 11 other recusants who were imprisoned in Chester Castle at this time.[3]

Hocknell was tactless not only in what he said but also in his choice of Sir Rowland Stanley as confidant. As Sir Rowland was the father of three well known Roman Catholic sons, William, the betrayer of Deventer, Edward, who served with him, and John, a Jesuit, he may have found it essential to disavow the sympathy that Hocknell assumed he would show far more vehemently and publicly than would have been necessary had he been the father of three eminent Anglicans. Hocknell paid a heavy price for all this, for he died in Chester Castle on 23 April 1590, from an injury inflicted by his gaoler, John Taylor, with a pitchfork. The circumstances which led to this tragedy remain unknown, but at the Assizes of 27 April, Taylor was found guilty of murder and sentenced to death.[4] Two and a half centuries later a Cheshire writer, George Bakewell, was to use Taylor's death by hanging as material in a pamphlet on 'The Impolicy of Capital Punishment Considered':[5] Hocknell's equally squalid end stands as a stronger indictment of religious persecution, however political its complexion.

[1] Chester, 29. 328, m. 18d.
[2] Under 5 Eliz., c. 15, an Act against the dissemination of false prophecies, whose maximum penalty was one year's imprisonment and a £10 fine.
[3] The usual nine prisoners in Chester Castle were accompanied by James and John (?) Longton when they were indicted at the Assizes in September 1589 (Chester 21, 1, f. 142v: though dated as September, 30 Eliz., judging by its position in the sequence of entries it would seem to be from September, 31 Eliz., i.e. 1589).
[4] Chester, loc. cit.
[5] Published Manchester, 1857. It is referred to in *Cheshire Notes and Queries*, II, 243.

Hocknell's death doubtless drew attention to the laxity and inefficiency of Taylor's regime, though even before the murder took place conditions in Chester Castle had been fastened on as the gravest weakness in the control of recusancy in Cheshire. In February 1590, 'An Information touching the Recusants of Lancashire', in which Cheshire conditions were also described, was drawn up.[1] Its writer asserted that in Lancashire few of the 800 recusants indicted actually stood trial because of kinship with and generous treatment by the justices, whose wives and children were often recusants: thus the county 'is mightely infected with popery'. The writer went on to describe Cheshire:

> The estate of that countie of Chester is much like to that of Lancashire, but not sore wounded with popery as is Lancashire. A direction for the owne will serve both the counties.
> There is one thing chiefly to be respected and with speede to be redressed. That is that those recusantes which lie in the Castell of Chester (uppon executions for greate somes of money forfeited to hir Majestie uppon that statute) may not have libertie to goe and ryde abroad at their pleasures as they now have, and not anie offence taken thereat at all, so that their imprisonment is to them libertie where they should be detayned untill the forfeitures were paied to hir Majestie.
> The keeper of the Castell, or the Constable of the same at Chester, for profitt neglecteth his dutie in this behalfe.
> It hath been of late vehemently suspected that massing preistes and suchlike resorte at their pleasures to the recusantes in the Castell of Chester. There is no restraint made of anie person at all by the keeper there.

This description of prison conditions is clearly substantiated by the events just described—the mass of 1588, which John Taylor was no doubt bribed to allow, and the murder of Hocknell, which is all of a piece with the general negligence. Like his predecessor, John Browne, Taylor had winked at Catholic practices. Similarly, the accusation that the authorities punished only a few of the recusants is largely borne out by the extant Quarter Sessions and Assize cases that have already been described. Along with the more general 'Observations in the offers of the recusantes'[2] this document appears to give an accurate account of the enforcement of the anti-recusant laws in Cheshire in the late 1580's.

Further confirmation of the picture presented in these documents is given in the correspondence between the Privy Council and the county authorities in 1590. Throughout there is a note of urgency. Spain was fitting out a new Armada, so that the recusants were seen as a military embarrassment. A general letter of 8 March to the Deputy Lieutenants of all counties set the tone.[3] It divided recusants into three groups, the 'principal recusants', the 'inferiour sorte', and those in between. After

---

[1] Cotton MSS., Titus B III, No. 20, f. 65.
[2] Supra, 63-4.
[3] A.P.C., 1589-90, 406.

F

asking for a return of the names and means of the principal and middling recusants it went on to state that

There are alsoe diverse of the inferiour sorte that are assessed at noe fines or penalties for theire recusancie whoe are likewise as evell affected in religion as the rest.

The Deputy Lieutenants were to send in their

names, disposicion and meanes, to the end there maie be order taken for the disarminge of them and the arming of other her Majestie's good subjects with their furniture.

At worst, where such a recusant possessed no armour or weapons, two or three might together furnish arms for a neighbour.[1]

As Sir William Stanley was expected to invade Anglesey, specific instructions were issued for Lancashire and Cheshire as adjoining counties and as areas where

the said Stanley doth assure himself, as we are likewise advertised, of good aide and assurance yf some timely prevencion be not used. And whereas also we are informed that there are many Seminaries and other evill affected persons in the said counties of Lancashire and Cheshire and the north parts of Lancashire, which are not so well looked unto as in respect of these doubtfull and daungerous tymes in reason they ought to be.

The Earl of Derby was ordered to commit to a safe place 'such suspected persons within your jurisdiction (and) aucthoritie as be of good habilitie and whose liberty maie breed daunger to the State'.[2]

Thus much of the correspondence of the Privy Council with the local authorities was a response to the threat of invasion. Alongside this the routine repression of recusancy was discussed, though with an urgency that reflected the atmosphere of crisis. This correspondence began in June 1589, when the Council advised Chadderton on how to make his visitation, due later in the year, effective. They wrote that they were

given to understand that there be within that countrie soundrie obstinate recusantes against whom noe execucion is used for lacke that the mynisters doe not in their severall cares presente them as they are by the statute prescribed.

Like the justices the clergy failed to take the most elementary steps to crush recusancy. The bishop was therefore ordered to make his clergy swear on oath to observe their duty in presenting recusants and to inquire into children instructed by papist teachers.[3]

This insistence on greater thoroughness in bringing recusants before the

[1] At least one Cheshire recusant, Hugh Erdeswick, was ordered to appear before the Council, on 29 March, 'to receave such order as was prescrybed to the rest of the recusants of the severall countyes', but because he was too ill to do so was instead confined under bond to his house at Leighton (A.P.C., 1590, 34).

[2] A.P.C., 1590, 155, dated 24 May.

[3] Ibid., 1588-9, 309-10.

authorities had no apparent effect. Not one recusant was named as such in the presentments to the visitors and only a handful of charges that might be related to recusancy were dealt with. Thomas Huxley and his wife, already excommunicate, were presented for not coming to church, as was Mary Lawton, whose husband appeared on her behalf before the visitors, who referred the case to the bishop. Ralph Langton and his wife were presented for absence from church and failure to receive the communion, and William Aire and his wife, Margaret, as non-communicants only: all four were ordered to comply with the law. These were all charged before the lay or ecclesiastical authorities on some other occasion as recusants or suspected recusants, or they were the wives or husbands of recusants; their presentment was as far as the visitation went in dealing with the problem of recusancy.[1]

Whatever the records of the visitation show, Chadderton was clearly perturbed by the extent of recusancy in his diocese, and he communicated his disquiet to the Council. An answer was delayed because of Walsingham's fatal illness at this time and it was not until after the Secretary's death on 6 April 1590, that Chadderton received his reply. Then, on 16 April, the Council informed him that

We have seene and read a letter written by your Lordship to Mr. Secretarie Walsingham concerninge divers abuses commytted in that your Diocesse and such recusantes as were presented in your Lordship's laste yeere's vysytacion. Whereunto you could not any aunswere receave from the said Mr. Secretarie by reason of his sicknes, who sythence is deceased . . . Forasmuch as we are not well acquaynted with the partycularyties of the contemptes, abuses, or the quallyty of the persons by your Lordship complayned of, we have thought good to praie and requyre your Lordship to enforme us with convenient expedicion at large as well of the names, livelyhoodes and dependaunce of the said recusantes, as of the contemptes and abuses comytted within your Lordship's said Dioces specyfied in your Lordship's said letter, that we take convenyente order for the repressing of those insolencies without delaie. And if your Lordship shall desyre to have the assistance of any gentlemen of calling therabouts to joyne with you for the examyninge, discoverie and punnyshment of those abuses, to advertyse us therof that we may give dyreccion for the same accordinglie.[2]

Evidently Chadderton was able to reply with a list of over 700 Lancashire and over 200 Cheshire names, but, despite its length, this was unsatisfactory, for the bishop had not 'sett downe the dwellinge places and quallities and livelihoode of the persons that wee might have ben more particulerly enformed of theire estates', as the Council wrote on 25 July.[3] Nevertheless, as recusancy in Lancashire and Cheshire was 'dailie increasing', an all-out attack was to be made at the next Assizes, about which the Council proceeded to send the most detailed instructions.[4]

[1] E.D.V., 1, 8, ff. 85v, 114, 128 & 136v. Cf. Appendix I for persons named.
[2] A.P.C., 1590, 66.   [3] Ibid., 342.
[4] Ibid., 335–42.

Every loophole by which the recusants escaped punishment was to be stopped up. In the first place, a new form of indictment was to be used; it had been drawn up expressly to avoid the flaws which made escape from punishment possible. Then, Derby was specially asked to be present or at least to confer with the bishop and the justices beforehand in order to make sure that ample information about the recusants was available. Half a score principal recusants should be made an example of by being sent before the Council, while the Bishop should provide instruction for their reformation. Nor should all this be merely an isolated skirmish, for the Justices of Assize were to command the J.P.s to see that the indictments continued to come up at every Quarter Sessions, while the principal convicted recusants who failed to conform within a year should be bound to good behaviour and disarmed.

Schedules of those in Chester Castle and the gaols at Lancaster and Manchester were to be drawn up by their keepers. These would show the causes of imprisonment and the amount of fines paid or outstanding. Negligence in allowing the visits of friends, who merely confirmed the perversity of the prisoners, should be ended along with all other liberties.

This considered instruction was contained in three separate letters of overlapping content, one to the Justices of Assize for Lancashire, another to Derby and the third to Chadderton. All were especially enjoined to be strict. Thus, in the letter to the justices the full penalties of the law were stressed, while Derby was told that 'it is more than time to take some speedy and strict order to see (the recusants) reformed or severely corrected and punished'. He was at least praised for setting a good example in this himself: 'We doe perceave the accustomed great care which your Lordship doth use in those thinges that concerne the publique service, and . . . we cannot but greatly commend the good order your Lordship hath lately begun to take amongst your owne servauntes, tenantes and retayners to bring them to conformitie or to see them punished.' Derby's zeal in this was compared to Chadderton's failure to provide anything but the names of the recusants in the lists he had sent to the Council, and sorrow was expressed to him at the increase in the number of recusants shown by these lists, 'and yet the nomber doubeted to be farre greater not to us certyfied', the Council pointedly added elsewhere. He was told that it was 'more than tyme to take some more sever course to see them punished, seeing the remysnes that hath ben used against them hath brought forth these nombers of recusants'. Chadderton had clearly annoyed the Council, so that the line they took in writing to him harked back to the days of his slack predecessor, Downham. It was Derby who was praised as the thorough and virtuous administrator.

The Bishop was expressly told to exercise the care now being demanded in Lancashire at the next Chester Assizes, about which he was to confer with the Solicitor-General when he came into those parts. In fact, a somewhat higher proportion of the 200 Cheshire recusants than of the 700 from Lancashire appear to have been convicted. Fifty-one from Cheshire and 126 from Lancashire had total fines of £15,440 and £21,953 11s. 8d. respectively levied upon them.[1]

A mere quarter of the Cheshire recusants known to the authorities had thus been convicted and the Privy Council had regarded the actual number as 'farre greater' than the known 200. But the document containing the information about the number convicted quietly conveys a harsher ignominy for the authorities than that.

Theare hath gone out Commissions into the saide Counties of Chester and Lancashire to finde goodes, landes and tenementes apon the saide convictions and the saide recusantes theare. But nought hath bene retorned upon theim all because manye of the said recusantes be indighted as the wifes of men and the daughters of men, and many be indighted as spinsters, yeomen, laborers, servingmen, priestes and men of occupacion. And sondrie of the said recusantes beknowen languid in prisona. So as of the said debtes and convictions to the Courte's knowledge there is not yet anye thinge leviable.

The only measure of success that could be claimed was in relation to six earlier convictions involving total fines of £260, on which

goodes are seased to the sum of £27 and landes to the sum of £117. 13. 4d. that will pay the saide debt in time if the said recusantes live so longe.

[1] Lansd. MSS., 64, no. 8, f. 21, 'Convictions and Debts of Recusants Com. Cestr. Lancastr. & Eborac., 1590'. Dated December 1590, this document is probably a summary of the work of the assizes in that year.

CHAPTER VII

THE EARLY 1590's

The first thing . . . in skilful cures is the knowledge of the part affected; the next is of the evil which doth affect it; the last is not only of the kind but also of the measure of contrary things whereby to remove it.

Hooker, *Laws of Ecclesiastical Polity*

At the end of 1591 a detailed report on the religious situation in Lancashire and Cheshire was submitted to the Privy Council by the Council of the North.[1] It provides a convenient introduction to Cheshire recusancy in the early 1590's, though at first glance it seems to spring from a later time, that of the Lancashire justices who were to lead James I to issue his Declaration of Sports a quarter of a century later, for it is passionate in its condemnation of 'the multitude of bastards and drunkards . . . many lusty vagrants . . . cockfights and other unlawful games'. The writer laid the blame for these moral lapses and for the extent of recusancy squarely on the clerical and lay authorities. Thus, on the one hand,

the preachers are few, most of the parsons unlearned, many of those learned not resident, and diverse unlearned daily admitted into very good benefices by the Bishop . . . the people who resort to church are so few that preachers who were determined to preach on Sundays and holidays have refrained, for lack of auditors; the people so swarm in the streets and alehouses during service time that many churches have only present the curate and his clerk, and open markets are kept in service time.

On the other hand, some of the justices and ecclesiastical commissioners did not merely wink at the abuses but even encouraged them:

Cockfights and other unlawful games are tolerated on Sundays and holidays, during divine service, at which justices of the peace and some Ecclesiastical Commissioners are often present (while) some of the Commissioners and Justices . . . have grants of the goods and lands of the recusants so that the recusants may not forfeit them, in case they are touched for any illegal cause . . . some of the coroners and justices and their families do not frequent church, and many of them have not communicated at the Lord's supper since the beginning of her Majesty's reign . . . the youth are for the most part trained up by such as profess papistry; no examination is had of schools and schoolmasters. The proclamation for the apprehension of seminaries, Jesuits and mass priests, and for calling home children from parts beyond the sea is not executed, nor are their Lordships' letters commanding the justices to call before them quarterly all parsons, vicars, curates, churchwardens and swornmen, and examine them on oath how the

---

[1] S.P., 12, 240, 138. It mentions the proclamation against Jesuits and seminaries issued late in 1591, and appears to date from a short time after that.

statutes of 1 and 23 Elizabeth as to resorting to churches are obeyed, that at the next quarter sessions information may be given against the offenders . . . the seminaries in many places have lately offered disputations against the settled religion, but nothing has been said to them.

Yet looking beyond the writer's pity for the preaching clergy and hostility to easy-going justices and commissioners, it is clear that recusancy had developed a vitality of its own in opposition to 'the settled religion'. Priests were active, carrying out marriages and baptisms 'in corners', and refusing to divulge information when apprehended,

so that the state of the country is not thoroughly known, and until their haunts have been discovered it is impossible to reform it. . . . The recusants have spies about the Commissioners to give intelligence when anything is intended against them, and some of the bailiffs attending upon the Commissioners are entertained for that purpose, so that the recusants may shift out of the way and avoid being apprehended.

The writer finally stated that even though 'great sums have been levied under pretence of the commission' to cure both moral laxity and recusancy, 'the counties are in worse case than before, and the number of those who do not resort to divine service greater'.

Of course, as a description of and a commentary upon conditions in Cheshire this report must be treated with great care. Not only should allowance be made for the writer's Puritanism, but, as with so much evidence that consists of generalisations about both Lancashire and Cheshire, the writer seems to have known most about Lancashire; in the concluding paragraph of the letter he comments on the difficulty of keeping the other northern counties in order so long as recusancy was so widespread in Lancashire, while the document that follows it in the State Papers[1] was written by the same person as the one under discussion and was about a purely Lancashire matter: the writer was clearly less familiar with Cheshire.

Fortunately, his generalisations can be tested against five important sources for the years 1590–3. The records of two visitations (the Metropolitan Visitation of 1590[2] and the Diocesan Visitation of 1592[3]), the indictments for recusancy at the Assizes,[4] the first Recusant Roll,[5] and the records of the examinations carried out by the Ecclesiastical Commission for Chester City at the beginning of 1592 in an attempt to enforce the proclamation against Jesuits and Seminaries of October 1591,[6] are all extant. The analysis of these documents tempers the pessimism of the report of the Council of the North so far as Cheshire is concerned.

[1] Ibid., 240, 139. [2] York, R.VI, A 12.
[3] E.D.V., 1, 10, 1592–3.
[4] Chester, 21, 1, f. 156v ff.: Chester, 29, 334, m. 11 & 17.
[5] Exchequer L.T.R., 22A, 377, Pipe Roll Series, 1, m. 6, printed in C.R.S., XVIII. Referred to hereafter as R.R. (Recusant Roll).
[6] Q.S.E., 4.

In so far as the Visitors dealt with a wide variety of other matters besides recusancy, which together reveal a good deal of the state of the church, these help to fill in the background to recusancy and provide a check upon the report of the Council of the North. In marked contrast to its sweeping assertions there were, however, few cases of clerical absenteeism before either of the Visitations, hardly any churches where the service was not said, the sacraments were not administered or in which preaching was wholly neglected.[1] Further, if in 1590 it was reported of the parish of Great Budworth that two of the swornmen had suppressed the presentments from their parish,[2] while in 1592 the churchwardens of St. Mary's, Chester, were presented for failing to take the names of absentees from service,[3] these were isolated cases in presentments from 101 parishes and chapelries in 1590, and 106 in 1592. Only one church was reported as being in obvious need of repair in 1590,[4] though the contrast with the 17 whose fabric was defective in 1592[5] gives one little confidence in the Visitation of 1590 in this particular respect, even if in general the two visitations are in broad agreement. In fact, there were only three parishes which were in such a condition as might allow recusants their head, that is, parishes like those described in the 1591 report; they were Stockport, Runcorn and Weaverham.

At Stockport, in 1592, the vicar, John Hilary

suffereth the churchyard to bee defiled and doth defile the same with horses, and maketh dunghills in everie corner, and doth not keep the Communion table and other ornamentes of the church as hee oughte . . .

He seems to be of a kind with the vicar of Runcorn who was presented, also in 1592, because

the vicarage howse (is) ruinated, and (he) doth not catechise; (he is) not residente at Ranucorne . . . hee abuseth the church yard and porch with sheepe . . .[6]

But it was Edward Shawcross, vicar of Weaverham, who alone appeared to be beyond redemption, just as had been the case with his parish 12 years earlier.[7] In 1590 he was presented as

not painfull in studie; he doth not (the) service accordinge to the order set downe; he goeth muche to the ailhouse and is a comon drunkarde.[8]

By 1592 this indictment had swollen in both substance and detail, so that the following presentment was brought against him:

[1] Most numerous were the seven cases of absenteeism and eight parishes where the vicar was said to be no preacher, all in 1592.
[2] York, R.VI, A 12, f. 81v.   [3] E.D.V., 1, 10, f. 24v.
[4] Harthill, actually a chapel (York, R.VI, A 12, f. 84).
[5] The worst case was Bromborough in the Wirral, where 'the chancell very ruinous insomuch they are not able to say service' (E.D.V., 1, 10, f. 38v).
[6] E.D.V., 1, 10, ff. 69 & 84v.   [7] Cf. supra, 16.
[8] York, R.VI, A 12, f. 78v. He was also dealt with as a drunkard and an adulterer by the High Commission in York in 1590 (York, H.C., 1585-91, f. 296v).

the chancel ruinated; (he is) negligent in his service, absent uppon Trinetie Sondaie last and the parish destitute that day of eveninge praier; he useth not the surples nor crosse; as they thincke, noe sermon (preached) there thees four yeares, but one hee readeth, and homelies; hee refuseth to goe the perambulation; hee resorteth much to alehowses and is often there, and bie reporte, one night cominge home fell into a dich and not able to rise without helpe; the vicarage oute of reparation (and) he tooke awaie chippes dew to the church; negligent in callinge to catechise, and gave noe monition to collectors. . . .[1]

Nevertheless, not a single recusant was presented from any of these three parishes during either of the visitations; instead in 1590 Stockport provided only 'William Coulsell . . . (who) usuallye goeth out of the churche when the sermon begynneth', which does not seem especially surprising in the circumstances.[2] No neat cause and effect of evident parochial weakness on the one hand and the presence of recusancy on the other can be traced in the records of the visitations.

At least, when the recusants were presented before the visitors they were called 'recusants', a significant development from the Metropolitan Visitation of 1578, which had singled out some 'papists' but did not make use of the term 'recusant' at all; it is, in fact, in the Visitation of 1588 that the term has first been found in use in the diocesan records.[3] As in the Recusant Roll the term would mean 'convicted recusant', as distinct from absentees or non-communicants who were also presented before the visitors.[4] The terminology of the visitation records is, in fact, with few exceptions, uniform and clear-cut. The exceptions are Barbara Ireland of Church Lawton, who, in 1590, was 'suspected of papistrie' but not described as a recusant,[5] Thomas Lawton of Bunbury, who was presented alongside but distinct from 33 recusants of his parish in 1592 as 'a notorious papist resorting to the recusant houses', and finally, Matilda, the wife of Richard Kelsall, Thomasina, the wife of William Hayward, and Elena Hayward, all of Daresbury, who were presented in 1592 as 'favourers of the Romishe Church and Religion'.[6] These were fine distinctions, especially so when it is noted that Matilda Kelsall was presented as a recusant at the Metropolitan Visitations of 1590 and 1595, both before and after the vaguer charge of 1592, while the way in which 'popery' might precede actual recusancy is clear in the case of Thomas Lawton, who was to be convicted as a recusant before long.[7]

As to the numbers of recusants dealt with both by the visitors and the

---

[1] E.D.V., 1, 10, f. 70v.   [2] York, R.VI, A 12, f. 102.
[3] E.D.V., 1, 7, f. 32.
[4] A further illustration of this is the way in which in several cases that came before the Diocesan Chancellor in 1592, absence from church for relatively trivial reasons unconnected with recusancy was dealt with by the imposition of a fine of 4d or 6d. (E.D.V., 1, 11, 1592–1620, ff. 13v, 19v & 20v).
[5] York, R.VI, A 12, f. 111.   [6] E.D.V., 1, 10, ff. 64v & 93.
[7] Cf. the relevant entries in Appendix I.

lay authorities between 1590 and 1593 they seem few when compared with the 200 listed by Chadderton in 1589 or in the light of the anguished description of their activities in the report of 1591. Sixty-nine people were presented as recusants at the Visitation in 1590[1], and 53 before the 1592 Visitation, while 31 were indicted at the Assizes in April 1591, and 76 in April 1593:[2] some 20 recusant prisoners are listed separately from the indictments in the Assize records and a further 20 recusants were dealt with by the Chester High Commission at the opening of 1592, including a few who were prisoners in the Northgate. What is perhaps striking about these figures is the contrast between the small number of recusants who appear in two or more of the sources involved, only 61, and the total of 150 that emerges as the number of recusants who were formally recognised as such by the authorities in these years; only this rather artificial total approaches that of Chadderton in 1589.

The most familiar of the recusants were those who were prisoners in Chester Castle. At the opening of the 1590's Alice, Richard and William Cheswis, Christopher Isherwood, Richard Massey, Thomas Maddocks, Thomas Trine, John Whitmore and Ralph Worsley were still there.[3] They were joined, temporarily, by Thomas Huxley, a staunch recusant from Alpraham, whose son, George, was to become a priest: he was imprisoned late in 1591, and early in the following year Margaret Massey joined her husband in the Castle after a sojourn in the Northgate prison. At the same time John Maddocks and Edward Probin, of the parish of Malpas, began an imprisonment of some two years, and William Stretbarrel and John Wilson, of the parish of Bunbury, an imprisonment of perhaps a year. All four were firm recusants, and, as is certainly the case with Mrs. Massey, were presumably imprisoned as a result of the inquiry into the activities of priests and recusants with which the year opened. In 1593 further recusant prisoners joined them: Gilbert Burscowe and Thomas Hesketh, both gentlemen, and Robert Ball, Nicholas Mawdesley and Thomas Stevenson. In all 20 recusants were imprisoned in Chester Castle for either a short or a long time in these years.[4]

Some of these prisoners were the leaders of large interrelated groups of recusants, as is especially obvious in the case of John Whitmore, whose family and relatives received a good deal of attention from the authorities.

[1] An undated return for the province of York, possibly from 1590, gives a total of 102 recusants from Cheshire (S.P., 12, 235, 25).

[2] Those indicted in 1593 are the recusants who appear on the Recusant Roll of 1592–3 as owing fines for absence. A few other names appear on the Roll in connection with sequestrated land.

[3] During 1590 Isherwood and Worsley, and, in the following year, Trine, disappear from the lists of prisoners recorded in the Crown Books, so that they may then have died or been released. However, each was indicted for absence and assessed for a fine of £240 at the April 1593 Assizes (Chester, 29, 334, m. 17; R.R., 1, m. 6), though in each case this was a final appearance in the existing records.

[4] Chester, 21, 1, ff. 146, 150, 152v, 155v, 159, 162. For Margaret Massey, cf. infra, 90 & 92.

Jane Whitmore, 'whose husband is in prison at Chester for not coominge to the church', was presented at the Visitation of 1590 because she 'cam not to there churche sence Easter laste' and 'had a childe sence Easter, not chrispenned in the parishe'.[1] She was John Whitmore's second wife and he had evidently married her and fathered her child while in prison, and both wedding and christening ceremonies had been performed by a recusant priest, as inquiries in 1592 by the Diocesan Visitors, before whom Mrs. Whitmore was presented as a convicted recusant,[2] and the Chester High Commission, who were given information about it,[3] make clear. John Whitmore's aunt, Alice, was presented as a recusant in 1590,[4] as an absentee in 1592,[5] and was assessed for a fine of £960 in the Recusant Roll of 1592-3.[6] In 1590 her husband, William Whitmore, was presented as one who 'doth not communicate', while John Whitmore's father- and mother-in-law, Henry Primrose and his wife, were presented as recusants, and their daughter, Elizabeth, was reported as an absentee.[7] Another group of recusants and Catholics probably centred on Mrs. Margaret Hocknell, who, in the year of her husband's murder, was perpetuating her faith by employing a recusant, John Cotgreve, to 'teach schoole privatelie' in her house: this was reported to the Visitors in 1590 along with her own negligent attendance at church.[8] As Margaret, wife of Edward Ravenscroft, whom she married after her first husband's death, she was assessed for a fine of £240 in the 1592-3 Recusant Roll.[9]

Mrs. Hocknell's schoolmaster, John Cotgreve, was himself a member of a family from Christleton that was firmly recusant. Margery Cotgreve, a widow, her son, Thomas, her daughter, Elizabeth, and her nephew, Randolph, were all presented before the Visitation in 1590 because they 'refuse to coom to churche'.[10] This was the first occasion when any member of the family appears to have fallen foul of the authorities and the charge fell short of recusancy in so far as they were not yet convicted recusants, though this appearance marked the beginning of just that, for three of them, Margery, Thomas and Elizabeth, were presented before the Visitors in 1592 as recusants 'for three yeares past',[11] and were to appear before the authorities as recusants on several occasions in future, though Randolph conformed to the extent that he was at least attending church by 1592.[12]

The government was slow to appreciate the importance of women like Jane and Alice Whitmore, Margaret Hocknell or Margery Cotgreve. They were regarded at first as susceptible to the discipline of their husbands if their husbands conformed, and did not share the imprisonment of husbands who were recusant. The only woman to be imprisoned for

[1] York, R.VI, A 12, f. 89.
[2] E.D.V., I, 10, f. 24v.
[3] Cf. infra, 95.
[4] York, R.VI, A 12, f. 88.
[5] E.D.V., I, 10, f. 39v.
[6] R.R., I, m. 6.
[7] York, R.VI, A 12, ff. 88-9, 95.
[8] Ibid., f. 87.
[9] R.R., I, m. 6.
[10] York, R.VI, A 12, f. 94v.
[11] E.D.V., I, 10, f. 19v.
[12] Q.S.E., 4, f. 3.

any length of time for recusancy by the Cheshire authorities in the 1580's was Alice Cheswis, a socially unimportant woman compared to Mrs. Hocknell and the Whitmores. Almost half of the recusants who were dealt with by the authorities between 1590 and 1593 were women; amongst the gentry women always predominated. Thus gentlemen like Randle Aldersey of Spurstow, George Egerton of Ridley, Hugh and Sampson Erdeswick of Leighton, William Golborne and Robert Jones of Chester, George Otley of Acton, Nantwich, and William Poole of Marbury were outnumbered by women like Lady Beeston and Lady Egerton, Katherine, the wife of Peter Dod of Shocklach, Katherine, the wife of John Golborne of Overton, Matilda, the wife of William Golborne of Chester, Mary, the wife of William Lawton of Church Lawton, Mary, the wife of John Massey of Coddington,[1] Margaret, the wife of Richard Massey of Waverton, and Alice Whitmore. Hooker's assessment of the role of women in Puritan circles was apt for female recusants too: '. . . diligent in drawing their husbands, children, servants, friends and allies the same way . . . bountiful towards their preachers who suffer want, apter . . . to procure encouragements for their brethren; apter . . . how all near about them stand affected as concerning the same cause'.[2] Their influence on their husbands is clear enough when the presentments before the visitors for 1590 and 1592 are compared: more of the husbands of these women were presented in 1592 than in 1590.

Other women who were presented as recusants ranged from Margaret, the wife of William Aldersey, the Chester linendraper, Anne, the wife of Thomas Moyle, a yeoman of Shocklach Oviatt, Joan, the wife of Owen Wilbraham, a smith of Malpas, Katherine, the wife of Richard Whitmore, a tailor of Guilden Sutton, down to Anne Crocket, servant to Margery Aire of Tilston, who was herself a recusant, and including even Elizabeth Bailey, a beggar from Prestbury.

Finally, as well as the gentry already named, the men included Richard, the son of John Eldershawe of Audlem, who, like his father before him was a physician, and husbandmen like Richard Probert of Malpas, Ralph Bushell of Tiverton and Randle Platt of Faddiley. There were yeomen like William Cooke of Tilstone Fearnall, who was presented with his wife, Isabel, and a miller, Robert Foster of West Kirby, a glover, Hugh Sim of Alpraham, a smith, Peter Somner of Haughton, and James and John Longton, skinner and labourer respectively. Thus the recusants were drawn from a wide social span, with the lesser gentry at one end and servants, labourers and a beggar at the other, though most of those from

---

[1] The Masseys of Coddington were probably Catholic in sympathy, though Mary, the fourth wife of John Massey, is the only one to emerge as a recusant in this period. Their influence may well explain the startling failure to remove Catholic furnishings from Coddington church that was reported to the visitors in 1592: 'the rood lofte standeth undefaced and full of Idolatrie pictures' (E.D.V., 1, 10, f. 53).

[2] Hooker, *Laws of Ecclesiastical Polity*, 104.

the lower orders were people of a certain independence; the very poor were few, possibly because the authorities were only concerned about them if they were particularly awkward.

This broad distribution among the various classes of society was not matched by a similar geographical scattering throughout the county. On the contrary, most of the recusants came from the west of the county, with a marked concentration in the south-west, close to the Welsh and Shropshire borders. Even greater precision is possible; the mass of the recusants came from two parishes, Bunbury and Malpas, while there were lesser concentrations elsewhere. Thus, in 1590, of the 69 recusants presented before the Metropolitan Visitors 23 were from Bunbury and 14 from Malpas, and a further 13 lived in or near the city of Chester. Similarly, of the 53 recusants before the diocesan authorities in 1592, 33 were from Bunbury alone,[1] and 11 from in or near Chester. Finally, all but 10 of the 78 men and women listed in the 1592–3 Recusant Roll hailed from the south-west of the county, 37 from Bunbury alone, with 10 from Malpas and three from Shocklach; apart from Ralph Worsley, listed as a prisoner in the Castle, though probably no longer alive, no Chester recusants were included. Bunbury's importance is perhaps made even clearer when the total number of recusants from that parish revealed in the sources under discussion is understood; there were 70 altogether, out of the total of 150 for the county as a whole, and the county total includes several people whose town, village or parish is unknown. This distribution confirms impressions derived from the examination of the sparser evidence from the earlier years of the Elizabethan Settlement.

So far the sources under discussion have been analysed simply to see what light they throw on the general pattern of recusancy in Cheshire, but they were, of course, the products of instruments for the repression of recusancy and we must now ask how far the local and central authorities were successful in this. For the Visitation of 1590, unfortunately, only the detecta survive, so that there is no indication about how the archbishop's visitors dealt with the accused; it can merely be observed that since 37 of them, over half of the total, were still recusants in 1592–3 (according to the Visitation and Assize records), the remedies of the visitors obviously had only a limited effect. However, the comperta have survived from the Diocesan Visitation of 1592, so that the methods then used by the Visitors in dealing with the recusants are apparent. They were straightforward enough, largely because most of the recusants were clearcut in their attitude to the Visitors; they did not answer their summons to appear before them and were therefore excommunicated for non-appearance; this happened to 35 of the 53 arraigned as recusants. Of those who appeared one was referred to the bishop and 11 to the ecclesiastical commis-

[1] There was also one 'notorious papist' from Bunbury, and six absentees and three non-communicants from Malpas; all these were certainly or probably recusants.

sioners.[1] The others were simply admonished and ordered to attend their parish churches, and in one case, that of Katherine Dunne of Bunbury parish, conformity was recorded. A mixture of threat and persuasion was also used in dealing with the absentees, non-communicants and 'papists' or 'favourers of the Roman Church and Religion' cited before the Visitors; John Street of Nantwich, presented in 1590 as a recusant and in 1592 as a non-communicant, was already in prison for recusancy, as was Anne Mallam, a widow of Grange, West Kirby, who was also presented as a recusant in 1590 but as an absentee in 1592, though in her case submission at a later date was recorded.[2]

The Recusant Rolls[3] raise more questions than they answer.[4] They are no more complete lists of the recusants in any given area than any other list we have encountered. They were lists of convicted recusants owing fines for church absence, so that their primary purpose was financial; the records of these debts were kept by the Exchequer in the general Pipe Rolls until they were extracted in the separate Recusant Rolls from 1592. From the early years of Elizabeth I's reign lists of religious dissenters, some scrappy, some more thorough, had been drawn up for government use; their 'object was to "count heads", if secondarily to ascertain incomes',[5] but the Recusant Rolls, whose main intention was financial, reversed this order of precedence.

Nevertheless, the national revenue appears to have gained little from the recusants of Cheshire. Seventy-five Cheshire recusants were listed as owing fines for church absence in the 1592–3 Roll, but in no case is there any indication that the fine was ever paid. Opposite unpaid debts in the roll appears the entry 'f.c.', short for 'fiat commissio', indicating that a warrant or order had been issued for proceedings for the recovery of the fine to be taken, and this entry appears beside the name of each of the Cheshire recusants listed as owing fines. Where the legal process thus initiated led to a satisfactory settlement, either by payment of the fine or by the discharge of the debtor without payment, the note 'deb' was added; this was not inscribed beside any of the names in the Cheshire section of the roll. Most of the fines were enormous when it is recognised that, with

---

[1] These would be the local (city or county) commissioners. The commission for Chester City and probably for the county also was renewed at the beginning of 1592 and both were active afterwards (cf. infra, 88 ff.). The recusant referred to the bishop was probably being sent before the Commission in fact, as well as the 11 who were referred directly to it; the relevant sentences are worded 'to appear before the Lord Bishop on the xiii October' or 'to appear before the Royal Commissioners on the xiii October': the bishop would preside over the local commission.

[2] E.D.V., 1, 10, ff. 42, 93 & 96.

[3] The Assize indictments from 1592–3 are not discussed separately here, as the long lists of recusants recorded there appear as the first Recusant Roll.

[4] The most recent discussion of them is by H. Bowler in C.R.S., LVII, in his introduction to Recusant Roll No. 2 (1593–4).

[5] M. M. C. Calthrop, C.R.S., XVIII, intro. xi. This volume reprints the Recusant Roll of 1592–3.

the exception only of the wives of two prominent local knights, Lady Frances Brereton and Lady Elizabeth Stanley, the wealthiest of the recusants listed in the roll were from the lesser gentry. Thus, if Lady Stanley owed fines totalling £960, so did two members of the lesser gentry, William Brereton of Shocklach, and Alice, the wife of William Whitmore of Neston, a yeoman, William Stretbarrel of Ridley, a husbandman, Randle Platt of Faddiley, and four members of the Cotgreve family, yeomen stock from Christleton, while Mary, the wife of William Lawton, a gentleman from Church Lawton, owed £1,440. The rest of the fines ranged from £720 to £20, the bulk of them, 44 in all, being the £240 fine for 12 lunar months' absence, and all alike distributed among the various social classes from gentry to labourers.

Ever since the passing of the act of 1581 which imposed the £20 fine for each lunar month's absence from church it had been obvious that this was not a levy that recusants could bear in full. It was more of a threat than a certain liability, extorted where the traffic could bear it, though failure to pay could be followed by any one of several more definite penalties. Imprisonment had been the fate of an increasing if small number of Cheshire recusants over the years; apparently haphazard in its incidence, it was experienced by relatively unknown recusants and avoided by some who were not unimportant, and it was more likely to be imposed in time of crisis. A further penalty was likely to be borne by convicted recusants whose fines were not paid, the seizure of their goods and two-thirds of their lands, as authorised by the act of 1587, and John Whitmore, Margaret Davenport, and Sampson Erdeswick, as well as the heirs of William Hough and John Hocknell had by 1592–3 suffered from this, to a limited extent at least. The 1592–3 Recusant Roll shows that lands of John Whitmore worth £15 7s. 10d. per year had been held from the crown by William Grafton since November 1588; tenants had held from the crown since September 1589, lands of Sampson Erdeswick worth £4 8s. 10½d. per year; tenants held lands, presumably part of her dowry, worth 66s. 8d. per year, which had been seized in September 1592, of the widow, Margaret Davenport. William Whitmore held lands of William Hough worth £26 13s. 4d. per year, and finally, John Hocknell held lands worth £10 per year of the former recusant of the same name, John Hocknell. The last two entries seem to illustrate the way in which, even though the rental value of the lands in question was lost, as this was paid to government by the holder of the lands, recusants attempted to ensure that land forfeited through failure to pay recusancy fines was at least controlled by a relative. A complaint making this point about the holding of Hough's lands by William Whitmore, his son-in-law, had been made many years before;[1] these lands had been sequestrated in March 1584, as it was possible for this to be done under common law before the

[1] Cf. supra, 58.

matter was put on a clearer, statutory basis by the act of 1587. There are no entries relating to the seizure of goods in this first roll, so that, as the fines do not seem to have been collected, the total income from the recusants of Cheshire in this year, £58 16s. 8½d., all from sequestrated land,[1] was small, not only in relation to the number of recusants listed in the roll, but also to the administrative effort involved in gaining the necessary convictions.

The Recusant Roll of 1592–3 was the first of its kind and was intended to strengthen the routine financial and administrative machinery of the realm; indictment at the Assizes was a judicial routine; the visitations were a normal exercise of the pastoral concern of the episcopate; but the last document against whose contents the report of the Council of the North at the end of 1591 can be tested is both more unusual and more interesting. This is the record of the inquiry made in Chester at the beginning of 1592: it reveals far more detail of the lives and personalities of at least some of the recusants of Cheshire than almost any other document we have examined.

The Council of the North had complained that 'the proclamation for the apprehension of seminaries, Jesuits and mass priests . . . is not executed'. This proclamation, issued towards the end of 1591,[2] reflected the current fear of a Spanish invasion and the consequent preoccupation with the political dangers of recusancy. One seminary had been imprisoned in Chester Castle earlier in the year; he was John Butler, alias Banister, and in the Spring the Privy Council had written to the Justices of Assize for Chester about him.[3] Evidence was being gathered for the trial of this 'bad member of this Commonwealth', who at that point was only under suspicion of being a seminary, which he evidently was.[4] Whether or not he had been active in Cheshire or was merely being kept in Chester Castle is not clear. The proclamation ordered that stricter inquiries be made into the ministrations of the priests and into church attendance; these were to be carried out by the local ecclesiastical commissions, which were first to be renewed in order to prune out those of unsound religion.[5] The commission was renewed for Chester City and 12 counties on 28 January 1592.[6] Thus, more slowly and deliberately than the Council of the North evidently liked, the hand of the Ecclesiastical Commission for Chester City was strengthened for a thoroughgoing inquiry on which it, as well as the county commissioners, had already embarked along the lines ordered in the proclamation.

The inquiry began with the examination in the Inner Pentice of the

---

[1] In each of the cases mentioned above the rent was duly paid; 'deb' is entered beside every one.

[2] S.P., 12, 240, 42, dated 18 October 1591, but not published till later (P. McGrath, *Papists and Puritans under Elizabeth I*, 256).

[3] A.P.C., 1591, 127, dated 16 May.   [4] Anstruther entry on Butler.

[5] A.P.C., 1591–2, 138–40.   [6] Ibid., 211.

City between 12 January and 5 February of 10 recusants or suspected recusants. They were interrogated on the basis of eight questions, three of which were asked under oath and five, including the so-called Bloody Questions, without oath, thus following the routine of examination by incriminating questions that had been developed since the early 1580's to deal with religious dissidents. The precise questions used by the Chester High Commission in 1592 were as follows:[1]

Questions to be mynistered by othe to any person that shal be verely suspected to have bene moved to geve assistance to the Pope or Kinge of Spaine.

1. Whether have you bene moved by anie and by whome and by what perswasion, to geve aide or releif, or to adhere to the forces of the Pope or Kinge of Spaine when they shuld happen to invade this realme for any cause whatsoever?

2. Item. Whether have you bene delte withall or moved, or have any perswasions bene used to you to withdrawe you from your allegeance and obedience to the Queene's Majestie, and to refuse or forsake the same and to adhere or favour the Pope or Kinge of Spaine or their doinges? Declare by whome and by howe manie you have bene so delte withall and what be their names and where every suche person is nowe at this present, to your knowledge.

3. Item. Whether do you know any Jesuit or Seminary prest, or are you acquainted with any of them, or with any prest that is under XXX yere old, declare where any such person is, to the best of your knowledge.

Questions to be mynistered without othe to wilfull recusantes.

1. Firste. Whether do you usuallie come to the Churche and why do you not?

2. Item. Whether do you thinke in your conscience that you ought to obeye the Pope's comandment if it be againste the Queene's Majesty or againste the realme?

3. Item. If the Pope or the Kinge of Spaine shall send an armye or any forces to invade this realme pretendinge to reforme religion, whether would you take parte with the Quene and the realme againste them to the uttermoste of your power or not?

4. Item. Whether you thinke in your conscience that the Kinge of Spaine, at suche tyme as he sent an navye to invade this realme in ano 1588, did well therein or not, and whether do you like of that attempt or favor the same in your conscience or conceite?

5. Item. Whether have you mayntained, aided or releived any Jesuite, Semynarie prist or other person sent from Rome or from beyonde-seas to disswade any of the Queene's subjectes from their obidience to her Majestie?

Ralph Langton, who had been in trouble with the city authorities over his beliefs in 1588, was the first suspect to be examined, on 12 January. He admitted that he had absented himself from church but answered 'directly and negatively' to all the other questions. On 17 January, Robert Browne and Elen Wilden, who were already prisoners for recusancy in the Northgate, were examined. Like Langton they confessed that they did not attend church and answered negatively to the other questions, which for Browne at least meant a significant change from the

[1] Q.S.E., 4, f. 16.

G

position he had taken up when examined in the previous August about the political implications of his recusancy.[1] Then, on 8 August 1591, Thomas Bennet, a Chester linendraper, claimed that Browne

. . . denieth to come to church or to communicate, and saith he taketh those that soe doe not to be the Quene's good subjects, and saith he aske(d) Browne towching the supremisy and he gave noe answer to that question.

Browne remained equally evasive about his precise attitude to the Queen's supremacy when examined before the justices about Bennet's accusations.

Robert Browne, examined who is the Quene of England, saith Quene Elizabeth is Quene and head of all England. Examined whether he doeth acknowledge that the Quene's Majestie that now is Supreme Governor in all causes spirituall and temporall, saith this he referred to the lerned to answer unto, and as for himself, he is not lerned and cannot otherwise answer for want of lerninge.[2]

Browne was a prisoner in the Northgate at the time of this examination and was evidently returned thither by the justices, as were both he and Elen Wilden after being examined in 1592; then, even though they took up a satisfactory attitude to the supremacy, 'for their recusancy' they were returned to prison, 'where they remayne, being but poor folkes'.[3]

Browne was, of course, the son of a former gaoler of Chester Castle and a convert of the seminary, Thomas Holford, while Elen Wilden was employed by a prominent recusant family, the Masseys of Waverton; she was maid to Margaret Massey, whose husband had been imprisoned in Chester Castle as a recusant since about 1584. Mrs. Massey was examined after Elen Wilden; she 'confesseth she doth not come to church and refused to take any othe, and therefore she was comitted to the Northgate', where she rejoined her maid. That night her house was searched,

wherin was fond divers ymages, bedes and popish bookes, among which one was an Inglish booke intituled, 'An epistle of the persecucion of Catholiks in England', conteyning many sclanderous thinges against Sir Roger Maneward, knight, Chief Baron, Sir Edmund Anderson, knight, his (?) Chief Justice, and the said (. . .?) and Mr. Sergeant Fletewood and others.[4]

This was at least the second time that the Massey household had suffered such intrusion, for a similar search had followed the return of Margaret Massey's son, Richard, from Rome in 1584, and was part of the train of

---

[1] Q.S.E., ff. 1 & 19. F. 1 is damaged, in parts badly, so much so that nothing can be learned of an examination that took place between that of Langton and that of Browne.

[2] Ibid., 5, f. 11.

[3] Ibid., 4, ff. 1 & 19.

[4] The book was an English translation of 1582 of a French version of Robert Person's 'De Persecutione Anglicana Epistola', with an accompanying address by the translator to the Lords of the Council: cf. A. C. Southern, *Elizabethan Recusant Prose, 1559–1582*, 319–22, 503–4 and 544. Sir Roger Manwood, Chief Baron of the Exchequer, and Sir Edmund Anderson, Chief Justice of the Court of Common Pleas, were two of the sternest judicial opponents of the recusants and sectaries. William Fleetwood, Recorder of London, was actually dismissed for slackness in proceeding against Catholics.

events that led to the prolonged imprisonment of her husband, Richard Massey the elder.[1]

Two days after Mrs. Massey's examination her passive resistance was emulated by another of her husband's servants, Joan Amos. She began by confirming that 'she hathe not comunicated these five yeares', but when 'further examined' made the sweeping admission that she 'hath not at any tyme donne at all'. She then 'refuseth to take othe that she knoweth eny Jesuite or priest to resorte to her master or mistress or s(ay) masse within one yere last past'. The Commissioners also followed the precedent set in their dealings with her mistress and imprisoned Joan Amos 'untill further order'.[2]

In between the examinations of Mrs. Massey and Joan Amos, on 18 January Sampson Erdeswick, the Staffordshire antiquary with land at Leighton in Cheshire, was examined. Not for him Mrs. Massey's refusal to take the oath: by answering the questions on oath 'directly and negatively' and the others 'fully and well' he avoided drawing further attention to himself and his household, so that even though he confessed that he did not attend church, he seems to have experienced no further trouble at the hands of the authorities on this occasion. They were out to unearth priests: Erdeswick had sworn on oath that he knew none, whereas Mrs. Massey and Joan Amos had drawn the line at this. When the authorities had carried out an immediate search of the Massey household at Waverton they had hoped to find more than seditious literature.

When the Commissioners next met, on 31 January, their clerk recorded in full the answers of Richard Spurstowe, a gentleman of Spurstow, Bunbury, whose uncle, Philip Spurstowe, was a recusant. The record may have been made simply because Spurstowe had plenty to say, as he had done when arrested; about that the swornmen later recommended that 'Mr. Hughe Starkey shoulde be examined, for that when Spursto was taken by the apoyntmente of the comesioners by the constable he gave hym verey bade speches and sayd he woulde be even with hym'. A more likely reason for the fulness of the record is that the answers bear the marks of careful consideration, for the issues at stake were important. They give a clear idea of a loyal recusant's way through the political issues in which his recusancy involved him. He answered the questions for which no oath was necessary in the following way:

1. To the firste (qu)estion: saith he doeth not use to c(ome to the) church, and only his consccience in th(at h)e is not perswaded it be the truth is the cause.

2. To the second question saith he is perswaded in conscience that he ought to obey the Quene's Majestie afore all others in all temporall causes.

3. To the third question saith that (he) wold take parte with the Queene againste all the worlde coming to invade this realme, what surmise or matter soever they wold pretende.

[1] Q.S.E., 4, ff. 1, 10 & 19.　　　　　　　　　　　　　　　[2] Ibid., f. 1.

4. To the fourth question saith he doeth think, and is perswaded in conscience that the Kinge of Spaine, at such tyme as (h)e sent a navy to invade this realme, 1588, did not well therin, neither doeth he like of that attempt nor never favored the same.

5. To the fifth question he saith he never maintand, aided nor releved any Jesuite, Seminary prest or other person sent from Rome or from beyond the seas to diswade any of these Quene's subjectes from ther obedience to her Majestie.

After giving these considered, succinct and forthright answers he refused to take an oath to those questions requiring it and was therefore committed to the Northgate, making the fifth recusant prisoner to be lodged there by the Commissioners at this time.[1]

If Margaret Massey's response to imprisonment in the Northgate was anything to go by (and it was) Spurstowe would soon reconsider the principles by which he stood, for on the day that he was committed to prison she reappeared before the Commissioners, because after

the said Margaret hath been two weekes in prison (she) desired to come before us agane, at which tyme she did take the othe conteyned in the Instructions and awnswered therto directly and negatively.

Not that this was enough to win her freedom:

Because she refused to come to church we, resolving to commit her, it was thought mete to send her to the Castell of Chester, where her husband is prisoner for his recusancy. And therefore she is comitted to the said Castell, to remayne ther with her husband, not having any other manteynance but at his handes.[2]

If she had actually wanted to share her husband's lot she could hardly have managed things better, and the sting at the end, whereby she was made wholly dependent on her husband, would make her life in prison little different from that of other prisoners of substance, who would normally live largely from their own means. She stayed with her husband for only a few months, for she was no longer there when the Assizes sat in October 1592.[3]

Strangers passing through a city like Chester would probably be businessmen on legitimate errands or troops on their way to or from Ireland, but some might be recusant priests or messengers, and useful sources of information about any on whom suspicion fell would be the innkeepers with whom they lodged. Thus Elizabeth, the wife of an inn-keeper, William Bostock, was next examined by the Commissioners.[4] She admitted that she had not been at church 'this six weekes paste', but the rest of the answers are not recorded, though a hint of what she might

---

[1] Q.S.E., ff. 2 & 14. Spurstowe was from Spurstow, Bunbury, and presumably came under the jurisdiction of the city authorities because he owned and lived in a house in Chester.

[2] Ibid., f. 19.

[3] Chester, 21, 1, ff. 159 & 162.   [4] Q.S.E., 4, f. 2.

have known is given in an unfinished sentence about her that was afterwards crossed out: 'Examined what gestes she hath lodged at her howse,
saith one Mr. . . .' Her husband later cleared the matter up.

These preliminary investigations ended on 5 February with the appearance before the Commissioners of Randolph Cotgreve, who, along with
his aunt and her son and daughter had been presented before the Archbishop's Visitors two years before for their refusal to attend church.[1] His
aunt and his cousins had not budged from this position, but Randolph,
'being examyned whether he dothe use to go to churche says he dothe butt
hathe not receyved the comynion this yere and more', and went on to
give just the kind of evidence about his relatives that the commissioners
were looking for.

And being forder examyned what Jesuittes and semynaris he hathe known or
byn acquanted withall sens Mychelmas was a yere past, saythe that he know one
Stones, a prist or semynary, before Christmas last (was) at one Wedow Cotgreve's,
his ante, at Christolton, where he sayd masse and mynystered the sacramentes.
And this was in company with the sayd wedow, her son, Thomas, and her doryter,
and one Mistress Whittmore of Sutton. And further saythe that he was in company whon one Davis, a semynary who was in Christolton a lyttell before Stone
the semynnari his being there, who did in lyke manner saye masse and used the
lyke order as the other at whose serves was the sayd widow, the sayd Thomas,
her sone, and her dorytyr.[2]

The investigations of the Commissioners were not to end for another
month, but this was the most important information that they unearthed:
two priests had been tracked down. Unfortunately, Christleton, two miles
away from Chester city, lay outside the jurisdiction of the city Commissioners, and further investigation and action would have to be made by
the county authorities. Action followed, but with such splendidly un-
hurrying haste as was bound to be fruitless. It was three days before
the city Commissioners wrote to their fellows of the county to ask for the
examination of those present at the masses;[3] an inquiry into one of the
masses (which was dated precisely as having taken place on 20 October
1591) was ordered at the April Quarter Sessions,[4] and ultimately Margery,
Thomas and Elizabeth Cotgreve were indicted at the Assizes for their
attendance at the mass, which had been celebrated by an 'unknown
priest'.[5] In April 1593 they were also convicted of absence from church,
and each was duly assessed on the Recusant Roll of 1592–3 as owing £960
in fines. But the original aim of the Commissioners had been primarily to
unearth priests and none of those involved seems to have been apprehended.
The stable door was bolted demonstratively but the horses had gone.

Meanwhile, the Ecclesiastical Commission for Chester had been

---

[1] Cf. supra, 83.
[2] Q.S.E., 4, f. 3.
[3] Ibid.
[4] C.S.F., 1592, F 2, D 4: F 3, D 1: F 4, D 4.
[5] Chester, 21, 1, f. 163v.

renewed,[1] and by it the Commissioners were required to empanel a jury to inquire about seminaries and Jesuits who had entered England since Michaelmas, 1590,[2] and the new Commissioners therefore set about making much more widespread inquiries than hitherto. They not only empanelled a jury of swornmen but on 10 February ordered the ministers, churchwardens and swornmen of all the parishes in the city to draw up lists of suspects by the 22nd of the month, and both sets of presentments have been preserved in full.[3]

The officials of St. Olave's presented only Mrs. Alice Stanley, as an absentee, and St. Bridget's Mrs. Margaret Aldersey and John Whitehead as absentees, with Whitehead as a non-communicant also 'these two yeres last past'. William Bostock was suspected to be a papist by the officials of St. Peter's, while 'Mr. William Golborne . . . coms not to his parish of St. Peter's and (is) well knowne to be an enymye to religion and a non-communicant two years and more'. Andreas Bredenam, the parson of St. John's, was more systematic in compiling his list. He set down four clear headings, thus: 'Recusants, Impotent, Negligent persons, and Indicted', providing names under the first two only, though those named as recusants, Ralph Langton and Margaret, his wife, and Alice Barker, were, in fact, suspects only. Under 'Impotent' was Lady Warburton, who was 'not able to go to churche, (but) hath service in her howse diverse times by Mr. Bredename'.

A scholarly caution marked the certificate from St. Oswald's:

Mr. Peter Dutton and his wife have bene in our parishe this halfe yeare or their-aboutes, but their is not any of us that dothe certainely remember ether hym or his wyfe to come to our parishe church to divine service according to the lawes in that behalfe provided, and therefore we referre them to your worships' examination.

These suspects were rightly distinguished from

Mrs. Massie and her maid, Elen Wilden, and Browne and Bloundell: they be in prison within our parishe and well knowen to your worshipes.

The officials of St. Michael's, St. Mary's and Trinity all wrote briefly and to the point. From St. Michael's William Helin was presented 'for not cominge to the church upon the Sabaoth dayes as he ought to doe' and Thomas Conghe 'for not coming to the church at all'. St. Mary's sent in just a tiny slip of paper on which was noted only, 'Widowe Browne suspected because she refuseth to come to churche', and finally, Trinity Church reported Mr. Richard Massey, James Hands of Blakenhouse and

---

[1] Cf. supra, 88. The aldermen and others who carried out the inquiry are referred to as Commissioners in the entries from 31 January onwards, but not before, i.e. only after receipt of the Commission.

[2] R. H. Morris, *Chester in the Plantagenet and Tudor reigns*, 83-4. Morris cites this Commission as from 1587-8, but it is, in fact, the Commission of January, 1592. It is directed to Thomas Lyniall, who was Mayor, 1591-2, and clearly follows from the proclamation against Jesuits and seminaries of late 1591. I have been unable to find the original.

[3] Q.S.E., 4 ff. 4-15. In what follows detailed references are not given.

his wife and maid, and Richard Norris and his wife as people who did 'not usually frequent the church nor communicatethe'.

These presentments from the individual parishes supplemented those from the jury of swornmen. Of the 24 suspects listed by the parish officials the jury named only six, namely Mrs. Margaret Aldersey, William Bostock, Mr. William Golborne, Ralph Langton, Peter Dutton and his wife, Elizabeth. They added not only 15 or 16 new suspects, but a far less inhibited account of the suspects than their more guarded parochial acquaintances.

We thinke mete that William Bostoke, inkeper, shoulde be examined for that he logethe such persons as are to be inquered of.

Allso we thinke mete that oulde Aldersea's wyfe should be examined, for that sence she was at churche, hit is credeble reporttede that her dochter Jane saythe that Mr. Massee's wife, the recusante, came unto her and toulde her that sence she hade bene at the churche she shoulde have no more releffe of the Katholykes.

We thinke mete that Mrs. Whytmore should be examined, for that hit is credeble reported that she was mareed by a semenary preste and she hathe chyldren and hit is not knowen howe they were crystened nor where.

Also, we thinke mete that John Hochton and his wyffe shoulde be examined, for that hit is well knowen that the(y) have receved into there house many suspected persons.

Also, we thincke mete that Gorge Ravenscrofte shoulde be examined, for we thinke that he knoweth that Mr. Edward Ravenscrofte was mareyde by a semenary preste.[1]

We thinke mete that Mr. Hughe Starkey shoulde be examined, for that when Spursto was taken by the apoyntmente of the comesioners by the constable he gave hym verey bade speches and sayd he woulde be even with hym.

We thinke mete that Mr. Thomas Gravenor shoulde be examined as a recussante.

We thinke mete that Henrey Primrosse and his fameley shoulde be examined, for the(y) are lyke to make knowne to you such persons as are to be inquered of.

Also, we thinke mete that Ralphe Lancton shoulde be examined, for that on Sundaie laste he was fonde in Blukenwode hymselfe alone, walkinge up and down, as certen yonge men of this cytty do reporte, and he is redy to goe into Iourlande.

We thinke mete that Gorge Wode's wyfe shoulde be examined, for she knoweth a seminery that ussethe the Castell and hit is thoughte he mareyd Mr. Whytmore.

Also, we thinke mete that Mr. Petar Dotton's wyfe shoulde be examined as a recussante.

Also, we thinke mete that Mr. Golborne shoulde be examined, for that he hath not ben in his pareshe churche for this longe tyme.

We of the Jury thinke mete that Mr. Pettar Dutton and his wyfe, his servante, Whydbe and his wyfe, Mrs. Dutton's mayde, and the reste of his famaley shoulde be examened, for that the(y) are verey lykly to make knowne shuche perssons as are to be inquered of.

We thinke mete that Mrs. Glacior that dwellethe nexte the Northegat shuld be examened: for she gevyth intertaymente to Browne and Ellin Wylden which are recussantes, and she comyth not to churche.

[1] He married the recusant, Mrs. Margaret Hocknell.

We thinke mete that Mr. Docter Renolde's wyfe shoulde be examened, for that she doth not comunykate and is inquered of in Spayne as a favorer of Papystree, as Hughe Moylde hathe reportted.

Lykewyse, we have credebly harde that on(e) Homfrey Hanmer, on(e) of Mr. Hanmer's sonnes, of Levadon Heath, is a Semenary preste[1] and usseth aboute Hanmer, Elsmear and Osester, and hathe bene oftentymes at Mr. Lloyde's house of Lloydamaine.

The Commissioners then had to decide where truth ended and gossip and malice began in all this. They had enlisted the aid of the diocesan Chancellor to find out 'what recusants are presented before the bysshop or the chancelor', and intended to sort out the sheep from the goats in yet another way, for they decided 'first to enquire what indictments ar agaynst any recusant prisoners and how the same hath passed'. On 22, 25 and 28 February, they re-examined several of those with whom they had already dealt in January and also interrogated 10 others, so that in all half the suspects named to them were actually examined. There is nothing in the records of the proceedings to indicate whether the rest were summoned to appear but did not do so or were simply ignored for one reason or another, though the Commissioners later declared that all suspects had been examined.[2]

The Northgate must have been a foul prison, for if only two weeks sojourn there had been enough for Mrs. Massey little more was needed to make Richard Spurstowe reconsider his initial refusal to take the oath. The record made by the clerk baldly stated that 'after he had remayned there (i.e. in the Northgate) three weekes and above he desired to be heard agane', but Spurstowe's plaintive 'petition to be heard againe' makes his discomfort plain. He wrote:

Mr. Maior, to you as the chife I humbley crave justice, that it maye please you and the rest of the Commissioners to heare me speake for my selfe, that I maye cleare me of those surmices that are thought to make againste me, and showe myselfe a true and faythful subjecte. Good Mr. Maior, famiche me not owte: I am content to yealde up the houlde with a better will than I extend (entered ?) yt. Consider, despite his extremities, for which he pleads relief, he is a true subject to the good and gracious Queen. Your prisoner, Richard Spurstowe.[3]

He seems to have been heard again on 28 February, 'at which time he did take the othe and aunswered to all the questions upon othe directly and negatively',[4] insisting thereby that he knew no Jesuits or Seminaries, but it was his answers ministered without oath that are more interesting.

---

[1] He was: cf. Appendix II.

[2] Q.S.E., 4, f. 17. Most of the records of the inquiry consist of rough, barely legible notes which briefly summarise the actual examinations. Some, recording two separate examinations of a suspect, were obviously written after the examinations had taken place, and in these cases it is not clear when the second examination occurred. Most of the interrogations were carried out on 28 February.

[3] Ibid., ff. 19v–20.　　　　　　　　　　　　[4] Ibid., f. 19.

They were again recorded fully and were signed by Spurstowe himself;
he was at pains to make both his recusancy and his loyalty unmistakably
clear. He stated that

... he doth not use to come to church, nor hath not done for these ix yeres last
past, and saith the cause is because if this be the true church, yet he is not yet
persuaded to come to church, and whatsoever is done against conscience he
holdeth it to be sin although the thing be good in itselfe.

And being demanded who hath so persuaded him he saith he hath not been
persuaded by any man nor drawn by the example of any, but by reading. And
being demanded whether he will now come to churche he saith he doth submit
himself to the Queen's mercy as one that doth offend the penal law in that behalf,
but is not yet resolved nor persuaded to come to the church.

Item. Being demanded whether he will take part with the Queene against the
Pope or King of Spaine, saith he will take part with the Queene against any that
shall invade the realm for any cause whatsoever.

Item. Being demanded whether he ought to obey the Queene's Majestie in all
causes whatsoever, saith that he ought to obey her in all causes, and saith that
wherin his former examinacion he saied that he ought to obey the Queene's
Majestie before all others in all temporall causes, his meaning therin and by this
word temporal was that his not coming to church was a spirituall cause. And
confesseth that her Majestie is Supreme Governor in her dominions in all causes
whatsoever.[1]

A sturdy individualism, so often regarded as a Protestant or even
Puritan phenomenon, marks his words; 'he hath not been persuaded by
any man nor drawn by the example of any, but by reading' sounds
remarkably like the Puritan Colonel Hutchinson on the eve of the Civil
War, as does his insistence that 'whatsoever is done against conscience he
holdeth it to be sin'. His attitude to Spain and to the royal authority places
him firmly on the side of those who wanted to find an acceptable relationship for Catholics with their Protestant ruler. However, read into his
answers what one may, the Commissioners stonily returned him to the
Northgate prison,[2] whence, as shall be seen, he soon found a quicker way
out than by petitioning the Mayor.

Joan Amos had also experienced the persuasions of the Northgate and
she too reappeared before the Commissioners on 22 February and evidently
gained her freedom after answering as follows:

... she hath not ben moved ... nor knoweth no Jesuit nor Seminarye prest,
nor any other prest under xxx yere ould, nor knoweth not where any of them is,
saving such as have ben in the Castell of Chester.

Item. She is content to come to the (divine ?) service, and to use herself ther
dutifully ...[3]

[1] Ibid., f. 2, sheet 2.
[2] Their decision is not recorded, but Spurstowe evidently returned to prison, to escape
on 6 March.
[3] Q.S.E., 4, f. 2, sheet 2. Again the Commissioners decision is not given, but this kind of
submission was accepted in other cases.

One more suspect, Alice, the wife of Robert Stanley, was examined on 22 February. She was a newcomer to the city, presented before the Commissioners as an absentee by the officials of St. Olave's Church. She quickly cleared herself of all suspicion. She

saithe she was at churche upon Sondaye at Evening Prayers and at other tymes, but hathe not bynne at any sermons since her cominge to Chester, where she hath remayned moste parte since Mydsummer laste. And examined what lykinge she hathe to the relygion now established by her Majestie, saythe she hath good lykinge to the same, and she hathe not bynne at eny masse or papishe service, nether hathe she bynne perswaded to adhere to the Pope or Kinge of Spaine, nor knoweth eny Jesuite, prest or semenarie.[1]

On 25 February a relative of three recusant prisoners in Chester Castle was questioned. This was Anne Dewsbury, who was related to Alice Cheswis and her sons, prisoners in the Castle for a decade or more after 1584. Most of her answers concerned visits to the Castle and her presence at the mass said there 'about four yeres paste',[2] and the Commissioners were eager to track down any priests she might have seen there. Anne Dewsbury declared that she had known only the unnamed Welshman who had celebrated the one and only mass she had attended in the Castle, though she did know 'one Fox, an old preste, who in the tyme of Mrs. Sevell used to repair to Woodhey'. All her information was necessarily out of date, for she insisted that 'sithens the said tyme', i.e. of the mass, four years before, 'she hath used and doeth use comenly to come to the church and has heard dyvine service'. She supported this by saying that Alice Cheswis, 'her said awnt, was angry with her, for that she . . . cometh to the church and heareth divine service'.[3]

Twelve further examinations, apparently crowded into 28 February, closed the Commissioners' investigations, apart from one which was delayed, that of

Margaret Aldersey, widow, an aged woman of eighty yeres and above, being imprisoned for a recusant, but so aged and weke that she is not able to come before us, wherupon three of the comyssioners are appoynted to examine her upon the questions befoure our next sitting.[4]

Unless there were two elderly Mrs. Alderseys the jury of swornmen had notified the Commissioners that she had been attending church, with the consequent threat of the loss of relief from her fellow-Catholics, according to the report of her daughter. A recusant for many years, she was not easily persuaded to conform; on 14 July, along with Mrs. Matilda Golborne, the wife of another suspect whose examination was recommended to the Commissioners, she was assessed by the Quarter Sessions for the old 12d. fine for absence from church.[5]

[1] Q.S.E., f. 23.
[2] Cf. supra, 71.
[3] Q.S.E., 4, f. 22.
[4] Ibid., f. 19.
[5] M.B., 1589–92, 14 July, 34 Eliz.

The aged Mrs. Aldersey might be regarded as a traditionalist in her Catholicism, a believer of the Old Faith rather than a product of the reformed Catholicism of the Counter-Reformation, unlike Mr. and Mrs. Peter Dutton, who were next examined. They were, perhaps, the newer type of Catholic. Indeed, Peter Dutton had been educated on the continent, but it was actually his wife, Elizabeth, who was most adamant as a recusant. Thus,

Peter Dutton, gentleman, sone and hyer apparent of John Dutton of Dutton, esquire, being accused to be a recusant, doth come sometymes to the church, and ther is hope of better conformity, and did answere to all the questions, as well to those without othe as upon othe, directly and negatively.

Peter Dutton promised, in fact, to attend church, but his wife would not do so. She admitted that she did not attend church, but 'will not as yet be content to come to church'. Consequently, Peter was bound in recognisance to the tune of £40 to ensure her future appearance before the Commissioners and, meanwhile, she was to attend church.[1] Peter's willingness to conform and his wife's refusal to do so is perhaps hardly surprising: Elizabeth Dutton was the daughter of Richard and Margaret Massey, prisoners for recusancy in the Castle, while her husband was the son of a man on whom no more than suspicion of Catholic sympathies ever fell. Peter Dutton died in the following year, but Elizabeth did not conform. After her husband's death she seems to have returned to the family home at Waverton, and was indicted for absence from church at the Assizes in 1594, apparently unsuccessfully;[2] later she resided at Walton, Lancashire.[3]

Ralph Langton, appearing for a second time, and Jane Andrews(?) were much more tractable. They 'confessed they had forborne to come to church, but upon persuasion yelded to come to church herafter, and have so done, and did answere directly and negatively as well to the questions without othe as upon othe'. Throughout the whole inquiry Langton had been dogged by curious rumours like the one repeated by the jury or another which went as follows:

Edward Stanley at Yoley (?) acquainted Raffe Longton and there had conference with a Semynary mett at Chester in the stretes and stayed in town all day. And after mett at Chester agayne the next daye at Chester, and so departed with him into the fyldes. And ther left him and had conference, and so departed. The semynaris name was one Cowper. This was about four yeres past.[4]

Along with Davies and Stone, whom Randolph Cotgreve had named in his examination, and the various references to an unnamed priest who had married Mr. and Mrs. Whitmore, this provided the Commissioners with knowledge, rumour or gossip, whichever it might be, of the presence

[1] Q.S.E., 4, ff. 19 & 24-5.   [2] Cf. infra, 114-15.
[3] Ormerod, I, 651.   [4] Q.S.E., 4, f. 18.

of four priests in the vicinity of Chester in the preceding three or four years. This was little enough reward for their efforts and the rest of their investigations of the 28 February were for the most part taken up with the attempt to gain more information about them.[1]

All the examinants denied any personal knowledge of any Jesuit or Seminary priest, and Alice Barker, the wife of Thomas Barker, innkeeper of the Unicorn, and Jane Brown, presumably the Widow Brown presented by the officials of St. Mary's, had nothing to say beyond just that. Anne, the wife of Thomas Powell, started the ball rolling with some comments on the priest who had married the Whitmores: 'she hath heard that an old man did mary Mr. Whitmore and his wif, but knoweth not what his name was'. Jane, the wife of George Woods, said that she had seen a priest 'in a white frese cote and a side bag, being like a fawkener, resort often to the Castell, and that Henry Pyncrose said to her, "That was the seminarye prest that maryed my sonne Whitmore and my daughter", and saieth the said seminary was abowt forty yeres of age'. Henry Primrose, the bride's father, immediately denied all this: 'he knoweth not who it was that maryed Mr. Whitmore and this the examinant's daughter, nor knoweth what his name is'. Adding a little more to the confusion Ralph Langton agreed with Anne Powell's belief that the priest was an old man, and not a mere 40 years old, but gave a description of him that partly tallied with what Jane Woods had said: he 'went like a surgoon in a long russet cote and a great bag'. He thought he was 'an old priest, but no Jesuit nor Seminary'; he did at least give him a name, 'Heth'.

Langton also added something about Davies: 'he has heard of one Davyes, a Jesuit or Seminary, who was about four yeres ago at the Hollandes ther in Chester, and had like to have been taken'. Davies was the only suspected priest whom anyone admitted they had seen, for William Bostock went so far as to say that 'ther hath one Davyes, a red sanded(?) man, about forty yeres of age, of a meane stature, lodged in this the examinant's house in Chester as a gest for one night within the space of a yere last past'. Bostock covered himself by saying that whether this Davies 'was a Jesuit or Seminary, or where he dwelleth, (he) cannot tell, and saith he did not see or know any man at Chester resort to the said Davyes while he was in (his) howse'. He denied any knowledge of Stone or Cowper.

Finally, John Houghton and his wife added even vaguer tales about a priest who sounds rather like the one who was said to have married the Whitmore's.

John Houghton being examined upon his othe saith (he) doth not know any Jesuit nor Seminary, but doth abhorr them. And (he) saith that he had a servant, which did in tymes past dwell with this deponent, called James Lawston, who

---

[1] The remaining examinations are all taken from ibid., f. 25.

said that ther was an old man that came from Christleton or therabout, with a white beard, that used to come to Mrs. Massie's house nere St. Oswald's (?) Church in Chester, and to say masse in that house while the master was at service in the said church, and saith that the said Lawston did once say he had been at masse in the said house and brought an old (?) with water in it, which he said was holi water. And (he) saith the speches were in Summer last and that the said Lawston went or ran away from this deponent's to Ireland about Barthomew-tide last.

Margery, wife to the said John Howghton, being examined upon his (*sic*) othe, saithe she knoweth no Jesuit nor Semenary, but saith that the said Lawston moved this deponent above halfe a yere past to have then a masse, which she did agree unto, therby to have defended those that shuld be at it, and that the said Lawston said he wold go to Christleton or Rowton to fetch an prest to say the masse, and in the meanwhile the said Lawston rane away. And (she) saith he did not tell her the preste's name.

The link with Christleton, where the Cotgreve's lived, is interesting.

A report now had to be drawn up for the Privy Council. Almost all the evidence at the disposal of the Commissioners was hearsay; only Randolph Cotgreve and Anne Dewsbury had described what they had actually seen of men they knew to be priests, and already the Commissioners had passed the buck in Cotgreve's case to their counterparts in the county, while the mass described by Anne Dewsbury lay outside their scope, as it had taken place before the time (Michaelmas, 1590) from which their inquiries were to date. They were thus able to write the following letter to the Council.[1]

May it please your honers to be advertised that by virtue of her Majestie's commission under the Great Seale of England to us lately directed for the dis-covery of Jesuites, Seminaryes and wilfull recusantes in this City of Chester, we have with all diligence, according to our bounden duties, spent many dayes at severall tymes in the said service, to trye and examine the said offenders as well by our owne knowledge as also by the othes and presentment of such choice men of good calling in this Citye, as for their zeale in religion and unfayned dealing now most fitte to be used in the same, who have very carefully and diligently done good service therin.

And therupon, we have called before us all such as were presented or thought meete to be examined, wherof we have sent a kalendar to your honours,[2] inclosed herein, conteyning the names of such recusantes as we found in the said city, of which some did reforme themselves and did come to church, and some others that will not yeld to come to church do remayne in prison, and some taken in bondes to appere agane, as by the kalendar may appere unto your honours.

We cannot find that any Jesuit or Seminary hath resorted to this city at any tyme since Michaelmas in the xxxiind. yere of her Majestie's reigne, but we find by the examinacion of one Cotgreve that ther have been two masses said by one Stone, a prest or Seminary, and by one Davyes, a Seminary, somwhat before Christmas last at the howse of one Widow Cotgreve in Christleton, which is in the

---

[1] Q.S.E., 4, f. 26, which is a rough draft of the letter.
[2] Unfortunately, not extant.

Countie of Chester, out of our jurisdiction; wherof we have written our letters to the Comissioners of that Countie.

And because this City is a port towne, and that diverse passengers take shipping here for Ireland, we have comanded the inkepers and others that kepe lodging in this City to kepe notes of the names and special markes of all strangers resorting to their howses for diet or lodging, and to geve us knowledge presently therof.

Thus, resting at your Lordships' further commands, we do most humbly take our leaves. From Chester, the first of March.

The work of the Commissioners is in one way extraordinarily irritating; it points to the existence in Chester in 1592 of some 20 recusants and 18 possible recusants, and of these 38 persons only 16 appear in all the other evidence that we have examined for the period 1590–3, a period which is especially well-documented by comparison with the rest of the reign of Elizabeth I. Not only does no single source give fully reliable information as to the number of recusants at any given time, but even when taken together over a short period of time for which they seem reasonably adequate several sources give nothing like a complete picture. This has to be borne in mind in assessing the significance of all the conclusions drawn from the evidence presented in this chapter. Only if the inquiry in the county that had run parallel to the city investigation that has just been reviewed remained extant would it be possible to make any very confident pronouncements.

While no record of the county inquiry has survived,[1] ironically enough the reply of the Privy Council to the report of the county Commissioners has been preserved while their reply to the city has not; perhaps the same letter, a conciliar round-robin, was sent to both. It ran:

Their Lordships received their letters of the first of this presente reporting the manner of their proceeding in the execution of her Majesty's commission addressed unto them for the inquiry of Jhesuites and Seminaryes within the countie of Chester, with the certificates of the recusantes presented in that countie, wherby yt appeareth they have taken paines to good effects. For the which their Lordships yelded them hartie thankes and allowed verie well of the course of their doinges therein, and expect the continuance of their dilligence in that service, that such as are evill affected maie be discouvered and they (be) either reformed or the lawe executed against them, the better to prevent the daily and dangerous falling away of her Majesty's subjectes from their due obedience growen by the secret practise of Jhesuites and Seminaryes . . .[2]

The Chester City authorities had not, in fact, wholly finished their investigations, for five days after they had written their complacent report to the Council a disturbing epilogue to their inquiry was enacted. In the evening of 6 March Richard Spurstowe escaped from the Northgate. An

---

[1] Some of its results appear to have done so, judging by the large number of recusants dealt with by the Assizes in 1592–3.

[2] A.P.C., 1591–2, 324, dated 8 March, 1592.

inquiry into the circumstances of his escape was held the next day; it revealed that the escape was carefully planned, probably with accomplices inside and outside the prison, and Spurstowe had got clean away.[1]

The escape itself was a simple matter. It was vividly described by Spurstowe's fellow-prisoner and recusant, Robert Browne. He said that

. . . in the beginning of the night yesterdaie night last[2] his fellow prisoner in the geate,[3] beinge overseem with drinke, did cry out and make an noice, he, this examinant, and the keper's wief being in the howse, and Spurstowe and the keper aslepe by the fieresside. Wherupon the Keper's wief bad this examinant to tak the keys of the geate and with light to see what aled the prisoner there, which this examinant did. And (he) came in and out twis or thris and did fetch him, the prisoner, aqua vita; and therupon, after this examinant came forth the same Spurstowe, and the Keper's wief folowed him. And Spurstowe loked to the walls as accustomed.[4] And the Keper's wief came into the geate and asked this examinant for Spurstowe, and this examinant said he was not ther, wherupon she retorned out and sought for Spurstowe and he was gone.

The account of Ellen Young, the underkeeper's wife, agreed with this.

Spurstowe's servant, Robert Barrow, was asked 'what he conceiveth of the crying out of the said person in the geate, whether of purpose to work this feat?' and replied that he 'doeth not think soe, for that the prisoner was dronk and semed sickley', and whether this illness was pre-arranged or not, escape under so slack a regime would not have been difficult for a determined man like Spurstowe. Much more important was the fact that he had arranged for the provision of a horse, saddle, bridle, spurs and boots for himself, so that even though Humphrey Young, the underkeeper, lost little time before he left in pursuit Spurstowe was not recaptured. Much of the questioning in the inquiry was directed to finding out who had aided Spurstowe.

He had enjoyed frequent visitors, especially William Bostock and his servant, Richard Wright. Bostock was the innkeeper who had been examined as a suspected recusant only the week before, and the officials of St. Peter's had reported him to the Commissioners as one 'whom we suspect to be a papist and, as well, fauvorer of papistes, dyvers weyes, in all ther affaires and busynes',[5] which would seem to be a fitting comment on his dealings with Spurstowe. In later years, when he was described expressively as 'with a bold head, somewhat talle . . . of a flaxen heare, and with a great rowling eie', he was a servant of Thomas Fitzherbert,[6]

[1] Q.S.E., 5, ff. 20–1, dated 7 March 1592. Robert Barrow, glover, Howell Edwards (both apparently Spurstowe's servants), Robert Browne, prisoner, William Bostock, innkeeper, his servant, Richard Wright, and Ellen Young, wife of Humphrey Young, the underkeeper, were examined by the justices.

[2] A little before 9 p.m., according to Ellen Young.

[3] His name is never given, nor was he examined by the Justices.

[4] i.e., he urinated.

[5] Q.S.E., 4, f. 7.

[6] S.P., 12, 268, 82, dated October 1598.

and as such lodged in the English College in Rome in 1600.[1] His Catholic sympathies are clear enough. According to Robert Browne, he 'used right certainly to be with Spurstowe every daie, and to be in (his) chamber with him and the dore thereof shut, and . . . Bostok's man hath bene with Spurstowe many tymes'. Bostock agreed that upon the previous Saturday and Sunday—the escape took place on a Tuesday—he was 'below in the (prison) howse, and sometyme hath ben in the chamber of Spurstowe, themselves together ther, walking and talking twis or thrise'. Robert Barrow stated that Spurstowe had sent him to Bostock's house on the day of the escape to ask Bostock and Wright to see Spurstowe, though he was not sure that they had done so.

Wright had acted as a messenger for Spurstowe, visiting Spurstowe's brother-in-law, Walley, at Tiverton, Mrs. Spurstowe in Lancashire, and possibly that unquenchable recusant, Lady Egerton. Mrs. Spurstowe had visited her husband at least once during his imprisonment, staying the night according to Barrow, so that some sort of escape plan might then have been arranged.

At all events, Spurstowe had gone, and all the examinations that followed his escape throw little light on how he had managed to do so. The examinations were conducted clumsily by the justices; many questions that could have been asked were not asked, for example, why Bostock maintained such close relations with Spurstowe and what the two of them discussed in their private conferences; neither Humphrey Young nor the sick and drunken prisoner whose cries had started off the events leading to Spurstowe's escape were examined; and finally, the examinations are extraordinarily confusing. This is all the more surprising in comparison with the undoubted thoroughness of the Chester authorities in a variety of administrative and judicial matters in the 1590's, not least where recusancy was involved.[2] It might be concluded that Thomas Lyniall, the Mayor at this time, was either slack or sympathetic to Catholicism, but he had after all shared responsibility as a High Commissioner for the imprisonment of several recusants, including Spurstowe, and he was thorough enough in following up the escape of another recusant prisoner, Thomas Stevenson, later in his mayoralty.[3] Is it possible that there was a certain reluctance to return a man of Spurstowe's calibre to prison? Spurstowe had told Richard Wright that 'if he had bene relessed he wold goe over into Ireland': if he in fact did so he might have ended his life most fittingly as an adventurer in the Irish Wars.

Spurstowe was a man of action whose disciplined words offered a

[1] H. Foley, *Records of the English College, S.J.*, VI, 571.

[2] For example, the case of Edward Cooper and his charges in 1594 (cf. infra, 108–10) or of Thomas Leake, the seminary, in 1601 (cf. infra, 124–6).

[3] M.L., 5, 100, which is a letter from Lyniall's successor as Mayor, John Fitton, in which Stevenson's escape is mentioned, though nothing further has been discovered about it.

coherent explanation of his political and religious convictions, but another prisoner in the Northgate, Ralph Langton, simply talked too much and too indiscreetly. In 1588 one of his conversations had been dangerous enough to lead to examination by the City justices, but in 1592 his words to the Mayor went so far as to land him in prison, from which, like Spurstowe, he petitioned the Mayor to release him:

In moste humble wise besecheth your woorship your suppliant, Rauffe Langton, that wheras your woorship have conceyved some displeasures towardes me concerninge some bad speches by me, to be uttered against yor woorship, I confesse and acknowledge mysellfe faultie, and that therein have abused mysellfe most badlie, for which I am moste hartely sory and doe wishe I had never ben borne, to comytt such an offence. Yet, seinge it is a thinge don and maie not be recalled I am willinge to accept of such ponishment as maie satisfy yor woorship . . . hopinge you will rather ascribe such my abuse to my owne follie then to take it upon anie cause of desert to your woorship. . . . And so moste humblie submittinge mysellfe to your good consideracons of me and of my humble suite, I rest your good pleasures, in this miserable state of ymprisonment. Northgate, this Sondaie, 23 of April, 1592.[1]

Langton and Spurstowe were two of several recusants who had been imprisoned by the city authorities in 1592, and these activities are the beginning in Chester of what Philip Hughes has called 'The Harrying of the Catholics in the North',[2] and they show what this meant in some detail at a local level. How this process continued in the county as well as in the city can be seen only to a much more limited extent. Two days after Spurstowe's escape and on the same day that they wrote to the Commissioners of the county to congratulate them on their diligence the Privy Council wrote also to the Justices of Assize for Chester County. The Earl of Derby and the Lancashire Commissioners had evidently questioned the Council about the correct way of dealing with obdurate recusants. Derby obviously favoured either imprisonment or custody with more orthodox people to provide instruction and win reformation. The Council stated that such recusants must be dealt with according to the law, and the Council be consulted about the best way to do this. The Justices were, finally, exhorted 'to be carefull in the execution of that charge against the recusant papist(s), in respect of the nomber latelie increased' through the work of Jesuits and Seminaries.

When the April Assizes met the law proved to be on the side of at least some of the accused, who were eight men from Ridley, Bunbury, charged with being absent from their parish church. All of them, William Cheidock, Henry and William Price, John Ridgeway, Peter Somner, William Stretbarrel, Robert Tatnall and Randle Wilson were recusants. Cheidock, Wilson and Somner appeared to answer the charge and complained that

[1] A.P., 1, 37. The date of his imprisonment, or release, is not known.
[2] P. Hughes, op. cit., III, 373.

H

the inquisition on which they were indicted was defective in law and their plea was allowed. A lengthy legal process had proved ineffective, though Cheidock, Somner, Stretbarrel[1] and Wilson did not escape the penalties of the law for long; all four were proclaimed in October and convicted at the Assizes of the following April, along with 72 other men and women, who were assessed for fines ranging from £1,440 to £20.[2]

These convictions have, in effect, already been analysed, as the recusants were those who were entered on the Recusant Roll for 1592–3. At the same time it is worth noting that on no previous occasion had so many recusants been indicted: earlier peaks in the rate of indictment had been 20 in 1587 and 51 in 1589. The rise to 76 is perhaps an indication of the steady growth of recusancy, for by the early 1590's, though not large in number, the recusants formed a recognisable community or series of communities, one of which was obviously in Chester, where financial relief was distributed by 'the Katholykes' to their poor brethren. There, the public face of the community was shown most boldly by the Massey family, drawing strength from hidden books and objects of personal devotion as well as from the priests who, saying masses, marrying Catholics and baptising their children, formed the private face of the community. What was open and what was secret joined hands in the county prison, Chester Castle, which clearly played an important part in keeping Catholicism alive, for its inefficiency and corruption offered wide scope to its inmates to practise and even spread their faith. Much of this was outside the knowledge of the authorities, but they knew enough to act confidently and firmly when they made their inquiry in 1592; they were firm enough to deal harshly with certain recusants and confident enough to make fine distinctions between them and those whose treatment was more lenient. Thus the rise in number of those indicted at the Assizes is not only an indication of the growth of recusancy or even of the increased activity of the authorities, but also of their increasing success in gaining convictions for recusancy; the growth of recusancy was paralleled by an increasing skill in the manipulation of the laws for their repression by the local authorities, who had steadily improved upon the fumbling, amateurish performance of earlier years.[3] When the Council of the North drew up its report in 1591 it had no confidence in the local authorities of Lancashire and Cheshire, but the extant evidence of their activities in Cheshire points to a real competence on the part of at least some of them; this is the central difference between the report of the Council of the North and the documentary evidence that has just been discussed.

In the summer of 1592 Derby's wish to deal with the more stubborn

---

[1] He was actually imprisoned in Chester Castle for much of 1592 (Chester, 21, 1, ff. 159 & 162).

[2] Chester, 29, 333, m. 11: 334, m. 17–20: Chester 21, 1, ff. 162–5.

[3] Doubtless assisted by the change in the method of convicting recusants introduced by 28 and 29 Elizabeth, c. 6: cf. supra, 68.

recusants by imprisonment had received government approval. As part of a general wave of restrictions, along with the other Lords Lieutenant he was instructed to commit the principal recusants in the counties in his charge to a safe place; this was because of 'the notable backwardness and defeccion in religion of late time growen generallie amongst her (Majesty's) subjectes of this realm, especiallie sithence the last libertie and leave graunted to such principall persons as were formerly comitted' to custody.[1] No clear evidence of action taken along these lines in Cheshire exists, though both the city and county Ecclesiastical Commissioners had been free enough in their use of imprisonment when they carried out their investigations at the opening of 1592.

The general tightening up of the restrictions on the recusants was further reflected in letters sent out by the Council to the Custos Rotulorum and Sheriffs in all the shires on 20 October 1592. All the justices were to swear an oath of loyalty and any who refused to do so were to be certified to the Council and replaced. The Council were sure that many existing justices were recusants and wanted them weeding out in order that the recusants as a whole might be brought to heel more speedily.[2]

It is right that the last word in all this should rest with the Privy Council. In 1592 the recusants of Cheshire received a rougher, more effective handling than ever before or ever after in the reign of Elizabeth I. The earlier drives to crush or reduce them, in 1581–2 or in 1589, and a later campaign of 1599–1600, were not so important. 1592 was the crucial year in the attempt to stem recusancy in Cheshire. The rest of the reign of Elizabeth is an anti-climax; never again was recusancy so strong and, in consequence, never again was so systematic a hunt needed. One looks in vain within Cheshire itself for any explanation of the scale and relative success of the activities of the authorities in 1592; Chadderton, the rod of iron, was ineffective by 1589, though, admittedly, Henry, fourth Earl of Derby, showed greater drive. But then, he was a member of the body that could claim credit for what success there was, the Privy Council. It was its unyielding pressure in advice, inquiry and reproof throughout the late 1580's and early 1590's that slowly pushed the local authorities into reasonably effective action.

[1] A.P.C., 1592, 110, dated 7 August.
[2] Ibid., 253.

CHAPTER VIII

THE FINAL DECADE OF THE REIGN

> Trusting upon shippes all them to convaye,
> Whiche was a riall rode that time, night and daye.
>
> H. Bradshaw, 'Legends of the Constable Sands'[1]

When the Irish Wars made Cheshire a base for reinforcements for the English army in Ireland a current saying in Cheshire was 'Better be hanged at home than die like dogs in Ireland'.[2] But while potential mustermen saw Ireland as a grave, it was more like a haven to the recusants, or at least a blessed stage in the tricky journey to Catholic France, Spain or the Netherlands, for which Chester offered itself as a port of exit. The Ecclesiastical Commissioners had been aware of this when making their inquiry at the beginning of 1592: 'because this City is a port towne, and that diverse passengers take shipping here for Ireland, we have comanded the inkepers and others that kepe lodging in this City to kepe notes of the names and special markes of all strangers resorting to their howses for diet or lodging, and to geve us knowledge presently therof', they wrote in their report to the Council.[3] These precautions echoed part of the Proclamation of 1591, while the Council, on 1 March 1594, ordered the Lords Lieutenant throughout the realm 'to take care about the landing of suspected persons not only at knowne and usuall portes but at creekes and by-places where no usuall landing is . . .',[4] and they had also sent specific instructions to the Mayor of Chester 'to serche for passengers into Ireland except they be knowen merchantes and suche like'.[5] Not only Chester, but the Mersey estuary and the broader estuary of the Dee would need some sort of watch maintaining over them if unlawful exits or entrances were not to take place. Almost immediately the examination took place before the Mayor of Chester of two boys and their guide who had been on their way to Ireland and beyond.[6]

Giving their names as Edward Cooper (or Cowper), John Warnford and Richard Thompson, the guide and the boys at first answered the Mayor's questions about their origins and purposes with an implausible

---

[1] E. Leigh, *Ballads and Legends of Chester*, 2.

[2] *Cal. S. P. Ireland, 1592–6*, XXVII, given in A. L. Rowse, *The Expansion of Elizabethan England*, 118.

[3] Cf. supra, 102. When a letter was sent to all counties at the end of 1593 for a list of the sons of gentlemen who had gone overseas unlicensed in the previous seven years (A.P.C., 1595–6, Appendix, 515, and Harl. MSS., 7042, f. 163), the Cheshire authorities replied with a nil return (Harl. MSS., 7042 f. 164v), as did Yorkshire, while Staffordshire reported five and Lancashire 32 (ibid., f. 164).

[4] A.P.C., 1595–6, Appendix, 516.

[5] M.L., 5, 220.　　　　　　　　　　　　[6] Ibid., 1, 59–62, 65–6 & 69–71.

mixture of truth and falsehood; in particular, it was claimed that the boys had been placed in Cooper's charge in Bedford in order that he should take them to Ireland to join Sir Richard Bingham, the notable soldier and governor of Connaught. Cooper, odd in appearance, with an 'artificiall lefte eie',[1] was first examined; then came the turn of 12-year-old John Warnford and lastly 11-year-old Richard Thompson, and it was not unnaturally from the younger boy that the Mayor gradually drew bits of the truth. After telling the Mayor, among other things, that 'he was at singing schole and doeth singe a treble parte', he was re-examined and confessed that recusancy lay at the back of their journey and that his true name was Richard Ody. Warnford was then re-examined and confessed the true nature of the journey. These examinations took place on 1 April; the next day the boys were thoroughly re-examined, and only then was Cooper seen again; doubtless confronted with the information drawn from the boys he at first largely 'saith as by his former speches he hath said', but on 3 April he too confessed.[2]

The boys were not going to join Sir Richard Bingham, though their journey had its beginnings in the actions of an equally remarkable Englishman, the former courtier turned Jesuit lay-brother, Thomas Pound. Ody, the son of Thomas Ody, a gentleman of Enmeth, which lay only a mile from Wisbech and its prison full of prominent priests and other recusants, described how

Mr. Thomas Pownde, nowe remeaning in Wissich prison for relygion, did send to this examinants father for this examinant to come unto hym about half yeres past, and at this examinant's comying to the prison the said Mr. Pownd sayd to this examinant that he wolde place this examinant in Ireland.

Later, Ody added that 'he hadde benne with Mr. Pownde five or six tymes'; it was Pound who advised him to 'turne his name' to Thompson 'that no man shall suspect him'. Warnford came from Limborne in Hampshire. His father, Oliver Warnford, was dead, and his mother, Elizabeth, a prisoner for recusancy in the London Fleet. Pound had arranged for the journey to Ireland, with the help of his own servant, Richard Baker, and Cooper's sister-in-law, Kathryn, as well as Cooper himself. Cooper

confesseth that the said two boies were delivered unto him at London by Richard Baker, servant to Mr. Pownde, which Baker doe ly in Alldegate Street, at the howse of one Kathryn Cooper, sister-in-law to this examinant, whose husband is in Dublin . . .

Financed by Pound, who gave to each boy through Baker enough money, mainly French, to see him through his journey, so that when searched Ody was found to have 'tenne French crownes and three duble pistolettes' and Warnford 'three French crownes and 4s. 6d. in silver in a little purse', they

[1] Ibid., 5, 218.　　　[2] Ibid., 1, 60–2.

seem to have travelled on horseback, with Cooper on foot, from London to Chester. Only en route for Chester did Ody learn of their final destination: he

confesseth that his fellow, John Warneford, as they came by the way, tolde him that they shall goe over into Spaine and reterne within five yeres, and before that this examinant did perceve none other but that they shall goe into Ireland and noe further.

Or so Ody claimed, while Warnford declared that 'one Richard Regby, a little boy' who had left them, 'whither this examinant knoweth not', had 'said that they shall goe over into Spain'.[1]

Cooper denied any personal knowledge of Pound or of the fathers of the boys. He claimed to be merely the guide, 'by the said Baker hyrrd for xs. in hand and xs. at his retern out of Ireland, to convey the said two boys into Ireland and to deliver them to one Mr. Cole dwelling in Dublin', though he did not know Cole, bore no letters for him and knew nothing of any directions that had been given to the boys. In fact, with his sister-in-law in London and her husband in Dublin, Cooper was the ideal go-between for the conveyance of Catholic boys to Ireland and was of greater importance than he was prepared to admit. This was clear to the authorities, for, from the very beginning of their investigation into the journey of Cooper and the boys they had been conducting a separate inquiry based on several letters found on Cooper.

One was from Cooper to Mrs. Agnes Mordant, a recusant who, like Cooper, lived in Bedford: Cooper informed her that he was about to travel to Ireland and asked if he might carry letters for her or be of service. Two further letters were from Mrs. Mordant to Robert Sefton of Mollington, near Chester: they asked if he had received a letter intended for the 'Lord Deputy of Ireland', if he would look after Cooper's horse in his absence, and if he would go to the house of Mrs. Mordant's son-in-law, Mr. Bold,[2] where he would find her nephew, Mr. Mordant, and Mr. Day, and pass on to them his answers to her inquiries. Finally, Cooper had carried a letter from Mrs. Mordant to her daughter, Mrs. Bold, which bore her greetings and commended Mordant and Day to her.[3]

The city authorities acted promptly on their discovery of these letters, for Mordant and Day might well be priests. On 2 April they examined Robert Sefton and wrote to Ferdinando, Lord Derby, informing him of the situation and asking him to examine Bold, who was outside their jurisdiction. Little was learned from Sefton, though he knew both Bold and Mrs. Mordant and was in correspondence with her. Derby acted even

[1] M.L., 59–61.
[2] Richard Bold of Bold, Prescot, twice Sheriff of Lancashire, though his wife and family were Catholic and he was sympathetic to the Catholic cause (V.C.H., Lancaster, III, 406).
[3] M.L., 5, 218–20 & 222.

more rapidly than the city authorities. Receiving their letter on the same day on which it had been written he visited Bold's home at Prescot, examined Bold, found Mordant and Day, whose presence Bold had at first denied, and sent them to Chester along with his reply to the letter from Chester. The date was still 2 April.[1]

Bold's family was Catholic, and his attempt to conceal Mordant and Day was suspicious enough, while Derby recollected that his father 'did much seek for such a man bearing such a name' (Mordant), but so far little of substance had resulted from the efficient action of the authorities. Nor did the examinations of John Mordant and Edmund Day, both from Bedfordshire, or a third man taken with them, Francis East, from Huntingdonshire reveal anything more; Mordant and Day insisted that they had journeyed north to buy cattle and East had joined them simply to enjoy their company. Thus, when the Mayor of Chester reported on the proceedings to the Privy Council he had to confess that 'as yet very little matter appeareth', and the suspects were eventually released.[2]

Anti-climax though this was, it had all followed from the apprehension of Cooper and his charges, and when the Mayor issued a warrant on 29 April for the execution of the Lord Treasurer's final instructions about them—the boys were to be separated, Ody being sent to the Bishop of Ely 'that suche order maie be taken for his educacon as shall be thought meete by his Lordship', and Warnford to the Lord Mayor of London—he saw the last of them,[3] but within little more than a month he had on his hands a larger group of boys bound on a similar errand, and they included another boy from Wisbech as well as the brother of John Warnford.

These were 'certen younge striplinges of England, under the chardge of one Bartholemew Wickam,[4] who had in purpose to transport themselves beyond seas to places of popishe religion'. They had been more successful in achieving their aim than the earlier trio, for they had got as far as Ireland before being apprehended; only there 'yt hath happened that their said intended voyadge is prevented'. Thus the Mayor was not called on to interrogate them but merely to hold them in Chester, whither they had been sent in June by the Lord Deputy of Ireland, until the wishes of the Council be made known to him, and early in July he was instructed to send them to appear before the Council, which was done by 8 July.[5]

[1] Ibid., 220–4.
[2] Ibid., I, 64 & 74: 5, 223 & 226–30.
[3] Ibid., I, 61, 65–6 & 69. But the last had not been seen of Cooper, who accompanied Warnford from Chester. He turned up in Chester on 28 September 1594, to declare that, under the Mayor's instructions, he and Warnford had been conveyed from constable to constable as far as Nantwich, whose constable refused to accept them. Cooper therefore took Warnford to London, where he eventually went to his mother in the Fleet (ibid., 5, 242–3).
[4] Son of Clement & Margaret Wickham of Newcastle-on-Tyne (ibid., I, 89); a Bartholomew Wickham of Geddinge, Suffolk, appears on the 1592–3 Recusant Roll (C.R.S., XVIII, 317).
[5] M.L., I, 89, 90, 96 & 102.

There is nothing to indicate that this second party had actually sailed from Chester or its neighbourhood in the first place, but wherever they had sailed from they had been assembled from over a very wide area of England. Henry and William Pownder, sons of Richard Pownder, a merchant, Robert Wall, son of John Wall, a draper, and Thomas Wylford, son of Robert Wylford, a lawyer, all came from London; Edward Warnford, whose brother had just been apprehended and whose mother was in the Fleet, was from Hampshire, John Hill, son of John Hill, was from Ayre in Suffolk, and Robert Colton was the son of Robert Colton, a Wisbech joiner; from the Midlands came Thomas Williamson of Tamworth, and the North was represented by Edmund Eymyng of Bashall, Whalley, Yorkshire, and Henry Kirckham, son of Thomas Kirckham, a husbandman of Hardhorne, Lancashire.[1] This was clearly a highly organised transit, and the presence of the second Warnford and a second boy from Wisbech makes one wonder whether Thomas Pound was behind it and also whether the first group was a trial run through Chester from which lessons were learned by the organisers of the larger party.

None of the boys came from Cheshire, but a year later, in July 1595, a Cheshire youth was arrested while attempting to make his escape abroad. He was George Huxley, son of a firm recusant, Thomas Huxley, a husbandman of Bunbury, by whose direction George

pretended to goe unto Spayne to some popishe universitie there and soe to become a Semenary priest contrary to his dutie to God and true religion and his allegeaunce to her Majestie, with lewde determynacon.[2]

Such, at any rate, was the blunt version of his aims as understood by the city authorities, but when he was examined by them the 15-year-old George tried to shift the responsibility for his journey away from his father. He said that he

was brought up at a school in Bunbury and left three weeks since, intending to go to France to learn the French language, though his father had appointed he should go to London to be apprenticed to such person as his brother, Thomas Huxley (a mercer in Cheapside), had provided, and gave him 20s. to pay expenses. He came to Chester to join a carrier to take him to London and met there Thomas Stevenson, who was known to his father, and was for some time in Chester Castle for recusancy; he advised the boy to go to France and promised, if he should do so and change his name, to place him better than he would be in London.[3]

Huxley was not arrested alone. With him was Thomas Cauze, the 17-year-old son of Richard Cauze of Drayton, Shropshire, another determined recusant. Thomas Cauze said that he had been sent by his father to journey with Stevenson to France, and while lodging at the Huxley's it

[1] M.L., 1, 89. [2] M.B., 1592–6, 11 August 1595.
[3] S.P., 12, 253, 22. This consists of the examinations of the youths, or rather, abstracts of them sent by the city council to the Privy Council.

had been agreed by Huxley that his son should accompany them, and so, the next morning,

Stevenson went to Chester to agree for the passage over and upon his return they left together. They lodged at Henry Primrose's house in Chester, (and) next day went to Batson's house at Neston and stayed a week. Stevenson agreed with a Frenchman there, laden with merchandise for France, for their passage for 10s. each. . . .[1]

Stevenson, who had escaped from the Northgate in 1592 and been imprisoned in Chester Castle for much of 1593-4, was, like Edward Cooper and Bartholemew Wickham before him, the all-important guide. Cauze had a letter in Latin from him, sewn into his doublet. The letter 'was to have been delivered to the chief of the university', while Cauze was told by Stevenson 'to call himself Banester, so that he might not be known'. Further, Cauze 'has heard Stevenson reprehend the religion used in England as false, and he promised to help (him) over the seas to learn the truth . . .'. According to Cauze, another boy, George Titley, should have accompanied them; he intended to go to Spain to enter a seminary there with Huxley, but after going into Chester the others never saw him again.[2]

'Being in Gode's good provedence prevented', the youths, but not the elusive Stevenson, were 'apprehended and therefore comitted to the gaole of the Northgate',[3] and on 19 July the incident was reported to Burghley by the Mayor, Fulk Aldersey, and Burghley's advice about what to do next was sought.[4] In accordance with his advice sureties for each of the youths were bound in recognisance. The youths were to attend church according to the law and to appear when required before the Mayor of Chester. Huxley was treated as a boy misled by his elders; it was partly because he

not only seemeth penitent and sorry for suche his degression but alsoe promyseth reformacion thereof . . . and of his tender yeares, not understanding to what end or purpose this lewde perswasion tended unto

that he was released from prison. Precautions were taken to prevent his future corruption, for he was not to

repayre, resort unto or have any conferaunce or talke with his said father so long as his said father shall contynue a recusant and an enemy to God and her Majestie.[5]

But Huxley's youthful contrition was misleading, for about two years later he escaped to Ireland and after spending a year or so there entered the

---

[1] Ibid. Primrose was a recusant (cf. Appendix I), but nothing is known of 'Batson'. After the silting up of the Dee estuary port facilities were built near Neston.
[2] Ibid. George Titley, a sherman of Wickstead, Malpas, and his wife, Gwen, were presented as recusants in September 1613 (Harl. MSS., 2095, No. 7, f. 10).
[3] M.B., loc. cit.   [4] S.P., loc. cit.
[5] M.B., loc. cit.

English College at Valladolid in January 1599, to re-enter England as a priest in 1607.[1]

Within little more than a year, between April 1594 and July 1595, three parties of youths attempting to escape overseas, where the Catholic faith could be freely practised, had been intercepted. These were the unsuccesful would-be escapers, and Chester obviously remained a port from which others might succeed where these had failed. Other youths or young men from Cheshire began to train abroad as priests in the 1590's—Peter Davenport, Frances Fitton, Edward Leigh and John Starkey—and though there is no evidence that any of them escaped via Chester such escapes continued to be organised through the port, as a letter written at the end of 1601 makes clear. It was written by a prisoner, James Feilde, to his captor, Mr. Preadis, outlining Feilde's life in order to win more lenient treatment after he had been captured with a group of youths attempting to escape overseas. Feilde stated that he had become acquainted with 'Mr. Physomans', the Jesuit, in Chester, and through him he met 'the guide of these youths'. He travelled with the guide to Tredach in Ireland. He possessed a Catholic book and beads and stated that he bought them in Dublin with the aid of the Jesuit.[2] The Jesuit would probably have been Henry Fitzsimon, the well-known priest who was sent on the Irish mission late in 1597 and was arrested in 1599, remaining in prison until 1604.[3] Feilde's letter indicates that Fitzsimon may have been in Chester in 1598 or 1599, in the brief spell of activity allowed to him before his capture, possibly organising the escape of Catholic boys and youths via Chester and Ireland.[4]

Dealing with would-be escapers was one of the duties that were carried out by the Chester authorities as a result of the particular position and function of the city, but the routine enforcement of the ordinary recusancy laws in the county as a whole also went on throughout the final decade of the reign of Elizabeth. It would be some years before an anti-recusant drive of similar magnitude to that of 1592 would again be needed, for what had then been uncovered and the convictions for recusancy that followed from it offered a firm foundation for future action. Thus few recusants were indicted during the rest of the 1590's. At the Assizes the first indictments for absence from church, in July 1594, were of Elizabeth Dutton and three of her servants, John, Alice and Eleanor Whitby,[5] though, like five men

---

[1] Cf. entry on Huxley in Appendix II.

[2] H.M.C., Salis. MSS., XI, 531, letter assigned to 1601, c. 25 December.

[3] D.N.B., VII, 209.

[4] This is speculative, of course, and, in fact, Fitzsimon led a very active, public life in Ireland which would seem to have offered little opportunity for such expeditions.

[5] Chester, 21, 1, f. 173. John and Alice Whitby were servants of the Massey family, and it is assumed that Eleanor Whitby was also. Elizabeth Dutton was the daughter of Richard and Margaret Massey and after the death of her husband in 1593 she seems to have returned to the family home at Waverton. All four were indicted as of Aldford parish.

who were indicted in the following October, they do not seem to have been convicted. The five men, Gilbert Burscowe and Thomas Hesketh, both gentlemen, Robert Ball, Nicholas Mawdesley and Thomas Stevenson had all been prisoners in Chester Castle earlier in the year[1] and were all indicted as 'of Chester' for absence from Backford parish church; only Robert Ball appeared to answer the ill-worded indictment and he was acquitted when it was shown that he belonged to neither Chester nor Backford.[2] Thomas Hesketh was, in fact, from Thurstaston, while Thomas Stevenson was well known as a recusant in Chester: he had escaped from imprisonment for recusancy in the Northgate in 1592 and was later to act as guide to George Huxley and Thomas Cauze when they tried to make their way abroad in 1595. The failure of these indictments of 1594 is reflected in the five successful indictments that followed in 1595, for they included Alice and Eleanor Whitby, and Thomas Hesketh and his wife Elizabeth. The fifth, Margaret Primrose, was a member of the Chester household at which Huxley and Cauze had lodged. Each of the five was assessed for a fine of £140 for seven months' absence from church.[3]

There would in fact be little need for action to be taken against recusants at the Assizes, for by the Act of 1587 convicted recusants who were not reconciled to the Anglican Church were to pay fines into the Exchequer twice yearly without further indictment, so that only newly emergent recusants or those who had conformed temporarily would be likely to appear. At the same time the Act of 1587 had severely circumscribed the role of the justices, for it limited the conviction of recusants to the King's Bench, the Assizes and the Gaol Delivery Sessions: convictions could no longer take place at Quarter Sessions, though presentments could still be made there. Thus, apart from the presentment of Richard Cheswis in July 1602,[4] the County Quarter Sessions were uninvolved in the repression of recusancy. Similarly, although the justices of Chester city were active in the oversight of suspicious strangers they dealt with very few presentments for recusancy. Robert Browne and Elen Wilden, the 'poor folkes' who spent several years in the Northgate for recusancy, were presented before the City Sessions on 21 January 1597, for absence from church for an unspecified period and were each assessed for the old 12d. fine.[5] Browne conformed in the autumn of 1598,[6] but Elen Wilden was presented for absence on two further occasions: on 7 November 1598, she was again fined 12d., and on 4 May 1599, along with Elizabeth Barton, who was presented for absence during the previous four years, she was

---

[1] Ibid., f. 172.
[2] Ibid., 29, 338, m. 16d.
[3] Ibid., 21, 1, f. 178. The fine is recorded on the Recusant Roll for 1596-7 (R.R., 5, m. 28).
[4] C.S.B., Indictments and Presentments, 1592-1617, f. 70v.
[5] M.B., 1596-9, 21 January, 39 Eliz.
[6] M.L., 1, 167: cf. infra, 122.

referred for punishment to the High Commission,[1] which had been renewed for Chester on 31 January 1599.[2]

Only in 1600 was there a major burst of anti-recusant activity, but the
one surviving trace of this is the large group of convictions, 51 in all, recorded in the Recusant Roll for 1599–1600; the convictions and assessments for fines of £240 for 12 months' absence from church had taken
place at the Assizes of September 1600.[3]

Of course, recusants continued to be presented to the bishop's or archbishop's visitors, but they occupied an increasingly subordinate role in the
repression of recusancy. Citation before them was not particularly daunt-
ing; as with earlier visitations most of those charged with an offence
against the ecclesiastical law did not trouble to appear to answer their
charges and such as did appear for recusancy or an allied charge received
little more than a warning. The visitors barked but did not bite, even if
those with whom they dealt could be involved in considerable expense.
Not one of the 18 men and women presented as recusants at the Metropolitan Visitation of 1595 appeared to answer the charge, though a witness
affirmed on behalf of Alice Yardley of Shocklach that she had told her that
she would attend church, and the judges therefore ordered that she do so
and that her attendance be certified to them. Similarly, Jane Davye of St.
Bridget's, Chester, who along with her husband, Edward, was presented
'for kepinge of popishe reliques (such) as a superaltare and popishe books',
was admonished as follows when she appeared:

. . . because she hath already delivered the said bookes in June(?) last(?);
therefore, being very pore, she is dismissed et monita est to be quiet towardes the
church wardens sub pena excommunication.

Two elderly ladies who were both presented as absentees from church
received lenient but very different treatment. Mrs. Alice Whitmore of
Neston 'hathe bene diseased these sex wekes last, and so not able to travel
at this time without danger', stated Richard Hough, who appeared on her
behalf, and he was told to signify to her the Visitors' pleasure that she
attend church. More striking was the comment on Lady Egerton: 'the
Lady (is) specially dispensed withall from her Majestie's (laws) and not to
be delt withall by the justices or ecclesiasticall judge'.[4] Throughout her
many years of opposition to the religious settlement she received favourable treatment, and if it occasions no surprise that she continued in her
long-standing recusancy, being presented as a recusant before the Diocesan Visitation in 1598, the year before her death, the ineffectual nature
of the ecclesiastical censures is clear in the fact that Alice Yardley, Jane

[1] M.B., 1596–9, 7 November, 40 Eliz., and 4 May, 41 Eliz.
[2] S.P., 12, 266, unnumbered.
[3] R.R., 8, m. 10d. A diocesan inquiry, made at the turn of 1603, gave the number of
recusants in Cheshire as 54 (S.P.D., James I, 9, 28).
[4] York, R.VI, A 14, ff. 2v, 6 & 14v: A 15, ff. 36v, 44v, 57 & 62.

Davye and Alice Whitmore were also presented as absentees at the same time, and it was then specified of Alice Yardley that she 'absenteth herself from the church since the laste visitation'.[1]

The Metropolitan Visitation had been made during the short vacancy between the end of Chadderton's episcopate in April 1595, when he passed on to the see of Lincoln, and the succession of Hugh Bellot in June. Bellot was reputed to be strict with recusants, but there is no record of his dealings with them in the short time that he filled the bishopric before his death in June 1596. The see then remained vacant until July 1597, when it was occupied by Richard Vaughan, who was associated with the Calvinist wing of the church and who was also said to be severe with the Catholics. He continued to occupy the see until the end of Elizabeth's reign, making diocesan visitations in 1598 and 1601.

In the Visitation of 1598, 55 recusants were presented, and what was perhaps most striking about it was the way in which greater pressure than ever before was put upon two interrelated family groups, the Masseys and the Duttons. Although suspicion of Catholic sympathies had long fallen on various branches of these families, only Peter Dutton and his wife, Elizabeth, her father, Richard Massey and his wife, Margaret, their eldest son, Richard, and Mary, the wife of John Massey of Coddington had actually been recusants. Of these, only the younger Richard Massey was presented as a recusant in 1598, though he was then joined by his wife, Jane (a Dutton), and along with them Thomas Massey, and Robert and William Dutton were presented for absence from Waverton church, and Hugh Dutton was presented there as a non-communicant, as were John Massey and his wife at Backford; the last two 'did not communicate at Easter laste but receyved at Potington, his brother's house'. Puddington Hall was a well-known Catholic centre in the early seventeenth century, though no signs of recusancy have been detected there in the reign of Elizabeth I. But it looks as though by the late 1590's the authorities were attempting to deal with the Catholicism that was probably widespread in these families as well as with their hard core recusants.[2]

Lady Egerton was presented as a recusant in 1598 along with a larger number of her household than on any previous occasion. Randolph Egerton, probably her grandson, and two servants, Cecily Buckley and William Chawver were presented as recusants, while the way in which her household acted as a Catholic centre was made clear in the presentment of Elena Greene, 'a younge woman corrupted at Ladie Egerton's howse'.[3]

Lady Egerton was presented as a parishioner of Astbury, where she resided in the closing years of her life and where she was buried after her death in 1599. Is it possible that her removal from Ridley was forced by the authorities in order to draw her away from the actively recusant southwest of the county? Eighteen 'obstinate recusants' were presented from

[1] E.D.V., 1, 12, ff. 13, 31, 43v & 56.   [2] Ibid., ff. 15v & 29v.   [3] Ibid., f. 56.

her former parish of Bunbury in 1598, and an added idea of the strength of recusancy there may be gained from the presentment of three of them, William Cheswis, Robert Longton and Thomas Smith (as well as of another recusant who was not actually presented as such on this occasion, John Langton), because they 'had children borne in the parish, not knowne where they were chrispenned'.[1] William Poole, the recusant of Marbury, was presented for the same reason, as had also been the case at the Metropolitan Visitation of 1595.[2]

Only 28 recusants were presented as such at Bishop Vaughan's second diocesan visitation in 1601, but the fall from the 1598 total of 55 is to some extent explained by the fact that no recusants were presented from Bunbury in 1601. However, 15 men and women were presented 'for not cominge to Church this last yeare and not receveinge the communion',[3] and in the case of the known recusants who made up most of the 15 this was only a terminological difference. But actively recusant though southwest Cheshire was, perhaps the most striking aspect overall of the visitations of 1598 and 1601 is the small number of recusants presented from Cheshire compared to the lengthy lists, often parish after parish, from Lancashire, with the exception of the Deanery of Manchester.

Many of the most determined recusants continued to be presented before the episcopal visitors, but the authority whose pressures they were most likely to feel was the High Commission. When Elen Wilden and Elizabeth Barton were presented for absence from church before the City Quarter Sessions in 1599 they were referred by the justices to the Ecclesiastical Commissioners, and the important role of the Commission can also be illustrated from the Recusant Rolls; there, during the decade, 1594–1603, 31 seizures of land or goods are recorded, and in 22 of these cases it is stated that they were ordered by the Ecclesiastical Commissioners. It is a pity that only such indirect evidence as this can be shown of the work of the body that was assuming an increasingly important role in the repression of recusancy.

In these years a total of 143 recusants can be traced, and their geographical distribution largely confirms that observed in earlier years. Over a third, in all 57, came from the parishes that had previously contained the most striking concentrations of recusants, Bunbury and Malpas, while the vast majority of the 143 were from the west of the county. The one surprise is that only 10 were from Chester city: is this a reflection of the success of the energetic city authorities in dealing with recusancy?

No surprise is occasioned by the social distribution of the 94 recusants whose status or occupation is known. Once more, the gentry (36 of them) form a disproportionately large group, while most of the rest—38 yeomen

---

[1] E.D.V., f. 64v.
[2] Ibid., f. 68v; York, R.VI, A 14, f. 10.
[3] Ibid., 1, 12a, f. 64v.

or husbandmen, one professional man, two businessmen and seven craftsmen—were men and women of a certain economic independence. There
were nine servants and one labourer, and at least two of the servants seem
to have been household officials of some importance rather than menials.

Rather more than half of the recusants were women, who, as a proportion of the total, continued to rise; of the 81 recusants who emerge as
such in these last ten years of the reign 49—three-fifths—were women.
Special attention had been drawn to them and to household servants by
the Council in August 1593, when instructions were sent out to all dioceses

to inquire of the wives and servantes of recusantes that refuse to come to the
Church, and to certify their names, with the qualitie of their husbandes.[1]

Though the government had eventually woken up to the importance of
women in the development of recusancy and advised more or less stringent
imprisonment for them[2] it was not long before this seemed an inadequate
answer to the problem that they presented, and Henry, Earl of Derby, had
been quick to see the provisions of the Act against Popish Recusants of
1593[3] as an alternative. Shortly before his death[4] he inquired of the
Council as to how the statute could be used against 'verie many widdowes
and others of accompt', whose obstinacy remained unaffected by imprisonment. The Council therefore instructed the Attorney- and Solicitor-
Generals to advise Derby on how it might be done,[5] though no evidence
that it was in fact used against Cheshire women has been found.

Such penalties as were borne by the recusants were fines, the loss of lands
or goods, or imprisonment. The Recusant Rolls record 56 fines in these
years, five of £140 that were levied in September 1595,[6] and 51 of £240
in September 1600.[7] Recusants from all levels of society were fined, but
there is no indication that any of these fines were ever paid or, at least,
paid in full,[8] and demonstrable financial loss, through the seizure of lands
or goods, was borne by a relatively small group, 28 in all.[9]

When the first Recusant Roll was drawn up all who had by that time,
1593, suffered sequestration were of the gentry. The Rolls then show how
in the following eight years, while more recusants of the gentry class were

[1] A.P.C., 1595–6, Appendix, 513.   [2] Ibid., 1592–3, intro. xxviii.
[3] 35 Eliz., c. 2.
[4] He died in September 1593, and was succeeded by Ferdinando, the fifth Earl, who
held the title for only a few months: on his death in April 1594, he was succeeded by
William, the sixth Earl (1594–1642).
[5] A.P.C., 1592–3, 234, letter dated 14 May 1593.
[6] R.R., 5, m. 28: cf. supra, 115.
[7] Ibid., 8, m. 10d: cf. supra, 116.
[8] Neither 'deb' nor 'quietus est' is entered beside any of the names of those assessed
for fines, whilst action ('fiat commissio') was ordered only in the cases of Elizabeth Hesketh
and Jane Whitmore.
[9] 'Deb', implying a satisfactory settlement of the matter, is inserted by most of these
and 'quietus est' by some.

penalised in this way, the lesser land-owners, yeomen and husbandmen freeholders, also lost land. Thus, while gentlemen like Randle Aldersey, William Poole and John Whitmore the younger lost land, so did four husbandmen or yeomen, Thomas Huxley, John Maddocks, John Whitby and John Wilson, and two women of the same social group, Katherine Crocket and Elen Wooley.

Losses from the forfeiture of goods ranged from one especially large seizure worth £45 suffered by William Poole in January 1593, to one of goods worth 12d. seized from Ralph Cooke in April 1594,[1] though the majority of seizures were in the range of £1 to £12. As might be anticipated recusants of middling status were penalised by this loss of goods to a greater extent than the land-owning gentry. Thus, while four of the gentry suffered from this, namely Peter Spurstowe (the brother of the Richard Spurstowe who escaped from the Northgate in 1592), John Whitmore the younger, and Richard and William Poole, so did 15 yeomen or husbandmen.

In all this two men seem to have attracted excessive attention from the authorities and suffered heavy penalisation. William Poole lost goods worth £45 and lands worth 41s. 8d. a year in 1593, lands worth 17s. 9d. a year and goods worth £20 18s. 4d. in 1595, goods worth £5 and lands worth 18s. 8d. a year in 1598, and lands worth £20 a year in 1599. Similar treatment was meted out to Thomas Huxley, whose son first failed and then succeeded in escaping overseas to train for the priesthood; goods of his worth 46s. were seized in 1594, 67s. 8d. in 1595, and £9 in 1598, while he also lost the rents of lands worth 22s. 4d. a year in 1595, and £4 in 1599.[2] No-one else was penalised so systematically.

As a means of penalising recusants who could not pay their fines the seizure of lands or goods was, for a government increasingly dominated by financial considerations in its attitude to recusancy, more satisfactory than the earlier alternative of imprisonment. Thus, if little mercy was shown to those long-standing, long-suffering inmates of Chester Castle, John Whitmore, Richard Massey, Thomas Maddocks and Alice, Richard and William Cheswis,[3] no-one else joined them for any length of time. In 1594 Edward Probin and John Maddocks completed the imprisonment that had begun for them in 1592, while Gilbert Burscowe, Robert Ball, Thomas Hesketh, Nicholas Mawdesley and Thomas Stevenson completed their rather shorter imprisonment. Mrs. Margaret Massey endured a short spell in the Castle in 1594 (her third), as did Richard Poole in 1596, and Eleanor Darme, Elmcott and Thomas Elmideth (?), Thomas Huxley, Henry Killiburne, John Maddocks, Jane Mellung, Edward Probin and

---

[1] R.R., 2, m. 6: 6, m. 12.
[2] Ibid., 2, m. 6: 5, m. 28: 6, m. 12: 8, m. 10d.
[3] Massey gained his release in 1595, as is shown in what follows, Whitmore seems to have died c. 1597-8 (cf. entry in Appendix I), and the Cheswises and Thomas Maddocks were still in prison in September 1598 (Chester, 21, 1, f. 198).

Peter Stoke in 1598.[1] Thus 22 recusants were imprisoned at one time or another from 1594–1603, though only six of them were long-term prisoners.

Richard Massey was fortunate enough to gain a respite under the terms of the Act against Popish Recusants of 1593,[2] which enabled limited freedom to be granted to irreconcilable recusants with little risk to the authorities. He had evidently made some sort of request under the terms of the Act and his case had been forwarded to the Council by the county authorities. The Council replied on 2 July, 1595 as follows:

Whereas one Richard Massy, gentleman, hath for the space of theise tenne yeares, as is alleaged, remayned prisoner in the Castle of Chester for matter of recusancie. Forasmuch as he is said to be verie aged, growen weake and full of infirmityes by reason of his close imprisonment, and that by the testimonye of the late Bushop of Chester he is a man simple and unlearned, and therefore not like to doe hurte to others by his conversation or persuasions, we are contented he be confyned to some certaine place of aboade, as by the late Statute is ordayned, and doe therefore praie and requier you . . . to give order for the same accordingly, and so sett him at libertie.

Massey was in consequence discharged from prison, receiving instead a freedom circumscribed by the five-mile radius around his home at Waverton, for the observing of which he was bound in the heavy recognisance of £200.[3]

By the following year, 1596, the substitution of confinement to the home for imprisonment was fairly general in the country as a whole, but it was only with bad grace that John Whitmore was allowed an even more limited freedom than Massey's. Only because he was so infirm that further unbroken imprisonment might put him 'in perill of his life' were the Council prepared to allow him, under bond, to visit 'the Bathe' for the sake of his health, and clearly this was much more than it was thought he deserved:

. . . by some good informacion we have receaved concerning the said Whitmore we find him verie unworthy of favour. Nevertheless, that nether himself nor any of his sort may justlie complaine of any straightnes used toward them for any meanes that may appertaine to their health, and that they may have cause to acknowledge more favour used toward them than they deserve . . .

he should be allowed to visit Bath, after which he should return to prison in Chester (where he had already spent about 12 years), which he evidently did, remaining a prisoner in all probability until his death.[3]

---

[1] Chester, 21, 1, ff. 172–98. Darme, the Elmideths(?), Killiburne, Mellung and Stoke are not known to be recusants but are assumed to be so as all other prisoners listed in this Assize book are recusants.   [2] 35 Eliz., c. 2.

[3] C.S.F., 1595, F 2, D 30–2 & D 66.

[4] A.P.C., 1595–6, 435, dated 6 June 1596 (letter from the Council to the Mayor of Chester). Committal to family custody for Whitmore had been thought of by the Council in 1592, but not carried out (H.M.C., Savis. MSS., IV, 240).

By the end of the next year, 1597, the Northgate was almost empty of recusant prisoners. A list of its prisoners from that time includes only one recusant, Robert Browne,[1] though Elen Wilden was presented with him as a recusant in prison before the Diocesan Visitation in September 1598.[2] Browne had been in the Northgate since at least 1591, and seems to have gained his release only when, on 20 October 1598, he joined three other men, Richard Maghull, Gabriel Chawe and Thomas Shelton, in promising conformity to the ecclesiastical law. First, Maghull acknowledged

... that I have highlie offended God and the Queene's Majesty in absenting myselfe from the Churche and the exercyses of religion nowe established within this realme, and am hertelie sorie for the same, and nowe doe humblie desier that my submission unto trew religion now professed and my renuntiation and abueration of all popery, popishe superstition and idolitry maye be admitted, and further doe promyse to contynue my obedyence to her Majesty and the present proceeding of the Churche of England as it is nowe governed, during my lief, by Gode's assistaunce ...

Chawe added his submission below, while Shelton and Browne, both apparently illiterate or semi-literate, were included by the addition of, 'We, whose names are underwritten, doe alsoe subscrybe to the submission above written, without fraud, with a syncere mynde'.[3] This presumably ended Browne's lengthy stay in the noxious Northgate, but unfortunately nothing can be said as to the way in which these promises of conformity were gained.

The pressure to conform was heavy and these four men were not alone in easing their lives in this way. Margaret Ravenscroft (formerly Mrs. Hocknell) was presented before the Metropolitan Visitation as an obstinate recusant in 1595, but by 1598 was before the Diocesan Visitation as a noncommunicant only, and she then promised to receive the communion. In 1595 Alice Yardley expressed her wish to conform, as did Henry Heape of Tarvin and Richard Longton of Bunbury in 1598, though all three absented themselves from church afterwards. Mary Massey of Coddington, and Anne Moyle and Katherine Dod of Shocklach all appear to have conformed to the extent of attending church by the late 1590's, though they drew the line at receiving communion. And, finally, the agony of choice facing the recusant is made abundantly clear in the case of Anne Mallam of West Kirby: an absentee in 1587, a recusant in 1590, by 1592 she was in prison, but then promised conformity: nevertheless, she was indicted for 12 months' absence and assessed for a fine of £240 in 1593: five years later when she was presented before the Diocesan Visitation as a noncommunicant she insisted that this was only 'by reason of the insuffiencie

[1] Q.S.E., 5, f. 108, undated, but almost certainly from late 1597.
[2] E.D.V., 1, 12, f. 16v.
[3] M.L., 1, 167. Browne's name is given simply as 'Browne', and it is assumed that this was Robert Browne, the recusant prisoner.

of the curate': yet she was presented as a non-communicant again in 1601 and, finally, indicted for six months' absence in 1610.[1]

To that extent only can the success of the authorities in inducing conformity be documented, but, judging by Chester city, they were much more aware of the problems associated with recusancy and active in dealing with them than they had been in the 1580's and before. At a time when the Irish War placed great administrative burdens on the city its officials were alert for suspicious strangers and meticulously thorough in examining and inquiring about them: this is especially clear in their dealings with the youths who were intercepted when trying to leave the country in 1594 and 1595. It was suspicion that they were priests that led to the prompt inquiries about Mordant and Day in 1594, and two similar and almost simultaneous inquiries took place. On 11 April Robert Allert, a yeoman of London and Staffordshire, was examined. Aged 61, he claimed to have been Registrar to the Dean and Chapter of Westminister for 12 years, and for further long spells to have served the Clerk of the Papers, and then Walsingham, abroad. He had been in Staffordshire for the previous year and a half, equipped with a warrant to search for his wife. Contact with Catholics had been considerable in at least two of these roles and it was evidently his dealings with the recusant prisoner, Richard Massey, that had aroused apprehensions about him. Allert claimed to have met Massey through his namesake, Richard Massey of Grafton,[2] and had known him for some three weeks, but had never talked with him on religious matters, and he denied any acquaintance with Whitmore.[3] There is nothing to show whether or not all or any of this was true, though at the end of 1595 a Jesuit prisoner evidently escaped from the castle: could this have been Allert?[4]

A month later, on 11 May, two men and a youth who had been detained by Randle Stanley, captain of the Isle of Man, were examined about their meeting together and their movements. One of them, Robert Barton, a Scot, had travelled widely in Europe to gain a knowledge of medicine, but in spite of this the Mayor decided that they were not priests or papists and merely detained them pending instructions from the Council, who ordered their release.[5]

The authorities not only watched closely for suspicious strangers but also observed any comings and goings at the prisons, as in the case of Allert, and two other inquiries took place in 1594 as a result of this. Ralph Horton, a sherman, was examined by the Mayor on 9 February on suspicion of giving aid to the recusant prisoners. He denied this, but admitted

[1] Cf. the relevant entries in Appendix A.
[2] In 1582 he was fined 40s. by the High Commission for 'setting fourth certeine papisticall plaies and showes call(ed) Tiroll(?)' (Ex. Dep., m. 7).
[3] Q.S.E., 5, f. 37.
[4] Ibid., f. 57. This is an examination about the escape; the Jesuit is not named and no information is given about the escape.   [5] M.L., 1, 84; 5, 235-41.

that he had not received communion for two years because he was at variance with Peter Jenkin, nor had he been to church because 'he hath not his ordenary usuall seate therein'; he promised amendment. Later, on 6 May, John Andrew, a shoemaker, was questioned about the behaviour of a fellow shoemaker, John Walker, who had evidently refused to receive the communion at his parish church at the previous Easter, saying that he would do so at Tattenhall. Andrew stated that when, he

about the feaste daie of the Purificacion of the Blessed Mary the Virgin laste paste was going to the Minster service to here service, and the said John Walker . . . in very bitter and hasty termes and contencions called this examinant back agane and asked this examinant whither he wold goe? And this examinant answered, 'To the Minster, to service'. And the same Walker asked this examinant what he wold doe ther? And this examinant said, 'To here the Word of God'. And therupon the said Walker said that the Word of God is not in England, and therupon this examinant said to the same Walker that he . . . was not the Queene's friend. And this examinant further saith that . . . Walker was accostomed to goe downe to the castle amongst the recusantes to serve them with shoes upon the Sondaie mornings, both to Mr. Whitmor and others.[1]

These routine inquiries seem to have led nowhere, but a striking success was gained by the city authorities in 1601, when, on 16 August, they were notified that a suspected seminary was in the vicinity. A hurried deposition was made by Robert Atkinson, a gentleman of Dublin, in which he said that he,

goinge this daie in the aforenoone betweene the cittie of Chester and Boughton did see Thomas Leeke, who as this deponent hath heard is a seminarie priest, rydinge towardes Boughton. And one other man in a cloake . . . whom this examinant knoweth not, rode in company with him. And after him there rode aboute ix or x persons whom this examinant knoweth by syght but knoweth not their names, and knoweth them all to be recusants . . .[2]

Action was evidently taken immediately, for Leake, the suspected seminary, and three of his companions, Bartholemew Brooksbie, a gentleman of Frisby on the Wreak, Leicestershire, his son, Gregory, and their servant, Matthew Green, were apprehended later on the same day in Nantwich by John Francis, postmaster of Chester.

They were examined punctiliously by the justices of Chester city the next day, 17 August. So many Catholic books and other objects had been found on them that it was impossible to deny their Catholicism.[3] Thus Bartholemew Brooksbie admitted that

the twoe bookes that were taken with him, thone named A Method to Meditate on the Psalter of Our Blessed Lady, and the other booke called Palestra Hominis Catholice were his bookes, and (he) useth them in his prayers.[4]

[1] Q.S.E., 5, ff. 35 & 39. [2] Q.S.F., 49, 85.
[3] Matthew Green made it clear that he attended church and received communion (ibid., 100, f. 2). [4] Ibid., 100, f. 1.

Similarly his son Gregory, at 16 just old enough to be penalised as a recusant, agreed 'that the book called *Modus Orandi Deo* is his booke'.[1] Leake admitted to being 'catholiquely affected and catholiquely perswaded', but his possessions clearly pointed to his being a priest: he had

a paier of beades . . . crucifixes and ringes of jett with the picture of Chryst uppon them, and three bookes, one called the Romane Breviary, another the Romane Catichisme, the third called the same(?) of Cases of Conscience, as he termeth them . . .[2]

When they were examined the main object of both Brooksbie and Leake was therefore to conceal Leake's priesthood while admitting to being Catholics.

Brooksbie claimed that what had begun as a journey 'to see Roger Hurleston, gentleman, and other of his freindes in the countie of Chester' had ended as a pilgrimage to the ancient shrine of Holywell in Flintshire when he and 'a gentleman who named himself Thomas Ratcliffe' met by chance in Newcastle, Staffordshire, and decided to travel together to Chester and thence to 'a well called Halliwel'. He readily admitted that 'he was not at the church nor receaveth the communion these twoe yeares last paste', but in describing his activities kept Leake's part in them to a minimum, just as he kept Leake's name out of his account. Ratcliffe was Leake, of course.[3]

When Leake was examined he was in a tight corner and knew it. Aged 33 or 34 he was born at Marston, Staffordshire, the son of Richard and Elizabeth Leake, and had been schoolmaster to the children of Adam Loftus, Lord Chancellor of Ireland,[4] for two or three years, and then became parson of Maynooth in Ireland and evidently preached on a well-known occasion in Dublin. His career was described by one Edward Burne of Dublin,[5] but Leake did not describe it in quite the same way, ascribing most of it to a fictitious brother of his, Thomas Leake, while persistently naming himself as William. He, William, had merely 'attended on his said brother' for three or four years and, after a spell in England, had spent another year or two in further attendance on his brother at the Lord Chancellor's in Ireland. Two years' service with Lady Malbie in Dublin followed 'and (he) only attended on her and did her noe other service'.[6] This was unconvincing enough, but when he came to answer questions about his more recent activities his explanations were more obviously self-incriminating.

He had spent the previous five or six years in England, mainly in London: when asked where he had stayed in London he 'refuseth to make

[1] Ibid., f. 2.   [2] Ibid., 101, f. 2v.   [3] Ibid., 100.
[4] Adam Loftus (1533?–1605), Archbishop of Armagh and Lord Chancellor of Ireland (cf. D.N.B., XXXIV, 73).
[5] Q.S.F., 49, 84, dated 19 August 1601.
[6] Ibid., 101.

answeare thereunto for feare of troublinge his Catholike frendes'. He was unable to offer satisfactory reasons for his visit to Holywell; he refused to disclose the names of those involved in providing him with the mare on which he rode or the horse for which he said that he exchanged it; he insisted that such prayers as he had said on Sunday morning in the Saracen's Head, Chester, had been 'private prayers . . . and that noe bodie was with him but himself at the same prayers'.[1]

Much of this was damning enough, but his answers to two especially crucial questions were unequivocally so. Firstly, asked 'what mainteynaunce of his own he hath to live uppon, saieth that he hath had mainteynaunce from some of his freindes, whose names he refuseth to descover'.[2] Secondly, he was asked how he had obtained an intriguing letter addressed to 'Mr. Stamford' that had been found on him and ran as follows:

Good Sir, I ame glad and more then gladd of your good happ in the late troblesome daungers, and wishe you to keepe yourselfe in in (sic) the safest harboure: our streates are boysterous and subiecte to stormes. Remember the tale in Isopp of the countrie and citty mouse. This ientleman your frende, I perceave, hathe benne well motioned by you; I pray you, goe forward in your porpose. I have written unto Winge not to hurt your desires; commend me kindly unto them all. My Cosen Ffranke was with me this morninge. Vale. Festo Sancti Petri.

Your old frend Mr. Kellet commendeth him unto you. He was with me when I writt this, and wishes you would play the countrie mouse a while.

Youre ever most assured, William Clerk.[3]

Leake lamely averred that he had found the letter 'in London, amongst other papers', but precisely where this was he refused to say. If he had in fact left London to 'play the countrie mouse a while' he had thereby set a nice trap for himself.

There was little doubt that Leake was a seminary, and on 23 August the Mayor was commended by the Privy Council for the care he had shown in

the apprehension of a suspected person that goeth under the name of Leake, whoe ys dyscovered and knowne to be Stamford, a Semynary preist, one that heretofore escaped out of pryson and therefore ys the more heedfullie to be looked unto.[4]

Leake was kept in close confinement in the Northgate[5] until the Council decided to have him dealt with at Chester Assizes and told the Mayor to put Brooksbie in bond to appear before the Council. But they immediately changed their minds about Leake, ordering in a postscript to their letter that he too should be sent to appear before the Council because of 'some other cause why he should be dealt withall here'.[6]

[1] Q.S.F., The authorities were eager to show that he had said Mass.
[2] Ibid., f. 2.
[3] Ibid., 83, undated.
[4] A.P.C., 1601–4, 179.
[5] Q.S.F., 49, 82.
[6] Ibid., 209, dated 15 September 1601.

Leake escaped execution but subsequently endured many years in the Clink and the Gatehouse.[1] Death or imprisonment was the price that any priest expected to pay if he were caught; these were the penalties of a harsher age than ours, as were diseases like the plague that swept through Chester, Macclesfield and Congleton in 1603, when 60 died weekly, 650 in all.[2] But what Protestant zealots regarded as the plague of recusancy was neither so devasting nor so ephemeral. By comparison with the neighbouring county of Lancashire its extent was slight, though it had taken deep root in certain areas and in particular families by the middle of the reign of Elizabeth I, and, even though the authorities had gradually built up a cumbrous legal and administrative machine whose effectiveness at the end of the reign was far greater than it had been 20 years earlier, it had come to stay.

Well aware of the crucial role of priest and seminary the authorities both tried to eradicate them and to provide a counterpart within the church in addition to the parochial clergy. Thus the end of the sixteenth century saw the institution of the Queen's Preachers in Lancashire, and in the year in which Queen Elizabeth died the Chester Assembly took a leaf from Lancashire's book by ordering that

the Treasurers of this City shall demand and receave of the severall Societies and Companies within this City the Somme of Thirteene Poundes Ten Shillinges to make upp the Somme of Twenty Poundes which is promised to be payed unto John Cryton(?), preacher of God's worde, whoe is retained in this City for one yeare nexte cominge.[3]

But he was to be on the cheap: each of Lancashire's preachers was to receive £50. In both the development of recusancy and the attempts to counter it, Lancashire, not Cheshire, set the pace.

[1] Anstruther.
[2] W.E.A. Axon, 'Chronological Notes on the Visitations of Plague in Lancashire and Cheshire', *Transactions of the Lancashire and Cheshire Antiquarian Society*, XII, 64.
[3] Chester Assembly Book, September 1603. There is a brief account of the city preachers of Chester in the seventeenth century by T. Hughes in *Cheshire Sheaf*, First Series, III, 234.

CHAPTER IX

CONCLUSION

This study has been partly a narrative based on the chief extant evidence of Cheshire Elizabethan recusancy and partly an analysis of the same material. Before drawing any final conclusions some account of the nature of the main sources should perhaps be given so that the basis of such conclusions can be clearly understood.

Almost without exception the sources from the years before 1580 are disappointing, so much so that it may be thought that the outline of the development of recusancy in the first 20 years of the reign of Elizabeth I that is given in Chapters I and II is more a reflection of the content of the available sources than of the actual development itself. Thus, if one begins a study of the source material by examining the records of the Ecclesiastical Visitations the early ones are found to be very scrappy,[1] though the complete Metropolitan Visitation Book of 1578 is the most important single source for the understanding of Cheshire recusancy before 1580,[2] even if it does not suggest any important conclusions that cannot be gleaned by piecing together evidence from other, more fragmentary sources. For the later years of the reign the visitation records are very rich sources indeed,[3] revealing a good deal about the names, number and distribution of recusants in the county. However, if, because the visitors dealt with the infringement of the ecclesiastical law generally, one looks for wider evidence of, say, the reasons for the growth of recusancy in a particular area or its absence in another, little of any importance is actually revealed.[4] Further, as the visitors were equipped chiefly with the ineffective penalty of excommunication they occupied a subordinate role in the repression of recusancy, referring the more intractable recusants who were presented before them either to the bishop or the commissioners.

On first sight the substantial records of the Ecclesiastical Commission offer just the evidence for the early years of the reign that is not available elsewhere. The Act Books of the Provincial High Commission at York begin in 1571, and with gaps from 1573-5 and 1581-4 run to 1595, while those of the Diocese go back even earlier, running from 1562-73. But since they frequently give no indication of the nature of the charges of those who were dealt with by the commissioners they are unilluminating.[5] A simple

---

[1] Cf. supra, 6-8.　　　　　　　　　　　　　　　[2] Ibid., 15-19.

[3] These are the Metropolitan Visitations of 1590 and 1595, and the Diocesan Visitations of 1592, 1598 and 1601. They are discussed in Chapters VII & VIII.

[4] Cf., for example, supra, 80-1.

[5] Cf. supra, 6. Some interesting Lancashire cases are included, especially E.D.A., 12, 2, 126v-30.

list of fines imposed by the Diocesan Commissioners from 1580–3 is almost as useful as the actual proceedings from other years, especially when combined with relevant correspondence containing in Peck's *Desiderata Curiosa*.[1] But the most interesting evidence of the work of the commissioners is to be found in what is ostensibly a file of the Quarter Sessions of Chester city, but which is in fact the record of two months of investigation into recusancy by the City Commissioners in 1592.[2] Hints from many quarters make it clear that the Ecclesiastical Commission occupied a crucial role in the repression of recusancy, so that the most important gap in the sources for the study of recusancy in Cheshire at this time is created by the weakness as evidence of its activities of most of its surviving records.

Certain other ecclesiastical records, namely the Parish Registers and the Bishops' Transcripts, provide little more than the confirmation of what can be found in several other sources in so far as parishioners are sometimes stated to be recusants. This is most often done when their burial without church rites is recorded, though only a minority of the recusants received this treatment.

Such drastic penalties as were meted out to the living are to a large extent apparent in the secular Recusant Rolls, which record sums owing to the Exchequer from fines for absence from church, the seizure of goods or the rents of sequestrated land.[3] They show how, if the heavy fines were, in most cases, never paid, the loss of lands or goods consequently followed for a small number of the recusants. In doing so the Rolls are at the same time a major source for the names of recusants, though those who appear on them as owing fines had in fact been convicted at the Assizes, whose chief records are the Plea Rolls and the Crown Books. The latter include lists of those indicted as recusants at the Assizes, while the Plea Rolls include the records of the indictments; the Crown Books also provide lists of recusant prisoners. Entries concerning recusancy begin in the early 1580's.

All these sources are supplemented by the Quarter Sessions' records, of which a good proportion for both Chester city and the county of Cheshire are available. Brief records of presentments and indictments before the Quarter Sessions of the City are contained in the Mayors' Books; entries begin in 1562 and cover about half of the total number of Sessions of the reign of Elizabeth I. They reveal the imposition of 43 small fines for absence from church scattered throughout the reign, though there is an unfortunate gap in the Books from 1580–2, and these were years in which the authorities were active in dealing with absentees from church and in which lay absentees were first dealt with at the County Quarter Sessions. Brief records of presentments and indictments from the county are contained in their Sessions' Books, though the Sessions' Files deal with them

---

[1] Cf. supra, 24–30.   [2] Q.S.E., 4.
[3] Cf. supra, 86–8, for a brief discussion of their nature.

much more fully. They are substantial from 1571, though almost all the presentments and indictments for recusancy are confined to the years 1581–4,[1] when the county justices dealt with three presentments and 86 indictments for absence from church, as well as an indictment for hearing a mass. But in both the city and the county much the most interesting material about recusancy is contained in the depositions, examinations and correspondence that have been preserved. In the county this can also be found in the Quarter Sessions' Files, while for Chester city it is divided between the Mayors' Letters, the Sessions' Depositions and Examinations, and the Sessions' Files. Thus, for example, the Mayors' Letters contain correspondence about the youthful escapers of 1594, while the Depositions and Examinations contain the records of the inquiry into the escape of the recusant prisoner, Richard Spurstowe.

Finally, any student of the history of Cheshire at this time is bound to make use of the State Papers Domestic, the Acts of the Privy Council, the Lansdowne and Harleian Manuscript collections, the Salisbury Papers,[2] Peck's *Desiderata Curiosa* and Strype's *Annals*. They contain a wide variety of correspondence between the national and local authorities and certificates and returns of ecclesiastical matters, which together offer a good deal of material similar in nature to what the more local sources contain and at the same time provide the wider framework within which this must be set.[3]

Taken all together these sources reveal only a minute portion of the activities of the recusants of Cheshire in the reign of Elizabeth I, though they reveal far more of what went on in the second half of the reign than in the first, and are substantial for the 1590's. Thus much of what has been concluded about the recusants rests on deduction and induction from such flimsy material as must make any conclusions little better than guesses. Bearing this in mind, what follows is a summary of them.

The main conclusion is a negative one: there were few recusants in Cheshire in the second half of the sixteenth century. In the whole of the reign of Elizabeth I only 302 recusants can be identified with any certainty, and, of course, at any given time even fewer can be found, for some of the 302 conformed temporarily or permanently, and many who were alive in, say 1582, must have died before the end of the reign. Thus 150 can be found in the records from 1590–2 and almost 200 in the longer period from 1590–1600, so that Chadderton was probably not wide of the mark when he sent the Council a list of 200 names in 1589. However, the basis of these figures should be clearly understood. They rest on a cautious,

[1] Indictments for absence were outside the scope of the Quarter Sessions after 1587.
[2] H.M.C., Calendar of the Salisbury MSS.
[3] Obviously, many secondary sources must also be consulted, as is made clear in the bibliography.

sceptical approach to the existing records: only those named as recusants, or dealt with as absentees on more than one occasion or in such circumstances as makes their recusancy more or less certain are included. This is done in order to distinguish recusants from those who were absent from church for reasons unconnected with recusancy, for the boldness of the recusant in defying ecclesiastical censure was far from unique; some parishioners were willing to absent themselves from church for trivial enough reasons. Further, these figures are derived from the surviving records, which are surprisingly full for the 1590's, when they suffer from only one important loss—most of the records of the Ecclesiastical Commission—but are less and less complete the further back one goes towards the beginning of the reign. At no point can completeness be claimed, and even in the 1590's it is possible for recusants to slip through the net represented by the available evidence. Thus Elizabeth Barton of Chester was presented for absence for four years in 1599, but no mention of her absence occurs in the records of those years. Similarly, as distinct from some 'recusants latelie reported' Maria Sutton of Daresbury was presented before the Diocesan Visitation of 1604 as an 'olde recusant', and yet no earlier mention of her occurs in spite of the fact that Matilda Kelsall who was presented alongside her in 1604 as an 'olde recusant' had been presented for recusancy with unfailing regularity in the previous 14 years—at the visitations of 1590, 1592, 1595, 1598 and 1601, as well as being indicted at the Assizes in 1600.[1] How many more recusants were overlooked in the same way as Maria Sutton? When the Chester Ecclesiastical Commission carried out its inquiry in 1592 it revealed the existence of some 38 recusants or probable recusants in the city, and yet only 16 of these emerge in the rest of the fairly ample evidence from the 1590's.[2] One of those who was then examined was Richard Spurstowe, and it would be difficult to imagine a man more firmly committed to recusancy: he told the Commissioners that he had not been to church for nine years,[3] and yet on only one occasion, and that in a national, not a local list of recusants, has mention of him been found in those years; in particular he was presented to neither the Visitation of 1590 nor that of 1592.[4]

Nevertheless, even if it is assumed that the loopholes in the system of reporting recusants to the authorities and the gaps in the records involve an error of as much as 50 per cent the total number of recusants remains small in relation to the population of the county. No-one would pretend that an accurate estimate of this can yet be given, but a figure against which the numbers of the recusants can be set can be derived, perhaps, from the number of households in the county and these were given in a

[1] Cf. the relevant entries in Appendix I.
[2] Cf. supra, 102.
[3] Ibid., 97.
[4] The number of priests born in Cheshire is also, at first sight, surprising (cf. Appendix II), but the vast majority bear the names of known recusant families.

diocesan report of 1563.[1] It gives a total of 12,773 households, and, judging by recent research on the size of households in the seventeenth century,[2] it would seem reasonable to multiply this by five to find some sort of figure for the total population, namely 63,865. In comparison with such a figure, even if it is remembered that children would form a much higher proportion of the whole than they do today,[3] the total number of recusants is so small as to be almost insignificant.

However, it must immediately be added that this was not true of every part of the county. The recusants were concentrated in Chester city[4] and the surrounding area, and especially in the south-west of the county, centred on the parishes of Bunbury and Malpas, whose villages and hamlets almost all contained recusants. Of the total number of 302 known recusants, 75 were from Bunbury and 53 from Malpas parish. Thus, even though these were very large parishes, each containing several townships, recusancy was clearly a grave problem in the south-west of the county. The Wirral contained several gentle families all or some of whom were recusant, but few others beyond these, while the Cheshire plain was almost empty of them. In fact, if the River Weaver be taken as dividing the county into roughly equal eastern and western halves, only 24 of those known to be recusants came from the eastern half.

If it is asked why recusancy was distributed in this way, no very satisfactory answer can be offered. If recusant gentry are looked for to provide hiding places for priests and some sort of protection or encouragement for recusant tenants and servants, even though little direct evidence in support of this can be given, there were certainly gentry enough for this in the neighbourhood of Bunbury and Malpas. Lady Frances Brereton, Hugh Bromley, Katherine Golborne and Elizabeth Dod all lived very close to Malpas, while William Brereton and Katherine Dod at Shocklach and, just over the Welsh border, Agnes Hughes and Thomas Crewe and his wife at Holt, were all within reach. Furthermore, it seems astonishing that Lady Egerton should have received lasting consideration from the authorities when recusancy developed so obviously around her in the parish of Bunbury, while George Egerton and his wife, Lady Beeston, and Randle Aldersey, Peter, Philip and Richard Spurstowe at Spurstow were all in the immediate neighbourhood, and the Erdeswicks and George Otley at Acton, Nantwich, were not far away. Nor were the many recusants who lived just across the nearby Welsh border. There, in several of the parishes of eastern Denbighshire and south-eastern Flintshire, recusancy was strong, so that south-west Cheshire and the neighbouring

[1] Harl. MSS., 594, No. 11, ff. 97–100.
[2] P. Laslett, *The World we have lost*, 64–9.   [3] Ibid., 103.
[4] Even though Chester was by far and away the most populous area of the county, its 49 recusants from nine parishes seem significant when compared to the numbers elsewhere, though it must be borne in mind that there is more evidence available for Chester city than for any other part of the county.

parts of the two Welsh counties perhaps formed a single area in which priests could function. Certainly, Edward Hughes, the priest who performed a mass at Wichaugh, Malpas, in 1586, was active in the nearby Welsh parishes.[1] Thus it may well be that the association of Cheshire with Lancashire that follows naturally from the structure of the sixteenth-century diocese of Chester should be abandoned in the study of recusancy and that Cheshire should in fact be seen in connection with North Wales. The famous shrine and well at Holywell and, no doubt, the lesser shrines at Tremeirchion and Bodfari on the eastern edge of the Vale of Clwyd, retained their devotees at this time,[2] and may have been near enough to western Cheshire to exercise a continuing influence there.[3]

However, as far as Bunbury and Malpas go, Mr. Geoffrey Chesters has suggested[4] that two 'old priests' were in part responsible for the development of recusancy there. John Busshell, a former chantry priest of the Collegiate Church there, may have been active in Bunbury, for his presence there was noted in the 1577 diocesan return,[5] while John Maddocks, who was later imprisoned as an 'old priest', was probably practising as a schoolmaster in Malpas in the early 1560's.[6] Each doubtless worked under the protective shadow of one or more of the local recusant gentry.

But the importance of the gentry in the development of recusancy is less obvious in the Wirral than in the south-west. In the Wirral 16 recusants from half a dozen gentry families, namely the Hocknells of Prenton, the Houghs and Whitmores of Leighton and Thornton, the Heskeths and Whitmores of Thurstaston and Lady Stanley and her daughter, Jane, at Hooton, together outnumbered the 12 other recusants who might be thought of as being dependent on them, and there is no known connection between any of the gentry families and recusants of lower status. In the case of John Whitmore, such of his tenants as are known were not recusants.[7] Admittedly, John Hocknell, William Hough and John Whitmore were among the first Cheshire recusants to be imprisoned and it may well be that this harsh policy successfully limited the spread of recusancy in the Wirral,[8] while the man whose social status and personal quality alike made

[1] E. Gwynne-Jones, op. cit., 115–18.
[2] Holywell continued to attract pilgrims, while there were many recusants in Bodfari and Tremeirchion (ibid., 120–1). Mr. T. M. Griffith suggested to me that the influence of Holywell might have been important in S.W. Cheshire.
[3] And farther afield: cf. supra, 124–5.
[4] In an unpublished paper, which he kindly made available to me.
[5] Cf. supra, 15.   [6] Cf. Appendix II.
[7] Several of them are named in connection with rents from his sequestrated lands in the Recusant Roll of 1599–1600.
[8] To imprison these men and leave their wives at liberty may have been courting disaster, but Hocknell's wife conformed in 1581 and does not seem to have returned to recusancy until after her husband's death in 1590, Hough's wife either conformed from the early 1580's or pre-deceased her husband, who died in 1585, and Whitmore's first wife died in 1584. The boldest recusant in the Wirral in the 1580's seems to have been Hough's daughter, Alice, but her husband, William Whitmore, was a conformist.

him the natural leader of the Catholic cause in the area, Sir William Stanley, was absent in Ireland in the crucial years of the 1570's and the early 1580's even before he assumed a politically disastrous role, thus leaving the dominance of his conforming father, Sir Rowland Stanley, unchallenged. His brothers, Edward and John, similarly left England for the service of Spain and Catholicism.

Of course, by no means all the lay leaders of the recusants were from the gentry. The probable importance of several of the more humble recusants who were imprisoned in Chester Castle in the latter half of the 1580's, in particular Thomas Trine, and of the Probin family of Malpas, has already been alluded to.[1] And what obviously led many people into recusancy or held them there was family or personal relationships. Of the former there is abundant evidence in the dozen and a half recusant families or kinship groups, where brothers, or mothers and daughters, or whole families were recusant together, quite apart from the greater number of husband and wife recusants. Such relationships are clear enough in the case of the Whitmores, the Houghs, the Cotgreves of Christleton, or the Maddocks or Probins of Malpas,[2] but the less obvious connections like the marriage of John Whitmore to Jane, the daughter of the Chester recusants, Henry and Margaret Primrose, were also important. When Anne Dewsbury visited her aunt, Alice Cheswis, in Chester Castle she was probably all but drawn into recusancy,[3] while it was the misleading persuasions of her godmother that led Anne Brereton to attend the mass at Agden, Malpas, in April 1582: most of those who attended the mass were friends, acquaintances or relatives of each other.[4] There were others who were the servants of recusants, as Anne Crocket was of Margery Aire, or Cecily Buckley of Lady Egerton. Quite apart from the work of priests and the personalities or organisational skills of outstanding individuals, some of the explanation of the development of recusancy lies in relationships of this kind.[5]

Whoever gave the lead, the recusants were drawn from most levels of society, along lines already indicated in some detail in the analysis of the recusants of the early 1590's.[6] The status or occupation of some two-thirds of the 302 known recusants has been ascertained, and they can be divided as follows: 63 were of the gentry, 31 were business, professional or craftsmen, 84 were yeomen or husbandmen, and 20 were labourers or servants

---

[1] Cf. supra, 65–6.
[2] Or the Eldershawes, the Cheswises, the Erdeswicks, the Huxleys of Alpraham, the Spurstowes, Jane Ball and her daughter, Mary Lawton and her daughter, the brothers Richard and William Poole, the Alderseys of Chester (even if in their case precise relationships are not always apparent), or the ubiquitous Duttons and Masseys (under their own surnames or those of the families their women married into, e.g., the Starkeys of Over).
[3] Cf. supra, 71.
[4] Ibid., 42–4.
[5] Ibid., 82–3.
[6] Ibid., 84–5.

—or, in each case, came from the families of such men.[1] They range from Lady Elizabeth Stanley or Lady Frances Brereton at one end to Elizabeth Bailey, a beggar, at the other, though these are the untypical extremes. By and large it was men and women of some substance and independence who were recusants. The very rich and the very poor were few, while the lesser gentry form a disproportionately large group. None of what Mr. B. Coward has called the 'Cheshire elite',[2] the most influential landowners of the county, was wholly committed to recusancy. Of the 12 families whom he regards as the landowning elite, suspicion of Catholicism clung to the Leighs of Lyme, and only the Stanleys of Hooton and the Duttons of Dutton were ever recusant, but in not one of them was the head of the family involved. Thus recusancy lacked a clear lead from the families whose influence was predominant in the county, and in this perhaps the Stanleys of Knowsley and Lathom, who exercised the Lord Lieutenancy, and the Stanleys of Hooton, whose junior male members exercised a great influence outside the county and none within it, had roles that were of decisive importance in limiting the extent of recusancy in Cheshire.

In the two elite families that contained recusants these were mainly women, and of the total number of 302 known recusants 142 were women. This figure seems surprisingly low, for as the reign went on more and more women were presented or indicted as recusants, and a higher proportion of the total might therefore have been expected in the light of the numbers that emerge in the 1590's. About half of the recusants presented or indicted in the early 1590's were women, and rather more than half in the decade that followed: and their importance is clear.[3] This is one respect in which the estimated total of recusants as 302 can almost certainly be faulted: the number of women should be higher than the 142 included. Before the 1590's their importance went largely unrecognised, so that until then they were not indicted to the extent that their menfolk were.

From the start, in the 1560's there appears to have been little opposition in Cheshire to the Elizabethan religious settlement. Very little is apparent in the records of the Ecclesiastical Commission[4] and in what scanty Visitation records survive from these years,[5] while the report of 1564 on the attitude of the justices indicates nothing much beyond the uncertainty of religious loyalties at that time.[6] Some attempt seems to have been made by the justices of Chester city in 1568[7] and by the diocesan and provincial

---

[1] These numbers are to some extent arbitrary. Some recusants are said to be, say, husbandmen on one occasion and labourers on another; the higher status has always been adopted here. Finally, the divisions between one social status and another are arbitrary and are adopted throughout this study only to illustrate broadly the social spread of the recusants.

[2] 'The Lieutenancy of Lancashire and Cheshire in the sixteenth and early seventeenth centuries', *Transactions of the Historic Society of Lancashire and Cheshire*, Vol. 119, 42–3.

[3] Cf. supra, 83–4.

[4] Ibid., 6–8.   [5] Ibid., 5–6.   [6] Ibid., 8–9.   [7] Ibid., 10.

ecclesiastical commissioners in 1570 and 1571[1] to curb what little recusancy was emerging by those years, but not until the second half of the 1570's was a further attempt made to deal with the recusants and then those who were most prosperous were singled out.[2] The authorities were mild in their methods, except in dealing with Marian or old priests, who were penalised by imprisonment.

The change in government policy that is marked by the enactment of the Treason and Seditious Words Act of 1581 symbolises a change in the attitudes of the local authorities also. By 1581 both the Ecclesiastical Commission and the Quarter Sessions were attempting to bring heavier pressure to bear on the recusants than ever before.[3] Those who could neither escape apprehension nor conform were imprisoned,[4] and if the success of the authorities in bringing the recusants to heel was limited,[5] their attitude towards them was clearly hardening.

By this time the recusants were being harried. Few suffered any demonstrable financial loss, though lands of John Hocknell and William Hough were sequestrated as early as March 1584, and this treatment was meted out to John Whitmore in November 1588, and to Hugh Erdeswick in September 1589.[6] Hough, Hocknell and Whitmore were also among the dozen or so recusants who spent much or almost all of the 1580's in prison, while a slightly larger number suffered at least a short term of imprisonment.[7] Prison conditions were tolerable enough for the wealthier ones,[8] as is clear from the correspondence between Robert Worsley of the New Fleet and the Privy Council[9] and from later complaints about laxity in the administration of Chester Castle,[10] even if maladministration or accident could result in the death of one of the prisoners.[11]

In the 1580's the local authorities had grappled with the problem oι recusancy under the incessant goading of the Privy Council, so that by the end of that decade they were dealing with a problem which was far better understood than it had been ten years earlier. It was not only the growth of recusancy but also the increasing efficiency of the local authorities that was registered by the steady rise in the number of recusants indicted between 1587 and 1593.[12]

Several recusants were imprisoned as a result of the inquiries that took place in 1592,[13] as were others as the decade wore on,[14] but as the years went by the authorities penalised those who failed to pay the fine of £20 a lunar month for absence from church by the loss of lands or goods

---

[1] Cf. supra, 12.   [2] Ibid., 19.   [3] Ibid., Ch. III.
[4] Ibid., 31 & 34.   [5] e.g., supra, 34–5.
[6] R.R., 1, m. 6.   [7] Cf. supra, 65 & 67.
[8] Though the poor prisoner could be much less fortunate. Thus, in 1592 Thomas Maddocks, who had been a recusant prisoner in Chester Castle since c. 1583, petitioned the justices for the food usually allowed to pauper prisoners, as he had become sick (J. Beck, *Tudor Cheshire*, 67).
[9] e.g., supra, 38–40.   [10] Cf. supra, 73.   [11] Ibid., 72.
[12] Ibid., 106.   [13] e.g., supra, 90–2.   [14] Cf. supra, 120–1.

rather than by imprisonment, and by the end of the 1590's this bitter medicine had been administered to at least 28 recusants.

Long before the end of the reign of Elizabeth I recusancy had developed a vitality that no penal law could crush, even if life must have been made all but intolerable for those on whom the authorities clamped down successfully, so that the real solution to the problem of recusancy lay a long way ahead in time, as the *modus vivendi* called toleration was evolved.

K

APPENDIX I

A list, in alphabetical order, of Cheshire recusants or probable recusants of the reign of Elizabeth I, with a brief summary of what is known of each. It includes some who were Catholic (Papist) in outlook rather than recusant and they are labelled 'Catholic'.

Margaret or *Margery Aire* (or *Eyre*), the wife of William Aire, a yeoman of Tilston, near Malpas. She was presented, along with her husband, as a non-communicant, before the Diocesan Chancellor, October 1589 (E.D.V., 1, 8, f. 128), as an obstinate recusant at the Metropolitan Visitation, 1590 (York, R.VI, A 12, f. 84v), and 'for not orderly frequenting her parish church' at the Diocesan Visitation, 1592 (E.D.V., 1, 10, f. 59). She was indicted at the Assizes for absence and assessed for a fine of £40, April 1593 (Chester, 29, 334, m. 17: R.R., 1, m. 6), presented as a recusant at the Metropolitan Visitation, 1595 (York, R.VI, A 14, f. 8v: A 15, f. 64) and the Diocesan Visitation, 1598 (E.D.V., 1, 12, f. 43v), and as an absentee at the Diocesan Visitation, 1601 (ibid., 1, 12a, f. 44v). Her servant, Anne Crocket, was a recusant (q.v.).

Fulk Aldersey of Trinity parish, Chester, appeared before the Diocesan High Commission on an unstated charge, December 1562 (E.D.A., 12, 2, f. 2), was fined 12d. for absence at Quarter Sessions, September 1568, May 1576 and September 1579. (M.B., 1567-8, 2 September, 10 Eliz.: 1572-7, 3 May, 18 Eliz.: 1578-81, 22 September, 21 Eliz.), was presented for absence and popish practices at the Metropolitan Visitation, 1578 (York, R.VI, A 7, f. 19v), and fined 20s. by the High Commission, February 1581, for 'dyvers contemptuous speeches' (Ex. Dep., m. 3). A Fulk Aldersey was a prominent Chester citizen, being Mayor in 1594.

Jane Aldersey, daughter of the recusants William and Margaret Aldersey (q.v.) was fined 12d. for absence at Quarter Sessions, September 1579 (M.B., 1578-81, 22 September, 21 Eliz.), but appears to have been conforming by 1592 (Q.S.E., 4, f. 14).

John Aldersey of Chester. Along with several other Alderseys who were recusants he was fined 12d. for absence at Quarter Sessions, September 1579 (M.B., loc. cit.).

Margaret Aldersey of St. Bridget's parish, Chester, wife of William Aldersey (q.v.), was before the High Commission for concealing an image and using a Latin Primer, November 1562, and as a non-communicant in April 1570, when she was ordered to bring in a Latin Primer that she used (E.D.A., 12, 2, ff. 81v & 132). She was presented as an absentee and non-communicant at the Metropolitan Visitation, 1578 (York, R.VI, A 7, f. 22v), fined 12d. for absence at Quarter Sessions, September 1579 (M.B., loc. cit.), indicted for absence at Quarter Sessions, May 1582 (S.P., 12, 153, 65), and fined 12d. for absence at Quarter Sessions, January 1584, and January, 1588 (M.B., 1582-4, 21 January, 26 Eliz.; Q.S.F., 37, 41). She was presented as a recusant at the Metropolitan Visitation, 1590 (York, R.VI, A 12, f. 98), and was aged, ailing, widowed and in prison when dealt with by the High Commission, February 1592 (Q.S.E.,

4, f. 19), but was fined 12d. for absence at Quarter Sessions in the following July (M.B., 1589–92, 16 July, 33 Eliz.).

Randle Aldersey of Spurstow, gentleman, son of John Aldersey of Spurstow, was presented as a recusant at the Metropolitan Visitation, 1590 (York, R.VI, A 12, f. 109), and the Diocesan Visitation, 1592 (E.D.V., 1, 10, f. 92v), indicted at the Assizes for absence, April 1591 (Chester, 21, 1, 156v), and April 1593, when he was assessed for a fine of £240 (Chester, 29, 334, m. 17: R.R.1, m. 6), had land worth 13s. 4d. a year seized, September 1593 (R.R., 2, m. 6), and was presented as an obstinate recusant at the Diocesan Visitation, 1598 (E.D.V., 1, 12, f. 64v). He was buried on 25 May 1600 (E.D.B., Bunbury, f. 146).

Thomas Aldersey of Trinity parish, Chester, was presented as an absentee at the Metropolitan Visitation, 1578, and as an irregular attender and non-communicant at that of 1590 (York, R.VI., A 7, f. 19v: A 12, f. 90v). His name was included in a rough list of suspected recusants drawn up for the High Commission, 1592 (Q.S.E., 4, f. 17), and he was presented as a non-communicant at the Diocesan Visitations, 1598 and 1601 (E.D.V., 1, 12, f. 13: 12a, f. 36).

William Aldersey of St. Bridget's parish, Chester, a linen-draper, whose wife and daughter were also recusants: cf. Margaret and Jane Aldersey. A sick man, he was listed as a recusant in the 1577 diocesan report (S.P., 12, 118, 49), presented as an absentee and non-communicant at the Metropolitan Visitation, 1578 (York, R.VI., A 7, f. 22v), fined 12d. for absence at Quarter Sessions, September 1579, and indicted at Quarter Sessions, January 1584 (M.B., 1578–81, 22 September, 21 Eliz.: 1582–4, 21 January, 26 Eliz.) and presented for absence at Quarter Sessions, January 1588 (Q.S.F., 37, 41). By 1592 he was dead, for his wife was then a widow. A William Aldersey who was Mayor of Chester in 1560, was listed as an unreliable justice in 1564 (*Camden Miscellany*, IX, 73) and died in 1577 may be the recusant of the 1577 reference.

Katherine Alger (or *Angyer*), wife of Robert Alger of Barthomley (q.v.), was presented at the Metropolitan Visitation, 1578, as an absentee (York, R.VI, A 7, f. 11v.), and indicted for absence at Quarter Sessions, May 1582 (C.S.F., 1582, F 1, D 6).

Robert Alger (or *Angyer*), husbandman of Barthomley: same as wife, 1578 (q.v.). He was presented before the Diocesan Chancellor as a non-communicant, June 1582, and November 1588 (E.D.V., 1, 6c, f. 72v: 7, f. 31v): on the second of these occasions he was described by another offender, perhaps maliciously, as a recusant (ibid., 7, f. 32). He was presented as a non-communicant at the Diocesan Visitation, 1592 (E.D.V., 1, 10, f. 90) and as a troublemaker at the Metropolitan Visitation, 1595 (York, R.VI, A 14, f. 14v). Catholic.

Thomas Ames of Bulkeley, Malpas parish, was presented as a recusant at the Metropolitan Visitation, 1590 (York, R.VI, A 12, f. 85v), and indicted for absence at the Assizes, April 1591 (Chester, 21, 1, 156v).

Joan Amos, servant to the recusant, Richard Massey, was examined as a suspected recusant by the Chester High Commission and imprisoned until she promised conformity, January to February 1592 (Q.S.E., 4, ff. 1, 2 & 19).

Elizabeth Andrew of Woodchurch was indicted for absence at Quarter Sessions, May 1582 (C.S.F., 1582, F 1, D 20).

Richard Anion (or *Onion*) of St. Peter's parish, Chester, was presented as a recusant at the Diocesan Visitation, 1592 (E.D.V., 1, 10, f. 29). He may have been related to the Robert Amnyon who was fined 12d. at Quarter Sessions, September 1568 (M.B., 1567–8, 2 September, 10 Eliz.).

James Apsden was imprisoned by the High Commission, February 1581, as 'an obstinate papist and a person of verie lewde demeanor' (Peck, I, 103). He may not be a Cheshire man. Catholic.

Elizabeth Bailey of Prestbury, a beggar, was presented as a recusant at the Metropolitan Visitation, 1590 (York, R.VI, A 12, f. 104v).

Katherine Baker of Wrenbury was presented as a recusant at the Diocesan Visitation, 1592 (E.D.V., 1, 10, f. 100).

Alice Ball of Trinity parish, Chester, was presented as suspected of popery and popish practices at the Metropolitan Visitation, 1578; she was then old (York, R.VI, A 7, ff. 19v–20). Catholic.

Jane (or Joan) Ball, wife of Thomas Ball of Bickley, Malpas parish, was fined 40s. for her failure to answer an unstated charge before the High Commission, February 1581 (Ex. Dep., m. 12); a widow, she was indicted for absence at Quarter Sessions, 1581 (C.S.F., 1581, F 3, D 20). Her daughter, Katherine Dod (q.v.) was a recusant.

Robert Ball was a prisoner in Chester Castle, 1593–4, and was unsuccessfully indicted at the Assizes, October 1594 (Chester, 21, 1, 166 ff.: 29, 338, m. 16d).

Francis Bamvell and his *wife* of Trinity parish, Chester, were presented at the Metropolitan Visitation, 1578, for popish practices and Francis was suspected of popery (York, R.VI, A 7, ff. 19v–20). Catholics.

Alice Barker, wife of Thomas Barker, innkeeper of Chester, was examined by the High Commission, February 1592, as an absentee suspected of recusant sympathies (Q.S.E., 4, ff. 8 & 25). Catholic.

Elizabeth Barton, spinster, was presented for absence at Chester Quarter Sessions, 1599 (M.B., 1596–9, 4 May, 41 Eliz.).

Lady Beeston, wife of Sir George Beeston of Beeston, was presented as a recusant at the Metropolitan Visitation, 1590 (York, R.VI, A 12, f. 109). She died, aged 86, in the following year (E.D.B., Bunbury, f. 124: Ormerod, II, 272). Her daughter-in-law, Lady Margaret Beeston, wife of Sir Hugh, second son of Sir George Beeston (Ormerod, loc. cit.), was presented for absence at the Assizes, September 1610 (Chester 29, 370, m. 9).

Thomas Benyon of Malpas, a drover, was indicted for absence and for hearing a mass, at Quarter Sessions, May, 1582 (C.S.F., 1582, F 1, D 13 & 27).

Jane Berry, wife of Roger Berry (q.v.), of St. Michael's parish, Chester, and Thurstaston, was presented as an absentee and non-communicant from St. Michael's parish, and as a recusant from Thurstaston, at the Diocesan Visitation, 1598 (E.D.V., 1, 12, ff. 12 & 31v), and was indicted and assessed for a fine for absence of £240 at the Assizes, September 1600 (R.R., 8, m. 10d).

Roger Berry, husband of Jane (q.v.), of St. Michael's, Chester, was presented as an absentee and non-communicant at the Diocesan Visitation, 1598 (E.D.V., loc. cit.). Catholic.

Geoffrey Bickley of St. Bridget's parish, Chester, was presented as an absentee at the Metropolitan Visitation, 1578 (York, R.VI, A 7, f. 22v), and fined 12d. for absence at Quarter Sessions, September 1579 (M.B., 1578–81, 22 September, 21 Eliz.).

Richard Bird, a tanner of Chester, and his *wife* attended masses said by the seminary, Thomas Holford, in Chester Castle, 1585 (Chester, 21, 100, examination dated 27 August 1585). Catholics.

John Birtles, a gentleman of Birtles, Prestbury, one of a long line of the same name. He was listed as a prominent recusant in the diocesan return, 1577 (S.P., 12, 118, 49), and indicted for absence at Quarter Sessions, May 1582, but conformed two months later (C.S.F., 1582, F 1, D 10). He was named in a list, probably from the early 1580's, of recusants at liberty in Cheshire (H.M.C., *Salis. MMS.*, IV, 265).

Nicholas Blundell of Wigland, Malpas, labourer, was indicted for hearing a mass, May 1582 (C.S.F., 1582, F 1, D 27). A 'Bloundell' was a well-known recusant prisoner in the Northgate, 1592 (Q.S.E., 4, f. 10).

Henry Bolton of Chester was presented to both the Diocesan Visitation and the High Commission for absence, 1562 (E.D.V., 1, 2b, f. 14: E.D.A., 12, 2, f. 81v), fined 12d. for absence at Quarter Sessions, September 1568 (M.B., 1567–8, 2 September, 10 Eliz.), appeared before the High Commission in York on an unstated charge (York, H.C., Box 25, 1571–2, A.B., 16, f. 74), and was fined 12d. at Quarter Sessions, September 1579 (M.B., 1578–81, 22 September, 21 Eliz.).

Margery Booth, wife of George Booth, yeoman, of Mottram, was indicted for absence at Quarter Sessions, May 1582 (C.S.F., 1582, F 1, D 11), presented as an obstinate recusant at the Metropolitan Visitation, 1590 (York, R.VI, A 12, f. 103), indicted for absence at the Assizes, April 1591 (Chester, 21, 1, 156v), presented for absence at the Metropolitan Visitation, 1595, by which time she was a widow (York, R.VI, A 14, f. 13v), and goods of hers to the value of 30d. were seized in April 1594, and, later, 30s. (R.R., 2, m. 6: 6, m. 12).

Elizabeth Bostock of Chester was examined by the High Commission, 1592, about those who had lodged at the inn kept by her husband, William (q.v.); she then stated that she had not been to church for six weeks (Q.S.E., 4, f. 2). Catholic.

William Bostock, innkeeper of Chester, was presented as an absentee and noncommunicant at Quarter Sessions, January 1588 (Q.S.F., 37, 41), examined as a suspected papist with whom priests might lodge by the High Commission, 1592, and was shortly afterwards examined about the escape of the recusant, Richard Spurstowe, from the Northgate, and may well have been privy to it (Q.S.E., 4, ff. 7, 14 & 25: 5, ff. 20–1). In 1598 he was a servant of Thomas Fitzherbert (S.P., 12, 268, 82) and as such lodged at the English College in Rome, 1600 (Foley, H., *Records of the English College, S.J.*, VI, 571). Catholic.

Margaret Bowker of Malpas was present at a mass, April 1582 (C.S.F., 1582, F 1, D 1 & D 3), indicted for absence at Quarter Sessions, May 1582 (ibid., F 1, D 13), presented as a recusant at the Metropolitan Visitation, 1590 (York, R.VI, A 12, f. 85v), and as an absentee at the Diocesan Visitation, 1592 (E.D.V., 1, 10, f. 56), indicted for absence and assessed for a fine of £40 at the Assizes, April 1593 (Chester, 29, 334, m. 17: R.R., 1, m. 6), presented as a recusant at the Metropolitan Visitation, 1595 (York, R.VI, A. 14, f. 8), and at the Diocesan Visitations, 1598 and 1601 (E.D.V., 1, 12, f. 41: 12a, f. 45v). She was probably the Margaret Barley of Malpas who was indicted and assessed for a fine of £240 at the Assizes, September 1600 (R.R., 8, m. 10d), and was presented for absence at Quarter Sessions, 1604–8 and 1613 (Harl. MSS., 2095, 7, f. 10).

Lady Frances Brereton, the wife of Sir Randle Brereton of Shocklach and Malpas, was indicted for absence and assessed for a fine of £180 at the Assizes, April 1593 (Chester, 29, 334, m. 17: R.R., 1, m. 6). Her husband (cf. Appendix III) was apparently removed from the Commission of the Peace *c.* 1587 because of her recusancy.

Jane Brereton of Malpas was presented as a recusant at the Diocesan Visitation, 1601 (E.D.V., 1, 12a, f. 45v).

William Brereton, gentleman, of Shocklach, was probably the William Brereton in a list, probably from 1583, of suspected persons (Harl. MSS., 6998, f. 244v). He was indicted for absence and assessed for a fine of £960 at the Assizes, April, 1593 (Chester 29, 334, m. 17: R.R., 1, m. 6). He was probably the 'Brewreton' who was to be examined, along with several other Cheshire gentlemen, about the education of their sons abroad, 1580 (Peck 1, 99–100); the son may have been the Jesuit whose presence in Scotland was reported in 1582 (*Cal. Border Papers*, I, 85, quoted A. L. Rowse, *The Expansion of Elizabethan England*, 36).

Hugh Bromley, gentleman, of Hampton Post, was presented at the Metropolitan Visitation, 1578, as a 'supposed Papist' (York, R.VI, A 7, f. 8v), named in a list, probably from the early 1580's, of recusants at liberty in Cheshire (H.M.C., *Salis. MSS.*, IV, 265), fined 20s. in April and 100s. in June 1581, for his failure to answer an unspecified charge before the High Commission (Ex. Dep., m. 4 & 5), indicted for absence at Quarter Sessions, October 1581, May 1582 and May 1584 (C.S.F., 1581, F 3, D 23; 1582, F 1, D 15: 1584, F 1, D 21), and at the Assizes, September 1587 (Chester, 29, 325, m. 17). He was accused of being a prominent papist and priest-harbourer, 1583 and 1584 (S.P., 12, 169, 27: 15, 27, 94).

Joan and *Anne Browne*, the wife and daughter of John Browne, gaoler of Chester Castle, attended masses said by Thomas Holford, seminary priest, while he was in prison there (Chester, 21, 1, f. 124v: 24, 100, examination dated 27 August 1585). Catholics.

Robert Browne, the son of John Browne, gaoler of Chester Castle; for his mother and sister, cf. Joan and Anne Browne. He seems to have been converted to Catholicism by Thomas Holford, the seminary, when he was a prisoner in Chester Castle, 1585 (Chester, 24, loc. cit.), and spent several years in the Northgate for recusancy. As a prisoner there, he was examined about his reported disloyalty by the Chester authorities in 1591 (Q.S.E., 5, f. 11), and as a recusant by the High Commission, 1592, and by the Mayor and aldermen about the escape of a fellow-recusant prisoner, Richard Spurstowe (Q.S.E., 4, ff. 1, 19 & 21). He was presented as a recusant prisoner at the Metropolitan Visitation, 1595 (York, R.VI, A 15, f. 33v) and the Diocesan Visitation, 1598 (E.D.V., 1, 12, f. 17), fined 12d. for absence at Quarter Sessions, January 1597 (M.B., 1596–9, 21 January, 39 Eliz.), and conformed, October 1598 (M.L., 1, 167).

Cecily Buckley, Lady Egerton's maid, was presented as a recusant at the Diocesan Visitation, 1592 (E.D.V., 1, 10, f. 93v), an absentee at the Metropolitan Visitation, 1595 (York, R.VI, A 14, f. 14v), and as a recusant and non-communicant at the Diocesan Visitation, 1598 (E.D.V., 1, 12, f. 56).

Alice Burrows, wife of John Burrows of Bunbury, was presented as an absentee and a non-communicant, along with several known recusants, at the Diocesan Visitation, 1601 (E.D.V., 1, 12a, f. 64v).

Ralph Burrows and his wife *Jane* (or *Joan*), of Bunbury parish were presented as recusants at the Metropolitan Visitation, 1590 (York, R.VI, A 12, f. 109). Jane, a widow, was presented as an obstinate recusant at the Diocesan Visitation, 1598, and as an absentee and non-communicant, 1601 (E.D.V., 1, 12, f. 64v: 12a, f. 64v). She was probably the Ann Burrows, widow, of Alpraham, Bunbury, who was indicted and assessed for a fine of £240 for absence at the Assizes, September 1600 (R.R., 8, m. 10d).

Gilbert Burscowe, gentleman, was a prisoner in Chester Castle, 1593–4, and was unsuccessfully indicted for absence at the Assizes, October 1594 (Chester 21, 1, 166 ff.: 29, 338, m. 16d).

Ralph Bushell, a husbandman of Tiverton, Bunbury, was presented as a recusant at the Metropolitan Visitation, 1590 (York, R.VI, A 12, f. 108v), and, along with his wife, Joan, was indicted for absence at the Assizes, September 1610 (Chester, 29, 370, m. 9).

Frances Calveley, wife of Ralph Calveley of Saighton, was indicted for absence at Quarter Sessions, October 1581 (C.S.F., 1581, F 3, D 18).

Alice Calveley of Peckforton, Bunbury parish, was indicted for absence and assessed for a fine of £160 at the Assizes, April 1593 (Chester, 29, 334, m. 17: R.R. 1, m. 6).

John Cane, husbandman, and his wife, *Elizabeth* of Wigland, Malpas, were indicted for absence and for hearing a mass, at Quarter Sessions, May 1582 (C.S.F., 1582, F 1, D 17 & 27). Elizabeth was imprisoned, and speedily conformed afterwards (C.S.B., 1576–92, Recognisances, f. 206, and C.S.F., 1582, F 1, D 17).

Dr. Cannon of St. Michael's parish, Chester, was presented as a recusant at the Metropolitan Visitation, 1590 (York, R.VI, A 12, f. 99v). His wife, as of St. Oswald's parish, Chester, was presented as a non-communicant at the Metropolitan Visitation, 1595 (ibid., A 15, f. 33v).

Anne Capper, wife of John Capper, husbandman, of Bunbury, was presented as a recusant at the Diocesan Visitation, 1592 (E.D.V., 1, 10, f. 93), indicted for absence and assessed for a fine of £180 at the Assizes, April 1593 (Chester, 29, 334, m. 17: R.R., 1, m. 6), and presented for absence, along with her husband, John, at Quarter Sessions, July 1610 (C.S.B., Indictments and Presentments, 1592–1617, f. 127v).

Margery Carison, wife of William Carison, yeoman of Wichaugh, Malpas, was indicted for hearing a mass, at Quarter Sessions, May 1582; the Grand Jury questioned her sanity (C.S.F., 1582, F 1, D 27–8). Catholic.

Richard Cawley of Bebington, yeoman or husbandman, was indicted for absence at Quarter Sessions, May 1582 (C.S.F., 1582, F 1, D 7), conforming 1585–6 (C.S.B., 1576–92, f. 207).

Richard Cawley of Woodchurch, yeoman, was indicted for absence at Quarter Sessions, May 1582, and, after imprisonment, promised conformity in the October following (C.S.F., 1582, F 1, D 19).

William Chadock (or *Cheidock*), yeoman, of Ridley, Bunbury, was unsuccessfully indicted at the Assizes, April 1591, and April 1592, and indicted and assessed for a fine of £100 in April 1593 (Chester, 21, 1, 156v: 29, 333, m. 11: 334, m. 17; R.R., 1, m. 6).

Gabriel Chawe, probably of Chester, promised conformity, October 1598 (M.L., 1, 167).

William Chawver(?), of Lady Egerton's household at Astbury, was presented as a recusant and non-communicant at the Diocesan Visitation, 1598 (E.D.V., I, 12, f. 56).

Alice Cheswis of Alpraham, Bunbury, was a prisoner for recusancy in Chester Castle *c.* 1585–97 (Chester, 21, 121v ff.: 29, 320, m. 13: 321, m. 14: 323, m. 11: 334, m. 17; R.R. 1, m. 6). She was presented as an obstinate recusant at the Diocesan Visitation, 1598 (E.D.V., I, 12, f. 64v), assessed for a fine of £240 at the Assizes, September 1600, and shared the loss of goods worth £6 13s. 4d. with her sons, Richard and William (q.v.), *c.* 1601–2 (R.R., 8, m. 10d: 10, m. 5).

Jane Cheswis, wife of John Cheswis, husbandman, of Bunbury, was presented as a recusant at the Diocesan Visitation, 1592 (E.D.V., I, 10, f. 92), and indicted for absence and assessed for a fine of £240, April 1593 (Chester, 29, 334, m. 17: R.R., 1, m. 6), at the Assizes.

Jane or *Anne Cheswis*, wife of William Cheswis (q.v.) of Alpraham, Bunbury, was presented as an obstinate recusant at the Diocesan Visitation, 1598 (E.D.V., I, 12, f. 64v), and indicted for absence and assessed for a fine of £240 at the Assizes, September 1600 (R.R., 8, m. 10d).

Richard Cheswis of Alpraham, Bunbury, son of Alice (q.v.) and brother of William Cheswis (q.v.), styled variously as labourer, husbandman, yeoman or tailor. He was indicted for absence at Quarter Sessions, May 1582 (C.S.F., 1582, F 1, D 5), and was a prisoner in Chester Castle along with his mother and brother *c.* 1584–97 (Chester, 21, 121v ff.: 29, 319, m. 18: 320, m. 13: 321, m. 14: 323, m. 11: 324, m. 14: 334, m. 17; R.R., 1, m. 6). He was presented as an obstinate recusant at the Diocesan Visitation, 1598 (E.D.V., loc. cit.), goods of his worth 20s. were seized, November 1599, and he was indicted for absence and assessed for a fine at the Assizes, September 1600, and shared the loss of goods worth £6 13s. 4d. with his mother and brother, *c.* 1601–2 (R.R., 8, m. 10d: 10, m. 5). He was presented as a recusant before the Quarter Sessions, July 1602 (C.S.B., Indictments and Presentments, 1592–1617, f. 70v).

William Cheswis of Alpraham, Bunbury, son of Alice (q.v.), brother of Richard (q.v.), and husband of Jane Cheswis (q.v.), styled variously as labourer, husbandman or yeoman. He was in prison with his mother and brother *c.* 1584–98 (for references, cf. Richard Cheswis), was presented as an obstinate recusant at the Diocesan Visitation, 1598, and for having a child of whose christening nothing was known (E.D.V., loc. cit.), was indicted, like Richard, 1600, and shared the loss of goods with him and his mother, *c.* 1601–2 (for references, cf. Richard Cheswis).

William Cocker (or *Cooker*), his wife, *Margery*, and *Elizabeth*, widow, of Great Budworth, were each indicted for absence at Quarter Sessions, July 1581 (C.S.F., 1581, F 2, D 12).

Elena Cooke, a servant of the Whitmores of Thurstaston, was presented as a recusant and non-communicant at the Diocesan Visitation, 1601 (E.D.V., I, 12a, f. 55).

Elizabeth Cooke, wife of Ralph Cooke of Haughton, Bunbury (q.v.), was presented as negligent in coming to church at the Metropolitan Visitation, 1590 (York, R.VI, A 12, f. 108v), as a recusant at the Diocesan Visitation, 1592 (E.D.V., I, 10, f. 93), and was indicted for absence and assessed for a fine of £240 at the Assizes, April 1593 (Chester, 29, 334, m. 17; R.R., 1, m, 6).

Isabel Cooke, wife of William Cooke (q.v.) of Tilstone Fearnall, Bunbury, was presented as a recusant at the Metropolitan Visitation, 1590 (York, R.VI, A 12,

f. 109), and the Diocesan Visitation, 1592 (E.D.V., 1, 10, f. 92v), and indicted for absence and assessed for a fine of £240 at the Assizes, April 1593 (Chester, loc. cit.; R.R., 1. m. 6).

Ralph Cooke of Haughton, Bunbury, a labourer or husbandman. Same as his wife, Elizabeth, 1590–3. Goods of his were seized worth 12d. in April 1594, 10s. in April 1595, and he was indicted for absence and assessed for a fine of £240 at the Assizes, September 1600 (R.R., 2, m. 6: 5, m. 28: 8, m. 10d). He was presented as an obstinate recusant at the Diocesan Visitation, 1598 (E.D.V., 1, 12, f. 64v), and, dying excommunicate, was buried without church rites, 29 April 1617 (E.D.B., Bunbury, f. 157).

William Cooke, yeoman, of Tilstone Fearnall, Bunbury, was indicted for absence at the Assizes, September 1587 (Chester, 29, 325, m. 16d). Same as his wife, Isabel, 1590–3, with the addition that he was charged with failing to have his children baptised, at the Diocesan Visitation, 1592 (E.D.V., 1, 10, f. 91). Goods to the value of 21s. were seized from him, April 1595 (R.R., 5, m. 28). Dying excommunicate, he was buried without church rites, 29 December 1600 (E.D.B., Bunbury, f. 146).

Anne Cotgreve of Christleton was presented as a recusant at the Diocesan Visitation, 1598 (E.D.V., 1, 12, f. 16), was indicted at the Assizes for absence and assessed for a fine of £240, September 1600 (R.R., 8, m. 10d), and was presented for absence at Quarter Sessions, April & December 1605 (Harl. MSS., 2095, 7, f. 10).

Elizabeth Cotgreve, of Christleton, daughter of Margery Cotgreve (q.v.), was presented for refusing to attend church, at the Metropolitan Visitation, 1590 (York, R.VI, A 12, f. 94v), was present at two masses, 1591 (Q.S.E., 4, f. 3; C.S.F., 1592, F 2, D 4), was presented as a recusant at the Diocesan Visitation, 1592 (E.D.V., 1, 10, f. 19), was indicted for absence and assessed for a fine of £960 at the Assizes, April 1593 (Chester, 29, 334, m. 17; R.R., 1, m. 6), was presented as a recusant at the Metropolitan Visitation, 1595 (York, R.VI, A 14, f. 3) and at the Diocesan Visitation, 1598 (E.D.V., 1, 12, f. 16), was indicted for absence and assessed for a fine of £240 at the Assizes, September 1600 (R.R., 8, m. 10d), was presented as a recusant at the Diocesan Visitation, 1601 (E.D.V., 1, 12a, f. 40), and was presented as a recusant at Quarter Sessions, November 1604 and, April and December 1605 (Harl. MSS., loc. cit.).

John Cotgreve, yeoman, of Christleton, was presented from Woodchurch parish as a recusant who taught school privately, at the Metropolitan Visitation, 1590 (York, R.VI, A 12, f. 87), and was indicted for absence and assessed for a fine of £960 at the Assizes, April 1593 (Chester, 29, loc. cit.; R.R., 1, m. 6).

Margery Cotgreve of Christleton, widow, mother of Elizabeth (q.v.) and Thomas (q.v.), and aunt of Randolph Cotgreve (p.v.). All entries for her daughter, Elizabeth, apply also to her. In addition, Margery had goods worth £11 seized from her, April 1594 (R.R., 2, m. 6). She died in 1608 (E.D.B., Christleton, loose folio).

Randolph Cotgreve, yeoman, of Christleton, nephew of Margery Cotgreve (q.v.), was presented for refusing to attend church, at the Metropolitan Visitation, 1590 (York, R.VI, A 12, f. 94v). Examined by the Chester High Commission, 1592, he admitted to being a non-communicant and gave evidence about two masses (Q.S.E., 4, ff. 3–4). He took the oath under 3 Jac. 1, in October 1606 (C.S.F., 1606, F 3, D 36).

Thomas Cotgreve, yeoman, of Christleton, son of Margery Cotgreve (q.v.). Entries for his sister, Elizabeth, 1590–3, also apply to him.

Anne (or *Katherine*) *Crocket* of Tilston, Malpas, a servant of Margery Aire (q.v.), was presented with her mistress as a recusant at the Metropolitan Visitation, 1590 (York, R.VI, A 12, f. 84v), and the Diocesan Visitation, 1592 (E.D.V., 1, 10, f. 59).

Katherine Crocket of Tilstone Fearnall, Bunbury, was presented as a recusant at the Diocesan Visitation, 1592 (E.D.V., 1, 10, f. 92v), indicted for absence and assessed for a fine of £40 at the Assizes, April 1593, and land worth 13s. 4d. a year was seized from her by 1594 (Chester, 29, loc. cit.; R.R., 1, m. 6: 2, m. 6). She was presented as a recusant at the Diocesan Visitation, 1604 (E.D.V., 1, 13, f. 12v). Was Ralph Crocket, the Cheshire-born priest who was taken *c.* 1587, a relative?

Eleanor Darme was imprisoned as a recusant in Chester Castle, September 1598 (Chester, 21, 1, 198).

Margaret Davenport, wife of William Davenport, gentleman, of Bramhall Hall (cf. Appendix III). She was the daughter of Richard Assheton of Middleton, Lancashire, and married in 1560 (Ormerod, III, 827). In 1581 the Privy Council ordered search to be made for her outside Chester diocese, while *c.* 1583 her family, 'greatly infected' with popery, were said to be taking refuge in Westmorland (S.P., 12, 151, 72: 27, 94). She was indicted for absence at the Assizes, April 1591 (Chester, 21, 1, 156v), and dower land of hers worth 66s. 8d. a year was seized, September 1592 (R.R., 1, m. 6). A priest, Peter Davenport, was probably her son, as, possibly, was another priest, John Damford (cf. Appendix II).

Edward Davye and his wife, *Jane*, of St. Bridget's parish, Chester, were presented for keeping popish relics, at the Metropolitan Visitation, 1595 (York, R.VI, A 14, f. 2v), and Jane Powell, alias Davies, of the same parish was presented as an absentee at the Diocesan Visitation, 1598 (E.D.V., 1, 12, f. 13). Catholics (?).

Anne Dewsbury, the wife of John Dewsbury, wiredrawer, of Chester, a niece of the recusant prisoner, Alice Cheswis (q.v.), gave evidence of a mass celebrated *c.* 1588 (Q.S.E., 4, f. 22), and from what she then said it is clear that she had been at least Catholic then, having afterwards conformed. Catholic.

John Didsbury of Mottram was presented as an obstinate recusant at the Metropolitan Visitation, 1590 (York, R.VI, A 12, f. 103), and as an absentee and noncommunicant at the Diocesan Visitation, 1598 (E.D.V., 1, 12, f. 76).

Elizabeth Dod of Edge, Malpas, the wife of Randle Dod of Edge, and mother of Katherine Golborne of Overton (q.v.), was presented as an obstinate recusant at the Metropolitan Visitation, 1590 (York, R.VI, A 12, f. 85v), and for absence at the Diocesan Visitation, 1592 (E.D.V., 1, 10, f. 55v). She was indicted for absence and assessed for a fine of £240 at the Assizes, April 1593 (Chester, 29, loc. cit.: R.R., 1, m. 6), and presented as a recusant at the Metropolitan Visitation, 1595 (York, R.VI, A 14, f. 8), and the Diocesan Visitations of 1598 and 1601 (E.D.V., 1, 12, f. 41: 12a, f. 45v).

Katherine Dod, the wife of Peter Dod, gentleman, of Shocklach, daughter of Thomas Ball of Bickley (Ormerod II, 638): her mother, Jane Ball, was a recusant (q.v.). She was presented as an obstinate recusant at the Metropolitan Visitation, 1590 (York, R.VI, A 12, f. 86), indicted for absence and assessed for a fine of £240 at the Assizes, April 1593 (Chester, 29, loc. cit.; R.R., 1, m. 6), and presented as a non-communicant at the Diocesan Visitations, 1598 & 1601 (E.D.V., 1, 12, f. 43v: 12a, f. 43v).

Margaret Dod, of Edge, Malpas, was presented as a recusant at the Diocesan Visitation, 1601 (E.D.V., 1, 12a, f. 45v).

William Dorington of Astbury was fined 40s. for failing to appear to answer an unstated charge before the High Commission, February 1581 (Ex. Dep., m. 3), and indicted for absence at Quarter Sessions, October 1581 (C.S.F., 1581, F 3, D 27).

Thomas Dowra, yeoman, of Neston, was indicted for absence and assessed for a fine of £240 at the Assizes, September 1600 (R.R., 8, m. 10d).

Katherine Dunne of Bunbury parish was presented as a recusant at the Diocesan Visitation, 1592, though her conformity was noted (E.D.V., 1, 10, f. 93).

Peter Dutton, gentleman, eldest son of John Dutton of Dutton (cf. Appendix III) and Eleanor Dutton, who may have been the Mistress Dutton of St. Peter's parish, Chester, who was accused of keeping Catholic objects, 1559 (S.P., 10, 134). He was educated abroad, possibly in Rome (ibid., 12, 27, 94), returning to England, 1583, when he enjoyed the patronage of Sir Christopher Hatton (Peck, I, 142). When examined by the Chester High Commission, February 1592, he promised conformity, but his wife, Elizabeth, refused to attend church (Q.S.E., 4, f. 10 ff.). He died in 1593 (Ormerod, I, 651).

Elizabeth Dutton, wife of Peter Dutton (q.v.) and daughter of the recusant, Richard Massey of Aldford (q.v.). See Peter Dutton, 1592. She was indicted for absence at the Assizes, 1594 (Chester, 21, 1, 173), and later resided in Walton Lancashire (Ormerod, I, 651).

Elizabeth Dytoe, spinster, of Edge, Malpas, was presented as an obstinate recusant at the Metropolitan Visitation, 1590 (York, R.VI, A 12, f. 85v), and for absence at the Diocesan Visitation, 1592 (E.D.V., 1, 10, f. 56). She was indicted for absence and assessed for a fine of £60 at the Assizes, April 1593 (Chester, 29, loc. cit.: R.R., 1, m. 6), goods worth 20s. were seized from her, April 1594 (R.R., 2, m. 6), she was presented as a recusant at the Metropolitan Visitation, 1595 (York, R.VI, A 14, f. 8), and the Diocesan Visitations of 1598 and 1601 (E.D.V., 1, 12, f. 41: 12a, f. 45v). She was indicted for absence and assessed for a fine of £240 at the Assizes, September 1600 (R.R., 8, m. 10d), and presented for absence at Quarter Sessions, April & December 1605, & September 1610 (Harl. MSS., loc. cit.).

Alice Eastham, wife of John Eastham of Tarvin, was presented as an absentee and non-communicant at the Diocesan Visitation, 1601 (E.D.V., 1, 12a, f. 34), and for absence at the Assizes, 1610 (Chester, 29, 370, m. 9).

George Egerton of Ridley, Bunbury, gentleman. His relationship to the Egerton family is obscure, though he was probably Lady Egerton's son. He was named on a national list of suspected persons, c. 1588 (Harl. MSS., 6998, f. 244v), presented as a recusant at the Metropolitan Visitation, 1590 (York, R.VI, A 12, f. 109), indicted for absence at the Assizes, April 1591 (Chester, 21, 1, 156v), and presented as a recusant and for not sending his children to be catechised, at the Diocesan Visitation, 1592 (E.D.V., 1, 10, f. 91v).

The *Wife* of *George Egerton* of Ridley, Bunbury (q.v.), was presented, along with her husband, as a recusant and for not sending her children to be catechised, at the Diocesan Visitation, 1592 (E.D.V., loc. cit.). Dying excommunicate, she was buried without church rites, 11 February 1618 (E.D.B., Bunbury, f. 158).

Lady Mary Egerton of Ridley, Bunbury, daughter of Richard Grosvenor of Eaton, gentleman; she married and outlived two husbands, Thomas Leigh of Adlington and Sir Richard Egerton of Ridley, and was already a widow for the second time when, in 1581, signs of her recusancy first appear; she was then indicted for absence, at Quarter Sessions (C.S.F., 1581, F 3, D 16), though proceedings against her were stayed by order of the bishop (C.S.B., 1576–92, Recognisances, f. 205). Further attempts were made to protect her from the penalties of the law by Sir George and Sir Thomas Bromley and Sir Christopher Hatton, who all tried to delay her appearance before the High Commission, 1582–3 (Peck, I, 117 ff.). C. 1583 as she was listed as a prominent papist and priest harbourer, an accusation that was repeated in 1584; when light-horse assessments were made, 1585, she was noted as a recusant and was willing to contribute £50, which she evidently paid; in 1586 she was willing to pay £30 to be relieved of the statutory penalties for recusancy. (S.P., 12, 27, 94: 169, 27: 183, 43: 184, 20: 189, 54: 200, 61). In 1588 she paid £50 for the national defence (*Cheshire Sheaf*, 1st Series, III, 157). She was presented as a recusant at the Metropolitan Visitation, 1590 (York, R.VI, A 12, f. 109), indicted for absence at the Assizes, April 1591 (Chester, 21, 1, 156v), presented as a recusant at the Diocesan Visitation, 1592 (E.D.V., 1, 10, f. 93v), and the Metropolitan Visitation, 1595 (York, R.VI, A 15, f. 57), receiving favoured treatment before the last two. She was presented as a recusant and non-communicant at the Diocesan Visitation, 1598 (E.D.V., 1, 12, f. 56). She died at Astbury on 26 March 1599.

Randolph Egerton, son of George Egerton (q.v.) of Ridley, was presented from Astbury parish as a recusant and non-communicant at the Diocesan Visitation, 1598 (E.D.V., loc. cit.).

John Eldershawe of Audlem, physician, was presented as a non-communicant, before the Diocesan High Commission, May 1564 (E.D.A., 12, 2, f. 72), and on unstated charges before the High Commission at York, 1571 and 1572 (York, H.C., Box 25, 1571–2, A.B., 16, ff. 78v & 140v). He was included in the diocesan list of recusants, 1577 (S.P., 12, 118, 49), and presented as an absentee and non-communicant at the Metropolitan Visitation, 1578 (York, R.VI, A 7, f. 12), by which he was again ordered to appear before the High Commission in York. He was indicted for absence and as a non-communicant at Quarter Sessions, June 1581, and for absence in October 1581, when his death was reported (C.S.F., 1581, F 2, D 12: F 3, D 25). His wife (q.v.) and son, Richard (q.v.) were recusants.

The *wife of John Eldershawe* of Audlem shared her husbands charges, etc., 1564, 1577 and 1578.

Richard Eldershawe of Audlem, physician, son of John Eldershawe (q.v.), was indicted for absence and for not communicating, at Quarter Sessions, June 1581 (C.S.F., 1581, F 2, D 12), indicted for absence at Quarter Sessions, July 1587 C.S.B., Indictments, 1565–92, f. 169), and at the Assizes, September 1587 (Chester, 29, 325, m. 16d). He was presented as a recusant at the Metropolitan Visitation, 1590 (York, R.VI, A 12, f. 109v), and the Diocesan Visitation, 1592, 1598 and 1604 (E.D.V., 1, 10, f. 89: 12, f. 69: 13, f. 44v). He was indicted for absence at the Assizes, September 1610 (Chester 29, 370, m. 9), and presented as a recusant before the Diocesan Chancellor, 26 February 1614 (E.D.V., 1, 11, 1592–1620, f. 37). He was doubtless the Richard Eldershawe, yeoman of Marbury, who was indicted for absence and assessed for a fine of £240 at the Assizes, September 1600 (R.R., 8, m. 10d).

Elmcott and *Thomas Elmideth* (?) were imprisoned as recusants in Chester Castle, September 1598 (Chester, 21, 1, 198).

Hugh Erdeswick of Leighton, near Nantwich, whose main estates were in Staffordshire, but, descended as he was from a Cheshire family of Minshull Vernon, still held lands at Leighton. He would normally have been dealt with by the Staffordshire authorities, but only references relating to Cheshire are given here. He was fined 166s. 8d. by the High Commission, February 1581, for failing to answer an unstated charge (Ex. Dep., m. 4), and indicted for absence at Quarter Sessions, October 1581 (C.S.F., 1581, F 3, D 21). In 1586 he was listed as a prominent recusant (S.P., 12, 193, 47), and again in 1587 (Lansd. MSS., 53, 69, f. 143v). Lands in Cheshire worth £4 8s. 10d. a year were seized from him, September 1589 (R.R., 1, m. 6), and he was presented as a recusant at the Metropolitan Visitation, 1590 (York, R.VI, A 12, f. 109v), and when too ill to answer an order to appear before the Privy Council, 1590, was ordered to be confined to his home at Leighton (A.P.C., 1590–1, 34). His son, Sampson, was also a recusant (q.v.).

Sampson Erdeswick, gentleman, son of Hugh Erdeswick (q.v.) was a noted antiquary (for his life, cf. D.N.B., VI, 806). Same as his father for 1581. He was indicted for absence, at the Assizes, September 1587 (Chester, 29, 325, m. 16d), presented with 'divers of his howsehode' as a recusant at the Metropolitan Visitation, 1590 (York, R.VI, A 12, f. 109v), examined as a suspected recusant by the Chester High Commission, 1592 (Q.S.E., 4, f. 1), and the sequestrated lands that he inherited from his father in Cheshire remained so (R.R., 1, m. 6: 2, m. 6). He died in 1603.

Elizabeth Evans of Leighton, near Nantwich, was indicted for absence and assessed for a fine of £240 at the Assizes, April 1593 (Chester, 29, 334 m. 17: R.R., 1, m. 6).

John Fisher, a lawyer of Trinity parish, Chester, was commended on religious grounds as being worthy of an aldermanship, 1564 (*Camden Misc.*, IX, 64), but was fined 12d. for absence at Quarter Sessions, August 1576 (M.B., 1572–7, 9 August, 18 Eliz.), presented for absence at the Metropolitan Visitation, 1578 (York, R.VI, A 7, 19v), and fined 12d. for absence at Quarter Sessions, September 1579 (M.B., 1578–81, 22 September, 21 Eliz.). He was a Councilman at his death, 1584 (Chester Assembly Book, 1, 197v).

Katherine Fisher of Bulkeley, Malpas, was indicted for absence and assessed for a fine of £240 at the Assizes, April 1593 (Chester, 29, 334, m. 17: R.R., 1, m. 6).

Robert Foster, miller, of Newhouse, West Kirby, was indicted for absence at the Assizes, September 1587 (Chester, 29, 325, m. 16d), and presented as a recusant at the Metropolitan Visitation, 1590 (York, R.VI, A 12, f. 88v).

Robert Fullyhurst, gentleman, of Barthomley, was presented as an absentee and non-communicant and for having put away his wife and keeping a woman in his house (York, R.VI, A 7, f. 11), was named, possibly maliciously, as a recusant when presented as a non-communicant before the Diocesan Chancellor, November 1588, and presented as a non-communicant and on suspicion of incontinence at the Diocesan Visitation, 1598 (E.D.V., 1, 7, f. 32: 12, f. 67v). Catholic(?)

John Fyncote of Barrow was indicted for absence at Quarter Sessions, October 1581, conforming, May 1583 (C.S.F., 1581, F. 3, D 32).

George Garnet of Spurstow, Bunbury, labourer, was fined 40s. for an unstated offence by the High Commission, February 1581 (Ex. Dep., m. 4), indicted for absence at Quarter Sessions, October 1581 (named as John Garnet of Barthomley), and May 1582 (C.S.F., 1581, F 3, D 29: 1582, F 1, D 5), and presented as a recusant at the Metropolitan Visitation, 1590 (York R.VI, A 12, f. 108v), and the Diocesan Visitation, 1592, to which his death was reported (E.D.V., 1,10, f. 92v).

Margery Garnet of Spurstow, Bunbury, was presented as a recusant at the Diocesan Visitation, 1592 (ibid., f. 92), indicted for absence and assessed for a fine of £240 at the Assizes, April 1593 (Chester, 29, 334, m. 17; R.R., 1, m. 6), and presented for absence at Quarter Sessions, September 1610 (Chester, 29, 370, m. 9).

Richard Garnet, husbandman, of Bunbury, was cited as an absentee before the Diocesan Chancellor, 1596, presented as an obstinate recusant at the Diocesan Visitation, 1598 (E.D.V., 1, 9, f. 60: 12, f. 64v), and indicted at the Assizes and assessed for a fine of £240, September 1600 (R.R., 8, m. 10d).

Thomas Gatlies(?) of Bunbury parish was presented as a recusant at the Diocesan Visitation, 1592 (E.D.V., 1, 10, f. 92).

Matilda Geste(?), wife of John Geste(?) of Hampton, Malpas, was presented as a recusant at the Diocesan Visitation, 1601 (E.D.V., 1, 12a, f. 45v).

Mrs. Glasier of Chester was recommended for examination by the Chester High Commission as an entertainer of two recusant prisoners (Q.S.E., 4, f. 15). This was probably Elizabeth, wife of William Glasier, Vice-Chamberlain of Chester (cf. Appendix III), though Mary, wife of his son, Hugh, of Backford, was presented as an absentee and non-communicant at the Diocesan Visitations, 1598 and 1601 (E.D.V., 1, 12, f. 29: 12a, f. 54). Hugh was Mayor of Chester, 1603. Catholic.

Katherine Golborne, wife of John Golborne, gentleman, of Overton, Malpas, and daughter of Randle Dod (Ormerod, II, 671) and Elizabeth Dod of Edge (q.v.). She was presented as an obstinate recusant at the Metropolitan Visitation, 1590 (York, R.VI, A 12, f. 85v), indicted for absence at the Assizes, April 1591 (Chester, 21, 1, 156v), presented for absence at the Diocesan Visitation, 1592 (E.D.V., 1, 10, f. 55v), indicted for absence and assessed for a fine of £240 at the Assizes, April 1593 (Chester, 29, 334, m. 17; R.R., 1, m. 6), presented as a recusant at the Diocesan Visitation, 1598 (E.D.V., 1, 12, f. 41), and indicted for absence and assessed for a fine of £240 at the Assizes, September 1600 (R.R., 8, m. 10d).

Matilda Golborne, wife of William Golborne of St. Peter's parish, Chester (q.v.), was presented as a recusant and non-communicant at the Diocesan Visitation, 1592 (E.D.V., 1, 10, f. 29), and fined 12d. for absence at Quarter Sessions, July 1592 (M.B., 1589-92, 14 July, 34 Eliz.).

William Golborne, gentleman, of St. Peter's parish, Chester, was presented as a recusant and non-communicant at the Diocesan Visitation, 1592 (E.D.V., loc. cit.), and as an absentee, enemy of religion and a non-communicant before the Chester High Commission, February 1592 (Q.S.E., 4, ff. 7 & 14).

Robert Granwall of St. John's parish, Chester, was fined 12d. for absence at Quarter Sessions, September 1568, and April and September 1579 (M.B., 1567-8, 2 September, 10 Eliz., where he is named as Robert Gronns: ibid., 1578-81, 22

April & 22 September, 21 Eliz.), and presented as an absentee and non-communicant at the Metropolitan Visitation, 1578 (York, R.VI., A 7, f. 20).

William Granwall of Brindley, Acton, was fined 40s. for failing to answer an unstated charge before the High Commission, February 1581 (Ex. Dep., m. 3), and indicted for absence at Quarter Sessions, October 1581 (C.S.F., 1581, F 3, D 20).

Elena Greene of Lady Egerton's household at Astbury was presented as an absentee and non-communicant at the Diocesan Visitation, 1598 (E.D.V., 1, 12, f. 56).

Anne Grosvenor, wife of Thomas Grosvenor of Eaton, gentleman (q.v.), and daughter of Roger Bradshaigh of Haigh, Lancashire (Ormerod, II, 842), was listed as conformable on the short diocesan list of leading recusants, 1576 (Harl. MSS., 360, 39, f. 68), and included in the similar list, 1577 (S.P., 12, 118, 49). She was presented, as Mistress Grosvenor, as an absentee and non-communicant at the Metropolitan Visitation, 1578 (York, R.VI, A 7, f. 21). Though she lived until 1599 no further references to her recusancy have been found.

Thomas Grosvenor, presumably eldest son and heir of Sir Thomas Grosvenor of Eaton, was presented as a probable recusant before the Chester High Commission, 1592 (Q.S.E., 4, f. 14). A great-aunt, Elizabeth, had been prioress of Chester St. Mary's Convent (Ormerod, II, 842).

Alice Hampton, wife of John Hampton senior, a yeoman of Hampton, Malpas, was presented as a recusant at the Diocesan Visitations, 1598 and 1601 (E.D.V., 1, 12, f. 41: 12a, f. 45v), indicted for absence and assessed for a fine of £240 at the Assizes, September 1600 (R.R., 8, m. 10d), and presented for absence at Quarter Sessions, April 1606 (Harl. MSS., 2095, 7, f. 10).

Thomas Hatton of Stockton was indicted for absence at Quarter Sessions, October 1581 (C.S.F., 1581, F 3, D 31). Was he related to the Marian priest, Richard Hatton? (Cf. Appendix II).

Roger Haye of Prestbury was indicted for absence at Quarter Sessions, May 1582 (C.S.F., 1582, F 1, D 10).

Henry Heape (or *Heypey*) and his wife, *Elena*, of Tarvin: Henry was a carpenter. They were presented for wilfully absenting themselves from church, but expressed readiness to conform at the Diocesan Visitation, 1598 (E.D.V., 1, 12, f. 19v). Nevertheless, Henry was indicted for absence and assessed for a fine of £240 at the Assizes, September 1600 (R.R., 8, m. 10d).

Ralph Hebarte of St. Martin's parish, Chester, was presented as a recusant at the Metropolitan Visitation, 1590 (York, R.VI, A 12, f. 95).

Thomas Hesketh, gentleman, of Thurstaston, was a prisoner in Chester Castle, 1593–4, was indicted for absence at the Assizes, October 1594, and April 1595, when he was assessed for a fine of £120 (Chester, 21, 1, 166 ff.: 29, 338, m. 16d; R.R., 5, m. 28). He and his wife were probably the Thomas and Elizabeth Hesketh of West Kirby parish who were presented as recusants whose child had not been christened at the parish church, at the Diocesan Visitation, 1604 (E.D.V., 1, 13, f. 17v).

Elizabeth Hesketh, wife of Thomas Hesketh (q.v.). Same as her husband for 1595 and 1604. Was she the Elizabeth Hesketh, spinster, of Tiverton, Bunbury, who was indicted for absence and assessed for a fine of £240 at the Assizes, April 1593 (Chester, 29, 334, m. 17; R.R. 1, m. 6)?

Katherine Hickson, wife of William Hickson of Tarvin, was presented as an absentee and non-communicant at the Diocesan Visitation, 1601 (E.D.V., 1, 12a, f. 34), and for absence, at Quarter Sessions, 1610 (Chester, 29, 370, m. 9).

Roger Higginson, yeoman, of Woodchurch, was indicted for absence at Quarter Sessions, May 1582, was imprisoned, and promised conformity in the following October (C.S.F., 1582, F 1, D 19).

John Hocknell, gentleman, of Prenton, son and heir of William Hocknell of Prenton and Margaret, daughter of James Hurleston of Chester; he married Margaret, daughter of Peter Hockenhull of Hockenhull (Ormerod, II, 532). In the diocesan return of recusants, 1577, he was listed as worth £10 a year in lands (S.P., 12, 118, 49). In 1581 he was fined £10 for failing to appear to answer an unstated charge before the High Commission (Ex. Dep., m. 5), by whom he was then imprisoned, and was indicted for absence at the October Quarter Sessions, where he was assessed for a fine of £120 and returned to Chester Castle (C.S.F., 1581, F 3, D 3). In December 1581 or January 1582 he was transferred from Chester Castle to the New Fleet, Salford (A.P.C., 1581–2, 279; Peck, I, 112), and his indictment, at the Assizes, along with William Hough's, as an 'obstinately disobedient' recusant, was ordered by the Privy Council in February 1582 (A.P.C., 1581–2, 329–30); when brought before the Summer Assizes he was listed as worth £20 in lands and goods (S.P., 12, 155, 35), and lands worth £10 a year were sequestrated from him, March 1584, and held in lease from the Queen by his brother-in-law, John Hocknell of Hockenhull (R.R., 1, m. 6). He remained in the Salford Fleet for some three years; by March 1585, he was a prisoner in the London Fleet, at liberty on recognisance, and unable to make any offer to compound for his recusancy fines: he then claimed that he had been in seven prisons in the previous five years. When a levy was laid on him in October 1585, although he had recently been 'disarmed' he offered a man and a gelding and his personal service. By June 1586 he was owing £600 in fines (S.P., 12, 167, 40: 183, 43: 184, 61: 187, 48 II & XII: 190, 43: 200, 59 & 61). When indicted for absence at the Assizes, September 1587, he refused to accept the indictment, and seems to have avoided imprisonment again until he was sentenced to a year's imprisonment for the dissemination of false prophecy in September 1589. On 24 April 1590, he died from an injury at the hands of John Taylor, the under-keeper of the Castle (Chester, 29, 325, m. 17: 328, m. 18d: 329, m. 20).

Margaret Hocknell, later *Ravenscroft*. Her first husband was John Hocknell, gentleman, of Prenton (q.v.), after whose death she married Edward Ravenscroft, gentleman. She was indicted for absence at Quarter Sessions, October 1581, when she agreed to conform (C.S.F., 1581, F 3, D 14), and not until about the time of her first husband's death does she seem to have fallen foul of the authorities again, when in 1590 she was presented at the Metropolitan Visitation as negligent in church attendance, while her children were taught by a recusant school-master employed by her (York, R.VI, A 12, f. 87). At the opening of 1592 the Chester High Commission was recommended to inquire into her second marriage, which had probably been conducted by a Seminary (Q.S.E., 4, f. 14). She was presented as an absentee at the Diocesan Visitation, 1592 (E.D.V., 1, 10, f. 41), and indicted for absence and assessed for a fine of £240 at the Assizes, April 1593 (Chester, 29, 334, m. 17; R.R., 1, m. 6). She was presented as an obstinate recusant at the Metropolitan Visitation, 1595 (York, R.VI, A 14,

f. 6), and at the Diocesan Visitation, 1598, for not communicating the previous Easter: she then promised to communicate (E.D.V., 1, 12, f. 28). At the same time she and her husband were presented for failing to cohabit.

Jane Hough, wife of William Hough, gentleman, of Leighton and Thornton (q.v.), was listed as an obstinate recusant in the 1576 diocesan list (Harl. MSS., 360, 39, f. 68), and was presented as an absentee and non-communicant at the Metropolitan Visitation, 1578, at which she was excommunicated for non-appearance (York, R.VI, A 8, f. 16v), and later absolved (Chester County, D.D.X., 43, 12).

Joan Hough of Spurstow, Bunbury, was presented as a recusant at the Diocesan Visitation, 1592 (E.D.V., 1, 10, f. 92v), and indicted for absence and assessed for a fine of £160 at the Assizes, April 1593 (Chester, 29, 334, m. 17: R.R., 1, m. 6).

William Hough, gentleman, of Leighton and Thornton, was the son of Alice, an illegitimate daughter of Thomas Cromwell, and Richard Hough, who had acted as his father-in-law's agent in the Dissolution, joining in the scramble for church property (R. V. H. Burne, *The Monks of Chester,* 166–7; Ormerod, II, 552). William was singled out as a stubborn recusant from the first time mention of him is found, in the 1576 short diocesan list of recusants (Harl. MSS., 360, 39, f. 68). In the 1577 diocesan return of recusants he was stated to have lands worth £50 of the 'ancient rent' (S.P., 12, 118, 49). He was presented as an absentee and non-communicant at the Metropolitan Visitation, 1578, excommunicated for non-appearance (York, R.VI, A 8, f. 16v), and later absolved (Chester County, D.D.X., 43, 12). He was imprisoned by the High Commission, 1581, and indicted for absence at Quarter Sessions, October 1581, when he was assessed for a fine of £120 and returned to Chester Castle (C.S.F., 1581, F 3, D 13). In December 1581 or January 1582 he was transferred to the New Fleet, Salford (A.P.C., 1581–2, 279; Peck, I, 112), where he remained as one of a group of determined recusants for most of the time until his death in February 1585 (S.P., 12, 183, 43). Along with John Hocknell (q.v.), his indictment as an 'obstinately disobedient' recusant at the Assizes was ordered by the Council, 1582 (A.P.C., 1581–2, 329–30), though he was then allowed to return home on recognisance for a short time (S.P., 12, 152, 48: 153, 6). When he was brought before the Summer Assizes he was stated to possess lands and goods worth £40 a year (ibid., 155, 35), and lands of his worth £26 13s. 4d. a year were sequestrated, March 1584, and held from the Crown by his son-in-law, William Whitmore (R.R., 1, m. 6). In the autumn of 1585 he was assessed, as a recusant, to bear the cost of a lance, but his death had occurred at the beginning of the year in the New Fleet; in June 1586, when the fact of his death had not yet penetrated to the government, he was stated to be owing £600 in recusancy fines (S.P., 12, 183, 15 & 43: 190, 43). His sole heiress, Alice (q.v., as Alice Whitmore), was a recusant, as was his wife, Jane (q.v.).

Elizabeth Humpston, wife of George Humpston, husbandman, of Tilstone Fearnall, Bunbury, was presented as a recusant at the Diocesan Visitation, 1592 (E.D.V., 1, 10, f. 92v), and indicted for absence and assessed for a fine of £240 at the Assizes, April 1593 (Chester, 29, 334, m. 17; R.R., 1, m. 6).

Elen Huxley of Bradley, Acton parish, near Nantwich, was indicted for absence and assessed for a fine of £240 at the Assizes, April 1593 (ibid.), and presented as an obstinate recusant at the Metropolitan Visitation, 1595 (York, R.VI, A 14, f. 9v).

Elizabeth Huxley, wife of Thomas Huxley of Alpraham, Bunbury (q.v.), was presented for absence to the Diocesan Chancellor, October 1589, and as an absentee and non-communicant at the Diocesan Visitation, 1601 (E.D.V., 1, 8, f. 114: 12a, f. 64v).

Margery Huxley, daughter of Thomas Huxley (q.v.) and Elizabeth Huxley (q.v.) of Alpraham, Bunbury, was presented as a recusant at the Diocesan Visitation, 1592, and as an absentee and non-communicant, 1601 (E.D.V., 1, 10, f. 92: 12a, f. 64v).

Ralph Huxley, labourer or husbandman, of Duddon, Tarvin, was presented as a recusant at the Metropolitan Visitation, 1590 (York R.VI, A 12, f. 96), indicted for absence and assessed for a fine of £60 at the Assizes, April 1593 (Chester, 29, 334, m. 17; R.R., 1, m. 6), presented as an absentee and non-communicant at the Metropolitan Visitation, 1595 (York, R.VI, A 14, f. 4), and as a wilful recusant at the Diocesan Visitation, 1598 (E.D.V., 1, 12, f. 20), and was indicted for absence and assessed for a fine of £240 at the Assizes, September 1600 (R.R., 8, m. 10d).

Thomas Huxley, yeoman or husbandman, of Alpraham, Bunbury, husband of Elizabeth Huxley (q.v.), and father of Margery (q.v.) and George Huxley, who became a priest (cf. Appendix II). He was indicted for absence at the Assizes, September 1587 (Chester, 29, 325, m. 17), presented for absence to the Diocesan Chancellor, October 1589 (E.D.V., 1, 8, f. 114), presented as a non-communicant at the Metropolitan Visitation, 1590 (York, R.VI, A 12, f. 108), and as a recusant and for not sending his children and servants to be catechised, at the Diocesan Visitation, 1592 (E.D.V., 1, 10, f. 92), and in that year he was imprisoned in Chester Castle (Chester, 21, 1, f. 155v). He was indicted for absence and assessed for a fine of £240 at the Assizes, April 1593 (ibid., 29, 334, m. 17; R.R., 1, m. 6), suffered the seizure of goods worth 46s. in April 1594, the sequestration of lands worth 22s. 4d. a year and the seizure of goods worth 67s. 8d. in April 1595, a further seizure of goods worth £9 in May 1598, and further lands worth £4 a year in November 1599, when he was also assessed for a fine of £240 for absence (R.R., 2, m. 6: 5, m. 28: 6, m. 12: 8, m. 10d). He was presented as an obstinate recusant at the Diocesan Visitation, 1598 (E.D.V., 1, 12, f. 64v); and was in that year again imprisoned in Chester Castle (Chester, 21, 1, f. 198). He was presented as an absentee and non-communicant at the Diocesan Visitation, 1601 (E.D.V., 1, 12a, f. 64v), and was indicted for absence at the Assizes, September 1610 (Chester, 29, 370, m. 9). When his son, George, was arrested when trying to travel overseas in 1595 he stated that his father was a tenant of Mrs. Prestland of Prestland Greeves (S.P., 12, 253, 22).

Christopher Isherwood (or *Usherwood* or *Underwood*), a yeoman or labourer, was prisoner for recusancy in Chester Castle, *c.* 1584–90 (Chester, 21, 1, 114 ff.: 29, 319, m. 18: 320, m. 13: 321, m. 14: 323, m. 11: 324, m. 14: 334, m. 17; R.R., 1, m. 6).

Henry Jones of St. Peter's parish, Chester, was presented as a recusant at the Diocesan Visitation, 1592 (E.D.V., 1, 10, f. 29).

Robert Jones, gentleman, of St. Bridget's parish, Chester, was presented as a recusant at the Metropolitan Visitation, 1590 (York, R.VI, A 12, f. 98). A

Robert Johns was listed as an alderman of Chester who was unfavourable to the religious settlement, 1564 (*Camden Misc.*, IX, 73).

Thomas Jugram, labourer, of Wybunbury, was indicted for absence at Quarter Sessions, May 1582 (C.S.F., 1582, F 1, D 12). A Thomas Jugram of Middlewich was presented as an absentee at the Diocesan Visitation, 1601 (E.D.V., 1, 12a, f. 74v).

Maude (or *Matilda*) *Kelsall*, wife of Richard Kelsall of Daresbury, was presented as a recusant at the Metropolitan Visitation, 1590 (York, R.VI, A 12, f. 82v), and as a papist at the Diocesan Visitation, 1592 (E.D.V., 1, 10, f. 64v), as a recusant at the Metropolitan Visitation, 1595 (York, R.VI, A 14, f. 16), as a wilful recusant at the Diocesan Visitation, 1598, a recusant in 1601, and an 'olde recusant' in 1604 (E.D.V., 1, 12, f. 46: 12a, f. 86: 13, f. 27). She was indicted for absence and assessed for a fine of £240 at the Assizes, September 1600 (R.R., 8, m. 10d), and indicted, as from Keckwick, for absence at the Assizes, March 1610 (Chester 29, 370, m. 9).

Henry Killiburne was imprisoned in Chester Castle as a recusant, 1598 (Chester, 21, 1, 198).

Hugo King, labourer, of Tarvin, was presented as a wilful absentee at the Diocesan Visitation, 1598 (E.D.V., 1, 12, f. 19v), and was indicted for absence and assessed for a fine of £240 at the Assizes, September 1600 (R.R., 8, m. 10d).

James Knowsley of St. John's parish, Chester, was presented as an absentee and non-communicant at the Metropolitan Visitation, 1578 (York, R.VI, A 7, f. 20), and was fined 12d. for absence at Quarter Sessions, April 1579 (M.B., 1578–81, 22 April, 21 Eliz.).

Mrs. Langton, the widow of a gentleman, was listed in the diocesan return of recusants, 1577 (S.P., 12, 118, 49).

John Langton of Thurstaston was presented as a recusant at the Diocesan Visitation, 1598 (E.D.V., 1, 12, f. 31v).

Margaret Langton, wife of Ralph Langton of St. John's parish, Chester (q.v.), was presented as an absentee and non-communicant at the Diocesan Visitation, 1589 (E.D.V., 1, 8, f. 136v), as a suspected recusant at the Chester High Commission, 1592 (Q.S.E., 4, f. 8), as an absentee at the Metropolitan Visitation, 1595 (York, R.VI, A 14, f. 2v), and, as a widow, as an absentee and non-communicant at the Diocesan Visitation, 1598 (E.D.V., 1, 12, f. 22v).

Ralph Langton, yeoman, of St. John's parish, Chester. Same as his wife, Margaret, 1589 and 1595. He was examined about suspected treasonable words, 1588 (Q.S.F., 37, 23), was presented as an absentee and non-communicant at the Metropolitan Visitation, 1590 (York, R.VI, A 14, f. 2v), was examined as a suspected recusant by the Chester High Commission, January and February 1592 (Q.S.E., 4, ff. 1, 8 & 19), and was shortly afterwards imprisoned for 'bad speches' against the Mayor, whom he petitioned for his release (A.P., 1, 37).

Maria Lawton, wife of William Lawton, gentleman, of Church Lawton, was reported to be taking refuge outside the diocese, July 1581 (A.P.C., 1581–2, 123), and in the October following was indicted for absence at Quarter Sessions and, again, in May 1582 (C.S.F., 1581, F 3, D 17: 1582, F 1, D 9). As Alice Lawton she was indicted for absence at the Assizes, September 1587 (Chester, 29, 325, m. 16d). She was presented to the Diocesan Chancellor as an absentee and referred to the bishop, October 1589 (E.D.V., 1, 8, f. 85v), presented as a recusant at the Metropolitan Visitation, 1590 (York, R.VI, A 12, f. 111), and as an absentee at the Diocesan Visitation, 1592 (E.D.V., 1, 10, f. 108v). She was indicted for absence and assessed for a fine of £1,440 at the Assizes, April 1593 (Chester, 29, 334, m. 17; R.R., 1, m. 6), and was presented as a recusant at the Metropolitan Visitation, 1595 (York, R.VI, A 15, f. 65v), and the Diocesan Visitation, 1598, and as an absentee at the Diocesan Visitation, 1601 (E.D.V., 1, 12, f. 55v: 12a, f. 72v).

Maria Lawton, daughter of William and Maria Lawton (q.v.) of Church Lawton, was presented as a recusant at the Diocesan Visitation, 1592 (E.D.V., 1, 10, f. 108v).

Randle Lawton, of Agden, Malpas, was indicted for attending a mass at Quarter Sessions, May 1582 (C.S.F., 1582, F 1, D 27). Catholic.

Thomas Lawton, tailor, of Tiverton, Bunbury, was presented as 'a notorious papist resorting to the recusant houses' at the Diocesan Visitation, 1592 (E.D.V., 1, 10, f. 93), and indicted for absence and assessed for a fine of £40 at the Assizes, April 1593 (Chester, loc. cit.: R.R., 1, m. 6).

Elena Leche (alias *Parturton*), knitter, of Malpas, was presented as a recusant at the Diocesan Visitations, 1598 and 1601 (E.D.V., 1, 12, f. 41: 12a, f. 45v), indicted for absence and assessed for a fine of £240 at the Assizes, September 1600 (R.R., 8, m. 10d), and presented as a recusant at Quarter Sessions, April and December 1605, and September 1613 (Harl. MSS., 2095, 7, f. 10).

Richard Ledsham, pewterer, of St. Peter's parish, Chester, was presented as a recusant at the Diocesan Visitation, 1592 (E.D.V., 1, 10, f. 29).

Mr. Litherland, tanner, of Chester, attended masses said by the seminary, Thomas Holford, in Chester Castle, 1585 (Chester, 21, 100, examination dated 27 August 1585). Catholic.

George Litherland, weaver, of Woodchurch, was indicted for absence at Quarter Sessions, May 1582, and, after imprisonment, conformed in the October following (C.S.F., 1582, F 1, D 21).

William Liverpool of Trinity parish, Chester, was presented for absence and as a non-communicant at Quarter Sessions, August 1588 (M.B., 16 August, 30 Eliz.), and at the Diocesan Visitation, 1601 (E.D.V., 1, 12a, f. 36). He was presented for refusing to go to church, at Quarter Sessions, 1603–4 (Q.S.F., 52, 42). His *wife*, Jane, was presented with him on the first and last occasion, and their daughter also on the last.

Thomas Lloyd, servant of William Brereton of Tushingham, Malpas, was indicted for attending a mass at Quarter Sessions, May 1582 (C.S.F., 1582, F 1, D 27). Catholic.

James Longton, skinner or husbandman, and *John Longton*, husbandman or labourer, of Tiverton, Bunbury, were imprisoned in Chester Castle, *c.* 1589. (Chester, 21, 1, 142v), presented as recusants at the Metropolitan Visitation, 1590 (York, R.VI, A 12, f. 108v), and indicted for absence and assessed for a fine of £240 at the Assizes, April 1593 (Chester, 29, 334, m. 17; R.R., 1, m. 6), and in September 1600 (R.R., 8, m. 10d). John was presented at the Diocesan Visitation, 1598, for having a child of whose christening nothing was known, and James as an absentee and non-communicant, 1601 (E.D.V., 1, 12, f. 64v: 12a, f. 64v).

Richard Longton, yeoman, of Bunbury, was presented as a recusant at the Metropolitan Visitation, 1590 (York, R.VI, A 12, f. 108v), indicted (as William Longton) for absence at the Assizes, April, 1591 (Chester, 21, 1, 156v), presented as an obstinate recusant, reported as reformed, at the Diocesan Visitation, 1598 (E.D.V., 1, 12, f. 64v), indicted for absence and assessed for a fine of £240 at the Assizes, September 1600 (R.R., 8, m. 10d), and goods to the value of £4 were seized from him by 1602 (ibid., 10, m. 5).

Robert Longton, yeoman or husbandman, of Bunbury, shared the charges of Richard Longton (q.v.), 1590 & 1598–1600, whilst he was also reported to the Diocesan Visitation, 1598, for having a child of whose christening nothing was known. Goods to the value of 6s. 8d. were seized from him, April 1594 (R.R., 2, m. 6).

Elen Maddocks, wife of Thomas Maddocks of Malpas (q.v.), was present at a mass, April 1582 (C.S.F., 1582, F 1, D 1), and indicted for absence at Quarter Sessions, May 1582 (ibid., D 13).

Eleanor Maddocks, daughter of John and Matilda Maddocks (q.v.) of Agden, Malpas, was indicted for absence at Quarter Sessions, May 1584 (C.S.F., 1584, F 1, D 21), imprisoned in Chester Castle, *c.* 1587 (Chester, 21, 1, 133v), and presented as a recusant at the Metropolitan Visitation, 1590 (York, R.VI., A 12, 85v).

Joan Maddocks, of Agden, Malpas, was indicted for hearing a mass at Quarter Sessions, May 1586 (C.S.F., 1586, F 1, D 10). Catholic.

Joan Maddocks, wife of Thomas Maddocks of Thurstaston (q.v.), was noted in the Parish Register as an absentee and non-communicant, 1581 (E.D.B., Thurstaston, 1581), indicted for absence at Quarter Sessions, May 1582 (C.S.F., 1582, F 1, D 25), conforming July 1582 (C.S.B., 1576–92, Recognisances, f. 209), and presented as a recusant before the Diocesan Visitation, 1592 (E.D.V., 1, 10, f. 24v).

John Maddocks, husbandman or yeoman, of Agden, Malpas, was indicted for hearing a mass and for absence at Quarter Sessions, May, 1582, and May 1584 (C.S.F., 1582, F 1, D 13 & 27: 1584, F 1, D 21), imprisoned in Chester Castle, *c.* 1587 (Chester, 21, 1, 133v), presented as a recusant at the Metropolitan Visitation, 1590 (York, R.VI A 12, f. 85v), imprisoned in Chester Castle, 1592–4 (Chester, 21, 1, 159 ff.), and, as from Wirswall, Malpas, was assessed for an unspecified fine, 1593 (R.R., 1, m. 6d). He was presented as a recusant at the Metropolitan Visitation, 1595 (York, R.VI, A 14, f. 8), suffered the sequestration of lands worth 21s. a year, April 1595 (R.R., 5, m. 28), and was imprisoned yet again in Chester Castle, 1598 (Chester, 21, 1, 198). John Maddocks, almost certainly his son, became a priest (cf. Appendix II).

Matilda Maddocks, wife of John Maddocks of Agden, Malpas (q.v.), shared her husband's charges, 1582, 1584 and 1590. She was presented as an absentee and non-communicant at the Diocesan Visitation, 1592 (E.D.V., 1, 10, f. 56), indicted for absence and assessed for a fine of £240 at the Assizes, April 1593 (Chester, 29, 334, m. 17; R.R., 1, m. 6), and presented as a recusant at the Metropolitan Visitation, 1595 (York, R.VI, A 14, f. 8), and the Diocesan Visitation, 1598 (E.D.V., 1, 12, f. 41).

Thomas Maddocks, yeoman, of Thurstaston, was possibly before the High Commission at York, styled 'gentleman', on an unstated charge, 1572 (York, H.C., Box 25, 1571–2, A.B., 16, f. 80), was noted in the Parish Register as an absentee and non-communicant, 1581 (E.D.B., Thurstaston, 1581), and fined 40s. for his failure to answer an unstated charge before the High Commission, February 1581, though the fine was remitted on conformity (Ex. Dep., m. 3 & 11–12); nevertheless, he was indicted for absence at Quarter Sessions, October 1581, and May 1582 (Q.S.F., 1581, F 3, D 30: 1582, F 1, D 24), and was a prisoner for recusancy in Chester Castle, c. 1583–98 (Chester, 21, 1, 110 ff.: 29, 319, m. 8: 320, m. 13: 321, m. 14: 323, m. 11: 324, m. 14: 334, m. 17). In 1592, a sick man, he petitioned the justices for the food usually allowed to a pauper (J. Beck, *Tudor Cheshire*, 67).

Thomas Maddocks, husbandman, of Malpas, was indicted for absence at Quarter Sessions, May 1582 (C.S.F., 1582, F 1, D 13), and at the Assizes, September 1587 (Chester, 29, 325, m. 17).

Richard Maghull, probably of Chester, promised conformity, October 1598 (M.L., 1, 167).

Anne Mallam, widow, of Grange, West Kirby, was indicted for absence at the Assizes, 1587 (Chester, 29, 325, m. 16), presented as a recusant at the Metropolitan Visitation, 1590 (York, R.VI, A 12, f. 88v), and for absence at the Diocesan Visitation, 1592, when she was unable to appear because she was in prison, though she later did so and submitted (E.D.V., 1, 10, f. 42); nevertheless, she was indicted for absence and assessed for a fine of £240 at the Assizes, April 1593 (Chester, 29, 334, m. 17; R.R., 1, m. 6). She was presented for failure to communicate at the Diocesan Visitation, 1598, claiming that it was only because of 'the insufficiencie of the curate', but was presented as a non-communicant at the Diocesan Visitation, 1601 (E.D.V., 1, 12, f. 30: 12a, f. 56v). She was indicted for absence at the Assizes, September 1610 (Chester, 29, 370, m. 9).

Mrs. Malpas, widow of Thomas Malpas, was listed as a recusant in the diocesan return, 1577 (S.P., 12, 118, 49).

Godfrey Manning of Wrenbury was indicted for absence at Quarter Sessions, October 1581 (C.S.F., 1581, F 3, D 28).

Katherine Mason of Bunbury parish was presented as a recusant at the Metropolitan Visitation, 1590 (York, R.VI, A 12, f. 109).

Margery Mason, widow, of Malpas, was indicted for hearing a mass, and for absence, at Quarter Sessions, May 1582, and speedily conformed, but was indicted again for absence in May 1584 (C.S.F., 1582, F 1, D 13 & 27: 1584, F 1, D 21). She was imprisoned in Chester Castle, c. 1587, and indicted for absence at the Assizes, September 1587 (Chester, 21, 1, 133v: 29, 325, m. 16d), and presented as a recusant at the Metropolitan Visitation, 1590 (York, R.VI, A 12, f. 85v).

William Mason, husbandman, of Alpraham, Bunbury, was indicted for absence at the Assizes, April 1591 (Chester, 21, 1, 156v), presented as a recusant at the Diocesan Visitation, 1592 (E.D.V., 1, 10, f. 91v), indicted for absence and assessed for a fine of £240 at the Assizes, April 1593 (Chester, 29, 334, m. 17; R.R., 1, m. 6), presented as an absentee at the Metropolitan Visitation, 1595 (York, R.VI, A 14, f. 10), and as an obstinate recusant at the Diocesan Visitation, 1598 (E.D.V., 1, 12, f. 64v). His wife, *Elena Mason*, was presented as an absentee and non-communicant at the Diocesan Visitation, 1601 (ibid., 12a, f. 64v).

Margaret Massey, wife of Richard Massey, senior (q.v.), gentleman, of Waverton, was imprisoned in Chester Castle, c. 1587 (Chester, 21, 1, 133v), presented as a recusant at the Diocesan Visitation, 1592 (E.D.V., 1, 10, f. 24v), examined and imprisoned in the Northgate by the Chester High Commission, January 1592, and the search of her house was ordered: shortly afterwards she was sent to join her husband in Chester Castle (Q.S.E., 4, f. 1, 10, 14 & 19), where she was imprisoned for a third time, 1594 (Chester, 21, 1, 172). She was presented as a recusant at the Diocesan Visitation, 1601 (E.D.V., 1, 12a, f. 37v).

Margery Massey, widow, of Bunbury parish was presented as an absentee and non-communicant at the Diocesan Visitation, 1601 (E.D.V., 1, 12a, f. 64v).

Mary Massey, fourth wife of John Massey of Coddington, gentleman (Ormerod, II, 732), was presented as a recusant at the Metropolitan Visitation, 1590 (York, R.VI, A 12, f. 89), indicted for absence at the Assizes, April 1591 (Chester, 21, 1, 156v), and presented as a recusant at the Diocesan Visitation, 1592 (E.D.V., 1, 10, f. 22v).

Richard Massey, senior, gentleman, of Waverton, was presented as a non-communicant at the Metropolitan Visitation, 1578, and ordered to attend conferences with local clerics (York, R.VI, A 7, ff. 10–10v). In 1583 he and his household were said to be 'greatlie corrupted' with popery (S.P., 15, 27, 94), and early in 1584 his house was searched after the return of his eldest son, Richard (q.v.), from Rome (Peck, I, 143–4), and, in spite of a plea for leniency from Sir Christopher Hatton (ibid., 150) it was not long before he was in prison in Chester Castle, where he remained, 1584–95 (Chester, 29, 320, m. 13: 323, m. 11: 324, m. 14: 334, m. 17; R.R., 1, m. 6). He was unable to compound for the fines that he incurred (S.P., 12, 189, 54). A petition for his release on account of his age and ill-health was presented and accepted, 1595, and he was confined to his house at Waverton and to the area around it under 35 Eliz., c. 2 (C.S.F., 1595, F 2, D 30–2), though a report that he was mixed up in an attempt to furnish horses to the Earl of Kildare reached the government in the following year (S.P., 12, 260, 65). When he was presented as a recusant at the Diocesan Visitation, 1601, he was recorded as deceased (E.D.V., 1, 12a, f. 37v). He was probably the Richard Massey of Churcheon Heath who was listed as a recusant worth £10 a year in lands in the diocesan return, 1577 (S.P., 12, 118, 49). His wife, Margaret, was a recusant (q.v.), as was his daughter, Elizabeth (cf. Elizabeth Dutton).

Richard Massey, junior, son of Richard Massey (q.v.), gentleman, of Waverton and Chester, was presented as an absentee at the Metropolitan Visitation, 1578, and ordered to attend conferences with local clerics (York, R.VI, A 7, ff. 10–10v). In 1583 he was reported as recently returned from Rome (S.P., 15, 27, 94), and his father's house was consequently searched in 1584 (Peck, I, 143–4). In 1592 he was reported to the Chester High Commission for his failure to attend church and communicate (Q.S.E., 4, f. 19). He was presented as a recusant at the Diocesan Visitation, 1598, and as an absentee and non-communicant, 1601 (E.D.V., 1, 12, f. 16: 12a, ff. 37–9).

Jane Massey, wife of Richard Massey, junior (q.v.), was a Dutton by birth. She was presented as a recusant at the Diocesan Visitations, 1598 and 1601 (E.D.V., loc. cit.).

Nicholas Mawdesley was a prisoner in Chester Castle, 1593–4, and was unsuccessfully indicted at the Assizes, October 1594 (Chester, 21, 1, 166 ff.: 29, 338, m. 16d).

Jane Mellung was imprisoned in Chester Castle as a recusant, September 1598 (Chester, 21, 1, 198).

Margery More (alias *Cayliffe*) was indicted for absence at the Assizes, April 1591 (ibid., 156v).

Christopher Morville, a merchant of Trinity parish, Chester. Though commended as worthy on religious grounds to be an alderman, 1564 (*Camden Misc.*, IX, 74), he was fined 12d. for absence at Quarter Sessions, August 1576 (M.B., 1572-7, 9 August, 18 Eliz.), and presented as an absentee at the Metropolitan Visitation, 1578 (York, R.VI, A 7, f. 19v).

Thomas Moulton of Faddiley, Acton, was indicted for absence at Quarter Sessions, October 1581 (C.S.F., 1581, F 3, D 10), and presented for absence, July 1610 (C.S.B., Indictments and Presentments, 1592-1617, f. 127v).

Anne Moyle, wife of Thomas Moyle, yeoman, of Shocklach, was presented as a recusant at the Metropolitan Visitation, 1590 (York, R.VI, A 12, f. 86), indicted for absence and assessed for a fine of £20 at the Assizes, April 1593 (Chester, 29, 334, m. 17; R.R., 1, m. 6), presented as a non-communicant at the Diocesan Visitations, 1598 and 1601 (E.D.V., 1, 12, f. 43v: 12a, f. 43v), and presented for absence at Quarter Sessions, December 1603 (Harl. MSS., 2095, 7, f. 10).

Elen Myers of St. Michael's parish, Chester, was presented for using a Latin Primer at the Metropolitan Visitation, 1578 (York, R.VI, A 7, f. 19). Catholic?

Alice Nevet, wife of John Nevet, husbandman, of Tushingham, Malpas, and daughter of the recusants Roger and Margaret Yardley (q.v.), was indicted for hearing a mass and for absence at Quarter Sessions, May 1582 (C.S.F., 1582, F 1, D 13 & 27).

Peter Orrell of St. John's parish, Chester, was fined 12d. for absence at Quarter Sessions, September 1568 (M.B., 1567-8, 2 September, 10 Eliz.), and presented as an absentee and non-communicant at the Metropolitan Visitation, 1578 (York, R.VI, A 7, f. 20).

George Otley, gentleman, of Acton, Nantwich, was presented as a recusant at the Diocesan Visitation, 1592 (E.D.V., 1, 10, f. 88).

Elen Owley, wife of Richard Owley of Malpas parish, was presented as a recusant at the Metropolitan Visitation, 1590 (York, R.VI, A 12, f. 85v).

John Owley of Bunbury parish was presented as a recusant at the Metropolitan Visitation, 1590 (ibid., f. 109).

Margaret Parson or *Pearson*, widow, of Audlem, was presented as a recusant at the Diocesan Visitations, 1598 and 1604, when she was noted as deceased (E.D.V., 1, 12, f. 69: 13, f. 44v). She was probably Margaret Parson of Marbury who was indicted for absence and assessed for a fine at the Assizes, September 1600 (R.R., 8, m. 10d).

Henry Pemberton of Chester was fined 6s. 8d. for absence at Quarter Sessions, August 1576 (M.B., 1572-7, 9 August, 18 Eliz.), and presented as an irregular attender and non-communicant at the Diocesan Visitation, 1601 (E.D.V., 1, 12a, ff. 38v-9).

Randle Platt, husbandman, of Faddiley, Acton, was presented as a recusant at the Metropolitan Visitation, 1590 (York, R.VI, A 12, f. 107), indicted for absence and assessed for a fine of £960 at the Assizes, April 1593 (Chester, loc. cit.; R.R., 1, m. 6), and indicted for absence at the Assizes, September 1610 (ibid., 29, 370, m. 9).

Richard Poole, gentleman, of Marbury, brother of William Poole (q.v.), was indicted for absence at the Assizes, April 1591, and indicted for absence and assessed for a fine of £240, April 1593 (Chester, 21, 1, 156v: 29, 334, m. 17; R.R., 1, m. 6). He was presented as an absentee at the Metropolitan Visitation, 1595 (York, R.VI, A 14, f. 10), suffered the seizure of goods worth £4 16s. 8d, April 1595 (R.R., 5, m. 28), and was imprisoned in Chester Castle, 1596 (Chester, 21, 1, 185). He may have been the Richard Poole, yeoman, of Marbury, who was bound in recognisance to live at the home of his brother, Thomas, in Bedale, Yorkshire, 1596 (C.S.F., 1596, F 4, D 33).

William Poole, gentleman, of Marley Green, Marbury, brother of Richard Poole (q.v.), was indicted for absence at the Assizes, April 1591 (Chester, 21, 1, 156v), presented as a recusant at the Diocesan Visitation, 1592 (E.D.V., 1, 12, f. 95), lost land by sequestration worth 41s. 8d. a year, January 1593, as well as goods worth £45 (R.R., 6, m. 12), was indicted for absence and assessed for a fine of £720 at the Assizes, April 1593 (Chester, 29, 334, m. 17; R.R., 1, m. 6). He was presented as an absentee, along with his wife, his brother, Richard, and two servants, and because he had not had his child baptised at his parish church, at the Metropolitan Visitation, 1595 (York, R.VI, A 14, f. 10), and the latter charge was repeated at the Diocesan Visitation, 1598, when, along with his wife, he was also presented as a recusant (E.D.V., 1, 12, f. 68v). In April 1595, goods worth £20 18s. 4d. and lands worth 17s. 9d. a year were seized from him, as were goods worth £5 and lands worth 18s. 8d. a year in May 1598, and lands worth £20 a year in November 1599, while he was indicted for absence and assessed for a fine of £240 in September 1600, at the Assizes (R.R., 5, m. 28: 6, m. 12: 8, m. 10d).

Mrs. William Poole: see the charges against her husband at the Visitations of 1595 and 1598.

Jane Prees or *Price* of Spurstow, Banbury, was presented as a recusant at the Diocesan Visitation, 1592 (E.D.V., 1, 10, f. 92), and indicted for absence and assessed for a fine of £160 at the Assizes, April 1593 (Chester, loc. cit.; R.R., 1, m. 6).

Henry and *William Price* of Ridley, Bunbury, were indicted for absence at the Assizes, April 1591, and April 1592 (Chester, 21, 1, 156v: 29, 333, m. 11).

John Price, joiner, of Cholmondeley, was indicted for absence at the Assizes, September 1587, while a John Price, husbandman, of Bunbury, was indicted for absence at the Assizes, April 1591 (Chester, 21, 1, 186v: 29, 325, m. 16d).

Widow Prickett of St. Oswald's parish, Chester, was presented for harbouring recusants at the Diocesan Visitation, 1598 (E.D.V., 1, f. 16v). Catholic.(?)

Henry Primrose, tailor, of St. Martin's parish, Chester, was presented for absence at Quarter Sessions, January 1588 (Q.S.F., 37, 47), presented as a recusant at the Metropolitan Visitation, 1590 (York, R.VI, A 12, f. 95), and he and his family were treated as recusant suspects at the inquiry by the Chester High Commission, 1592 (Q.S.E., 4, f. 14). Catholic youths who were trying to escape overseas lodged at his house, 1595 (S.P., 12, 253, 22). His daughter, Elizabeth, was presented as an absentee at the Metropolitan Visitation, 1590 (York, loc. cit., f. 89), while Jane, another daughter, evidently married John Whitmore (cf. Jane Whitmore).

Margaret Primrose, wife of Henry Primrose of Chester (q.v.); the same as her husband, 1590 and 1592. She was indicted for absence and assessed for a fine of £120 at the Assizes, September 1595 (R. R., 6, m. 12).

Edward Probin, husbandman, of Wichaugh, Malpas, son of Randle Probin (q.v.), was indicted for hearing a mass and for absence at Quarter Sessions, May 1582, and for absence, May 1584 (C.S.F., 1582, F 1, D 16 & 27: 1584, F 1, D 21), and for hearing mass in his house, May 1586 (C.S.B., 1576–92, Recognisances, f. 209v). He was imprisoned in Chester Castle, *c.* 1587 (Chester, 21, 1, 133v), presented as a recusant at the Metropolitan Visitation, 1590 (York, R.VI, A 12, f. 85v), imprisoned in Chester Castle, 1592–4 (Chester, 21, 1, 159 ff.), presented as a recusant at the Metropolitan Visitation, 1595 (York, R.VI, A 14, f. 8). In 1598 he was again a prisoner in Chester Castle (Chester, 21, 1, 198), and goods to the value of 20s. were seized from him (R.R., 6, m. 12).

Gwen Probin, widow of Wichaugh, Malpas, was indicted for absence at the Assizes, September 1587 (Chester, 29, 325, m. 16d).

Joan Probin, wife of Edward Probin of Wichaugh, Malpas (q.v.); the same as her husband, 1582 and 1584. She was imprisoned in Chester Castle, *c.* 1587 (Chester, 21, 1, 133v), presented as a recusant at the Metropolitan Visitation 1590 (York, R.VI, A 12, f. 85v), indicted for absence and assessed for a fine of £240 at the Assizes, April 1593 (Chester, 29, 334, m. 17; R.R., 1, m. 6), presented as a recusant at the Metropolitan Visitation, 1595 (York, R.VI, A 14, f. 8), and the Diocesan Visitation, 1598 and 1601 (E.D.V., 1, 12, f. 41: 12a, f. 45v). As a widow she was indicted for absence at the Assizes, September 1610 (Chester, 29, 370, m. 9), and presented for absence at Quarter Sessions, April 1613 (Harl. MSS., 2095, f. 10).

John Probin, husbandman, of Malpas, was indicted for absence at Quarter Sessions, October 1581, submitting a year later (C.S.F., 1581, F 3, D 33: 1582, F 1, D 52).

John Probin, son of William Probin (q.v.) of Malpas, was presented as a recusant at the Diocesan Visitations, 1598 and 1601 (E.D.V., 1, 12, f. 41: 12a, f. 45v), indicted for absence and assessed for a fine of £240 at the Assizes, September 1600 (R.R., 8, m. 10d), and presented for absence at Quarter Sessions, December 1605 (Harl. MSS., 2095, 7, f. 10).

Margaret Probin of Malpas was presented as a recusant at the Diocesan Visitation, 1601 (E.D.V., 1, 12a, f. 45v).

Mary Probin of Malpas, ibid.

Randle Probin, husbandman, of Malpas, father of Edward Probin (q.v.). A mass was held in his house, *c.* 1580, he was indicted for absence at Quarter Sessions, May 1584, and for hearing a mass, said at Edward Probin's house, May 1586 (C.S.F., 1582, F 1, D 1: 1584, F 1, D 21: 1586, F 1, D 9; C.S.B., 1576–92, Recognisances, f. 209v). He was imprisoned in Chester Castle, *c.* 1587 (Chester, 21, 1, 133v), and was presented as an absentee and non-communicant at the Diocesan Visitation, 1592, to which his death was reported (E.D.V., 1, 10, f. 56).

Sybil Probin of Malpas was presented for absence at the Diocesan Visitation, 1592 (E.D.V., 1, 10, f. 55), and indicted for absence and assessed for a fine of £20 at the Assizes, April 1593 (Chester, 29, 334, m. 17: R.R., 1, m. 6).

William Probin, husbandman, of Malpas, was presented as a recusant at the Diocesan Visitations, 1598 and 1601 (E.D.V., 12, f. 41: 12a, f. 45v), indicted for absence and assessed for a fine of £240 at the Assizes, September 1600 (R.R., 8, m. 10d), and presented for absence at Quarter Sessions, April 1605, September 1610, April 1613, and April 1621: his wife, *Elena*, was presented along with him in 1610 and 1613 (Harl. MSS., loc. cit.).

Ralph Radford of Trinity parish, Chester, was fined 12d. for absence at Quarter Sessions, August 1576 (M.B., 1572-7, 9 August, 18 Eliz.), and presented for absence at the Metropolitan Visitation, 1578 (York, R.VI, A 7, f. 19v).

Roger Radford of St. John's parish, Chester, was fined 12d. for absence at Quarter Sessions, September 1568 (M.B., 1567-8, 2 September, 10 Eliz.), and presented as an absentee and non-communicant at the Metropolitan Visitation, 1578 (York, loc. cit., f. 20).

Margaret Ravenscroft: cf. Margaret Hocknell.

William Ravenscroft, husbandman, of Newhall, Over, was indicted for absence at the Assizes, September 1587 (Chester, 29, 325, m. 17).

John Ridgeway of Ridley, Bunbury, was indicted for absence at the Assizes, April 1591 and April 1592 (Chester, 21, 1, 186v: 29, 333, m. 11).

John Ridley of Wistaston: cf. supra, 25-6. Catholic.

Elen Robinson of Bunbury was indicted for absence at Quarter Sessions, May 1582, and May 1584 (C.S.F., 1582, F 1, D 5: 1584, F 1, D 19), conforming October 1585 (C.S.B., 1576-92, Recognisances, f. 209v), though she was imprisoned in Chester Castle, *c.* 1587 (Chester, 21, 1, 133v).

Elizabeth Robinson, wife of Randle Robinson, yeoman, of Tilstone Fearnall, Bunbury, was presented as a recusant at the Diocesan Visitation, 1592 (E.D.V., 1, 10, f. 92v), indicted for absence and assessed for a fine of £60 at the Assizes, April 1593 (Chester, 29, 334, m. 17: R.R., 1, m. 6), and indicted, a widow, for absence, at the Assizes, September 1610 (Chester, 29, 370, m. 9). She and Elen Robinson (q.v.) may have been the same person.

John Royle, yeoman, of Darley, Over, was indicted for absence and assessed for a fine of £240 at the Assizes, September 1600 (R.R., 8, m. 10d).

Elizabeth Salisbury, wife of John Salisbury of Farndon, was presented as an absentee at the Diocesan Visitation, 1598, while she and her husband, John, were reported as recusants whose child had not been christened at the parish church to the Diocesan Visitors, 1604 (E.D.V., 1, 12, f. 42v: 13, f. 4v). In 1590 widow Salisbury of Farndon, aged 80, was presented for seldom coming to church at the Metropolitan Visitation; she may have been John Salisbury's mother (York, R.VI, A 12, f. 98v).

Robert Sefton of Mollington acted as intermediary in correspondence between Mrs. Mordant, a Bedford recusant, and Ireland, 1594 (M.L., 5, 220-2). Catholic?

John Shaw of Trinity parish, Chester, was presented as suspected of popery at the Metropolitan Visitation, 1578 (York, R.VI, A 7, f. 20): Catholic?

Thomas Shelton, probably of Chester, promised conformity, October 1598 (M.L., 1, 167).

Hugh Sim, glover, of Alpraham, Bunbury, was presented as a recusant at the Metropolitan Visitation, 1590 (York, R.VI, A 12, f. 109), and the Diocesan Visitation, 1592, to which it was also reported that he had a child christened, but not at the parish church (E.D.V., 1, 10, f. 92v & 94). He was indicted for absence and assessed for a fine of £240 at the Assizes, April 1593 (Chester, 29, 334, m. 17: R.R., 1, m. 6), and 30s. worth of his goods were seized, April 1595 (R.R., 5, m. 28).

Ralph Sim and *his wife* of Bunbury parish were presented as recusants at the Metropolitan Visitation, 1590 (York, loc. cit.), and Ralph was indicted for absence at the Assizes, April 1591 (Chester, 21, 1, 156v).

Elen Smith, wife of Thomas Smith of Tiverton, Bunbury: the same as her husband, 1591, 1601 and 1610.

James Smith, labourer, of Tiverton, Bunbury, was presented as a recusant at the Diocesan Visitation, 1592 (E.D.V., 1, 10, f. 93), and indicted for absence and assessed for a fine of £240 at the Assizes, April 1593 (Chester, 29, 334, m. 17; R.R., 1, m. 6). Was he the Robert Smith, husbandman, of Bunbury, who was indicted for absence at the Assizes, April 1591 (Chester, 21, 1, 156v).

Joanna Smith of Darley, Over, was indicted for absence and assessed for a fine of £240 at the Assizes, September 1600 (R.R., 8, m. 10d).

Richard Smith, cutler, of Chester, was fined 12d. at Quarter Sessions, September 1568 (M.B., 1567–8, 2 September, 10 Eliz.), and was presented as an absentee and non-communicant at the Metropolitan Visitation, 1578 (York, R.VI, A 7, f. 20).

Susan Smith of Tiverton, Bunbury, was indicted for absence and assessed for a fine of £240 at the Assizes, April 1593 (Chester, 29, 334, m. 17; R.R., 1, m. 6). She may well be the Susan Smith of Beeston who was indicted for absence at the Assizes, September 1610 (Chester, 29, 370, m. 9).

Thomas Smith, husbandman or labourer, of Tiverton, Bunbury, was indicted for absence at the Assizes, April 1591, and April, 1593, when he was assessed for a fine of £240 (Chester, 21, 1, 156v: 29, 334, m. 17; R.R., 1, m. 6), presented as a recusant and one whose child had not been christened at the parish church, at the Diocesan Visitation, 1598, and as an absentee and non-communicant, 1601 (E.D.V., 1, 12, f. 64v: 12a, f. 64v). He was indicted for absence and assessed for a fine of £240 at the Assizes, September 1600 (R.R., 8, m. 10d), and indicted for absence at the assizes, September 1610 (Chester, 29, 370, m. 9).

Peter Somner or *Sumner*, smith, of Haughton, Bunbury, was presented as a recusant at the Metropolitan Visitation, 1590 (York, R.VI, A 12, f. 109), and the Diocesan Visitation, 1592 (E.D.V., 1, 10, f. 93), indicted for absence at the Assizes, April 1591, April 1592, and April 1593, when he was assessed for a fine of £240 (Chester, 21, 1, 156v: 29, 333, m. 11: 334, m. 17; R.R., 1, m. 6). Alice Somner of Haughton, Bunbury, who was indicted for absence at the Assizes, September 1610, may well have been one of his family (Chester, 29, 370, m. 9).

Katherine Sparrow of Rushton, Tarporley, was presented as a recusant at the Diocesan Visitation, 1592 (E.D.V., 1, 10, f. 31), indicted for absence and assessed for a fine of £60 at the Assizes, April 1593, and indicted again, September 1610 (Chester, 29, 334, m. 17: 370, m. 9; R.R., 1, m. 6).

Thomas Sparrow, yeoman, of Bickley, Malpas, was indicted for absence at Quarter Sessions, May 1582 (C.S.F., 1582, F 1, D 17).

Philip Spurstowe, gentleman, of Spurstow, Bunbury, second son of Randle Spurstowe of Spurstow (Ormerod, II, 294), was listed in a national list of leading recusants at liberty, *c.* 1581 (H.M.C., *Salis. MSS.*, IV, 265), was fined 40s. by the High Commission for failure to answer an unstated charge, February 1581 (Ex Dep., m.3), and was indicted for absence at Quarter Sessions, October 1581, and May 1582 (C.S.F., 1581, F 3, D 24: 1582, F 1, D 8). He was buried at Bunbury, 10 July 1586 (Ormerod, loc. cit.). Peter and Richard Spurstowe (q.v.) were his nephews.

Peter Spurstowe, gentleman, of Spurstow, Bunbury, son of Richard Spurstowe of

Spurstow, who died 1571, nephew of Philip Spurstowe (q.v.) and brother of Richard Spurstowe (q.v.), was named in a list of recusants, etc., compiled for the government, 1586 (S.P., 12, 193, 47). He was indicted for absence and assessed for a fine of £160 at the Assizes, April 1593 (Chester, 29, 334, m. 17; R.R., 1, m. 6), and goods of his worth £17 16s. 8d. were seized, April 1595, and by the time this was recorded on the Recusant Roll, 1596–7, he was dead (R.R., 5, m. 28).

Richard Spurstowe, gentleman, of Spurstow, Bunbury; for his family, cf. Peter Spurstowe. He was named on the same list as his brother, Peter, 1586, was examined as a suspected recusant by the Chester High Commission, January–February 1592, and imprisoned in the Northgate, from which he escaped, March 1592—for details and references, cf. supra, 91–2, 96–7, 102–4.

Lady Elizabeth Stanley, daughter of John Egerton of Egerton and second wife of the well-known Catholic, Sir William Stanley of Hooton, Eastham. Sir William had seen long and distinguished service in Ireland before his notorious surrender of Deventer at the opening of 1587, and Lady Stanley and her children only then took up residence in Cheshire in the household and under the charge of Sir Rowland Stanley, father of Sir William (A.P.C., 1587–8, 5). She was presented as an absentee at the Diocesan Visitation, 1592 (E.D.V., 1, 10, f. 38v), indicted for absence and assessed for a fine of £960 at the Assizes, April 1593 (Chester, 29, 334, m. 17; R.R., 1, m. 6), presented as an absentee at the Diocesan Visitation 1598, and as a recusant, 1601 (E.D.V., 1, 12, f. 28: 12a, f. 55v), and indicted at the Assizes for absence and assessed for a fine of £240, September 1600 (R.R., 8, m. 10d). She joined her husband in the Spanish Netherlands, 1606, after which their grandson, William, aged 17, was baptised into the Catholic faith (A. J. Loomie, *The Spanish Elizabethans*, 130 & 179).

Jane Stanley, daughter of Sir William and Lady Elizabeth Stanley, was presented for not communicating the previous Easter at the Diocesan Visitation, 1592, and as a recusant, 1601 (E.D.V, 1, 10, f. 39: 12a, f. 55v).

Alice Starkey, wife of John Starkey of Oulton (Ormerod, II, 192), daughter of Ralph Dutton of Hatton, who was himself suspected of Catholicism, and Anne Townshend, who was of a Catholic family (cf. supra, 23). She was presented as an absentee, along with her daughter, Amy, at the Metropolitan Visitation, 1595 (York, R.VI, A 14, f. 15), and indicted for absence, September 1610, at the Assizes (Chester, 29, 370, m. 9). Her third son, John, became a priest (cf. Appendix II). Was she the Eleanor Starkey, wife of John Starkey of Darley, Over, who, along with her daughter, Anne, was indicted for absence and assessed for a fine of £240, September 1600 (R.R., 8, m. 10d)?

Hugo Starkey, gentleman, and *Dorothy*, his wife, of Knights Grange, Whitegate, were presented as absentees and papists at the Diocesan Visitation, 1601 (E.D.V., 1, 12a, f. 73). Catholics.

Thomas Stevenson, probably of Chester, was a prisoner for recusancy in the Northgate, from which he escaped, 1592 (M.L., 5, 100), and in Chester Castle, 1593–4, while he was indicted for absence, October 1594, at the Assizes (Chester, 21, 1, 168v & 172: 29, 338, m. 16d), and in the following summer acted as guide to two Catholic youths trying to escape overseas (S.P., 12, 253, 22).

Peter Stoke was imprisoned as a recusant in Chester Castle, September 1598 (Chester, 21, 1, 198).

John Street, yeoman or husbandman, of Woolstanwood, Nantwich, was presented as a recusant at the Metropolitan Visitation, 1590 (York, R.VI, A 12, f. 109v), and as a non-communicant at the Diocesan Visitation, 1592, when it was stated that he was in prison for recusancy (E.D.V., 1, 10, f. 96). He was indicted for absence and assessed for a fine of either £60 or £720 at the Assizes, April 1593 (Chester, 29, 334, m. 17; R.R., 1, m. 6–6d), goods to the value of £12 were seized from him, April 1594 (R.R., 2, m. 6), and he was presented as recusant and excommunicate at the Diocesan Visitation, 1598, and as a 'knowne recusant', 1601 (E.D.V., 1, 12, f. 65: 12a, f. 67v). He took the oath under 3 Jac. 1, in October 1606 (C.S.F., 1606, F 3, D 36). When his wife was presented with him on a minor charge at the Diocesan Visitation, 1592, she was reported to be of sound religion (E.D.V., 1, 10, f. 96).

William Stretbarrell or *Stretbarrowe*, yeoman, of Ridley, Bunbury, was presented as a recusant at the Metropolitan Visitation, 1590 (York, R.VI, A 12, f. 109), indicted for absence at the Assizes, April 1591 (Chester, 21, 1, 156v), imprisoned in Chester Castle (ibid., 159) and indicted at the Assizes for absence and assessed for a fine of £960, 1592 (ibid., 29, 334, m. 17; R.R., 1, m. 6).

Maria Sutton, widow, of Daresbury, was presented at the Diocesan Visitation, 1604, as an 'olde recusant' (E.D.V., 1, 13, f. 27v).

Robert Tatnall of Ridley, Bunbury, was indicted for absence at the Assizes, April 1591 and April 1592 (Chester, 21, 1, 156v: 29, 333, m. 11).

Mary Tatton, wife of William Tatton, gentleman (cf. Appendix III), of Northenden, was described as a 'conformable' absentee in the diocesan return of recusants, 1576 (Harl. MSS., 360, 39, f. 68), presented as an absentee and non-communicant at the Diocesan Visitation, 1578, as was her servant, Anne Dickinson (York, R.VI, A 7, f. 6), as a recusant for 16 years at the Metropolitan Visitation, 1590 (ibid., A 12, f. 105), and she was indicted for absence at the Assizes, April 1591 (Chester, 21, 1, 156v).

Richard Thatcher (or *Ap Robert*), husbandman, of Malpas, was fined 40s. for failing to answer an unstated charge before the High Commission, February 1581 (Ex. Dep., m. 4), indicted for absence in May 1582 and May 1584 at Quarter Sessions (C.S.F., 1582, F 1, D 13: 1584, F 1, D 21), imprisoned in Chester Castle, *c.* 1587 (Chester, 21, 1, 133v), and presented as a recusant at the Metropolitan Visitation, 1590 (York, R.VI, A 12, f. 85).

Ursula Thickness of Barthomley was indicted for absence, October 1581, at Quarter Sessions (C.S.F., 1581, F 3, D 19).

Elen Tilston of St. Martin's parish, Chester, was presented as a recusant at the Metropolitan Visitation, 1590 (York, R.VI, A 12, f. 95).

Thomas Trine, yeoman or labourer, of Whitchurch, Shropshire, was active in Cheshire and was dealt with by the Cheshire authorities. He was of some importance in organising a mass held at Agden, Malpas, April 1582, and was indicted for absence, July 1582, at Quarter Sessions (C.S.F., 1582, F 1, D 1–4: F 2, D 13). He was a prisoner in Chester Castle, 1582–*c.* 1591 (C.S.B., 1576–92, f. 209; C.S.F., 1584, F 1, D 20; Chester, 21, 1, 110 ff.; Chester, 29, 319, m. 18: 320, m. 13–14: 323, m. 11: 324, m. 14: 334, m. 17; R.R., 1, m. 6). While there he was accused of uttering a disloyal prophecy (Chester, 24, 100, examination of 27 August 1585). It is possible that he was a priest (cf. supra, 44, n. 2).

Hugh and *Richard Vernon*, yeomen, of Darley, Over, were each indicted for absence and assessed for a fine of £240 at the Assizes, September 1600 (R.R., 8, m. 10d).

For *Walley* see *Wooley*.

William Watson, husbandman, of Alpraham, Bunbury, was indicted for absence and assessed for a fine of £240 at the Assizes, September 1600 (ibid.).

John Weston, ibid.

Alice Whitby, wife of John Whitby of Aldford parish, a servant of Peter Dutton and the Massey family; the same as her husband, 1590–2. She was unsuccessfully indicted at the Assizes for absence, 1594 (Chester, 21, 1, 173), but was indicted and assessed for a fine of £140, September 1595 (R.R. 5, m. 28), presented as an absentee and non-communicant at the Metropolitan Visitation, 1595 (York, R.VI, A 14, f. 8v), and as a recusant at the Diocesan Visitation, 1598 (E.D.V., 1, 12, f. 43).

Eleanor Whitby of Aldford parish was indicted for absence at the Assizes, July 1594, and September 1595, and assessed for a £140 fine (Chester, 21, 1, 173; R.R., 5, m. 28). She was almost certainly a servant in the Massey household.

John Whitby, husbandman, of Spurstow, Bunbury, was presented as a non-communicant at the Metropolitan Visitation, 1590 (York, R.VI, A 12, f. 108v), and as a recusant at the Diocesan Visitation, 1592 (E.D.V., 1, 10, f. 92). He was indicted at the Assizes for absence, April 1591, and April 1593, when he was assessed for a fine of £240 (Chester, 21, 1, 156v: 29, 334, m. 17; R.R., 1, m. 6). Goods worth £10 and lands worth 26s. 8d. a year were seized from him, April 1594 (R.R., 2, m. 6), and goods worth £13 6s. 8d, May 1598 (ibid., 6, m. 12). As of Beeston he seems to have been presented as an absentee at the Diocesan Visitation, 1598, and as an absentee and non-communicant, 1601 (E.D.V., 1, 12, f. 64: 12a, f. 64v). Joan Whitby of Spurstow, Bunbury, who was presented for not sending her children to be catechised, at the Diocesan Visitation, 1592, may have been his wife (ibid., 10, f. 91).

John Whitby of Aldford parish, a servant of Peter Dutton and the Massey family, was imprisoned in Chester Castle, 1586 (Chester, 21, 1, 127v), presented as an absentee at the Metropolitan Visitation, 1590 (York, R.VI, A 12, f. 86), and as a non-communicant at the Diocesan Visitation, 1592 (E.D.V., 1, 10, f. 92). He was examined as a recusant suspect by the Chester High Commission, 1592 (Q.S.E., 4, f. 15), was unsuccessfully indicted at the Assizes for absence from church, 1594 (Chester, 21, 1, 173), was presented as a non-communicant at the Diocesan Visitation, 1598 (E.D.V., 1, 12, f. 43), and was presented at Quarter Sessions for absence, 1604 (Q.S.F., 53, 1–2).

Richard Whitby, husbandman, of Spurstow, Bunbury, was presented as a recusant at the Diocesan Visitation, 1592 (E.D.V., 1, 10, f. 92), indicted at the Assizes for absence, April 1591, and April 1593, when he was assessed for a fine of £240 (Chester, 21, 1, 156v: 29, 334, m. 17; R.R., 1, m. 6).

Robert Whitby of Thornton le Moors was presented as a recusant at the Metropolitan Visitation, 1590 (York, R.VI, A 12, f. 96).

Nicholas White of Trinity parish, Chester, was presented for popish practices and suspicion of popery at the Metropolitan Visitation, 1578 (York, R.VI, A 7, f. 19v). Catholic?

John Whitehead, baker, of St. Michael's parish, Chester, was presented for using a Latin Primer at the Metropolitan Visitation, 1578 (ibid, f. 19).

Catholic? A John Whitehead of St. Bridget's parish was presented as an absentee and non-communicant to the Chester High Commission, 1592 (Q.S.E., 4f.).

William Whitehead of St. Oswald's parish, Chester, servant of Ralph Worsley (q.v.), was indicted at Quarter Sessions for absence, May 1582 (S.P., 12, 153, 65).

One —— *Whitese*(?) of St. Olave's parish, Chester, was presented as a recusant at the Metropolitan Visitation, 1590 (York, R.VI, A 12, f. 95).

Alice Whitmore, wife of William Whitmore, gentleman, of Leighton, Neston, daughter and sole heiress of William Hough (q.v.), and aunt of John Whitmore (q.v.). She was noted as an absentee and non-communicant in the Parish Register, 1581 (E.D.B., Thurstaston, 1581), indicted at Quarter Sessions for absence, May 1582 (C.S.F., 1582, F 1, D 23), and at the Assizes, September 1587 (Chester, 29, 325, m. 16d), presented as a recusant at the Metropolitan Visitation, 1590 (York, R.VI, A 12, f. 88), and as an absentee at the Diocesan Visitation, 1592 (E.D.V., 1, 10, f. 39v). She was indicted at the Assizes for absence and assessed for a fine of £960, April 1593 (Chester, 29, 334, m. 17; R.R., 1, m. 6), presented as an absentee at the Metropolitan Visitation, 1595 (York, R.VI, A 14, f. 6), and the Diocesan Visitation, 1598 (E.D.V., 1, 12, f. 31), indicted at the Assizes and assessed for a fine of £240 September, 1600 (R.R., 8, m. 10d), and presented as a non-communicant at the Diocesan Visitation, 1601 (E.D.V., 1, 12a, f. 56). She was presented as an absentee and non-communicant at the Diocesan Visitation, 1605 (W. N. & Q., II, 66), and indicted for absence, September 1610, at the Assizes (Chester, 29, 370, m. 9). Her husband, William Whitmore, the second son of Thomas Whitmore of Thurstaston (Ormerod, II, 552), did not wholly conform to the law but was never clearly a recusant: presented as a non-communicant to the diocesan authorities on several occasions, and in 1605 as an absentee as well (W. N. & Q., II, 66), he nevertheless protested, when ordered as a recusant to furnish a light horse, that 'he is no recusant, but a dutifull subject to her Majestie' (Chester County, D.D.X., 43, 10, n.d.). Indeed, from March 1584, he held the sequestrated lands of his father-in-law, William Hough, in lease from the Crown (S.P., 12, 183, 43; R.R., 1, m. 6).

Christina, Eleanor and *Jane Whitmore*, daughters of William and Alice Whitmore, of Leighton, Neston (q.v.), were presented as absentees at the Diocesan Visitation, 1598 (E.D.V., 1, 12, f. 31), and indicted for absence and each assessed for a fine of £240 at the Assizes, September 1600 (R.R., 8, m. 10d). Christina and Eleanor were presented as non-communicants at the Diocesan Visitation, 1601 (E.D.V., 1, 12a, f. 56), and as absentees as well in 1605 (W. N. & Q., II, 66).

Elen Whitmore, first wife of John Whitmore, gentleman, of Thurstaston (q.v.), daughter of Richard Done of Flaxyards (Ormerod, II, 508), was named as an obstinate recusant in the diocesan list, 1576 (Harl. MSS., 360, 39, f. 68), presented, along with her husband and family, as an absentee and non-communicant at the Metropolitan Visitation, 1578 (York, R.VI, A 7, f. 15v), listed in the same way in the Parish Register, 1581 (E.D.B., Thurstaston, 1581), and indicted for absence, May 1584, at Quarter Sessions, but died before her trial could take place (C.S.F., 1584, F 1, D 23; C.S.B., 1576–92, Recognisances, f. 209).

Jane Whitmore, second wife of John Whitmore, gentleman, of Thurstaston (q.v.), daughter of Henry and Margaret Primrose of Chester (q.v.), was imprisoned in Chester Castle, *c.* 1587 (Chester, 21, 1, 133v), presented for absence and for not having her child christened in the parish church at the Metropolitan

Visitation, 1590 (York, R.VI, A 12, f. 89), presented as a recusant and adulterer, as her 'popish marriage' would be invalid, before the High Commission in York (York, H.C., A.B., 7, 50, 1585–91, f. 297), while the Chester High Commission, 1592, inquired into her marriage by a recusant priest and the christening of her children in Chester Castle (Q.S.E., 4, ff. 14 & 25), and she was presented as a recusant at the Diocesan Visitations, 1592 and 1601 (E.D.V., 1, 10, f. 24v: 12a, f. 55).

John Whitmore, gentleman, of Thurstaston, eldest son and heir of John Whitmore of Thurstaston and Katherine, his first wife (Ormerod, loc. cit.). His first wife, Elen, and his second wife, Jane (q.v.) were both recusants. As early as 1570 he twice appeared before the diocesan High Commission on unstated charges (E.D.A., 12, 2, f. 133v), and before the High Commission in York in 1571 and 1572, again on unstated charges (York, H.C., Box 25, 1571–2, A 16, ff. 80 & 141). In 1576 he was named as an obstinate recusant in the diocesan list (Harl. MSS., loc. cit.), and was listed as worth £60 of ancient rent in lands in the diocesan return, 1577 (S.P., 12, 118, 49). Along with his wife and family he was presented as an absentee and non-communicant at the Metropolitan Visitation, 1578, and was ordered to answer these charges before the High Commission in York (York, R.VI, A 7, f. 15v: H.C., A.B., 6, 26, 1576–80, f. 172v). These years marked him out as the leading Cheshire recusant, except perhaps for Lady Egerton, but it was not until the 1580's that the authorities dealt severely with him. Summoned before the Diocesan High Commission, February 1581, he was fined £10 for failing to appear to answer an unstated charge, though £5 was later remitted (Ex. Dep., m. 4 & 11), but he was imprisoned in Chester Castle in June by the Commissioners and indicted, as a prisoner, in October, at Quarter Sessions for absence, and, although the recusants who had been with him in Chester Castle were returned there, he was not (C.S.F., 1581, F 3, D 11 & 61). In May 1582, he was indicted for absence again (ibid., 1582, F 1, D 22), while in June the Council expressed their amazement at the continued liberty of this 'verie daungerous practising Papist' (A.P.C., 1581–2, 447). Ten years later a Warrington man, Humphrey Cartwright, reported seeing a priest at Whitmore's house about this time (Strype, *Annals*, IV, 261). However, from *c*. May 1584–*c*. 1597 he was a prisoner in Chester Castle (C.S.F., 1584, F 1, D 23; Chester, 21, 1, 114 ff.: 29, 319, m. 18: 320, m. 13: 321, m. 14: 323, m. 11: 324, m. 14: 325, m. 17: 334, m. 17; R.R., 1, m. 6), appearing regularly before the Assizes to be assessed for fines, while he was also assessed to bear the cost of a lance in 1585, though he does not seem to have done so, offering a mere £10 'to be dismissed of the penalties of the Statute', in May 1586; a month later he still owed £200 in fines (S.P., 12, 189, 54: 190, 43: 200, 61: 206, 8). However, he suffered the sequestration of lands worth £15 7s. 10d. a year in November 1588 (R.R., 1, m. 6). A mass was said in his room in the Castle, *c*. 1588 (Q.S.E., 4, f. 22), perhaps one of many, judging by the slack regime that then prevailed at the Castle (cf. supra, 73). His first wife, Elen, died in 1584, and he married again before 1587. His marriage to Jane, daughter of Henry Primrose, and the christening of their subsequent children appear to have been celebrated by recusant priests in Chester Castle (cf. entry on Jane Whitmore). However, he was no longer young, and in 1592 it was recommended that he should be placed in the custody of his family (H.M.C., *Salis. MSS.*, IV, 240), though this was not adopted, and by 1596 he was infirm enough to be 'in perill of his life' from further captivity, so that he was granted leave to visit Bath (A.P.C., 1596–7, 435), but afterwards seems to have been returned to prison, dying *c.* 1597, when he last appears in the Assize records as a prisoner (Chester, 21, 1, f. 187), while lands and goods were seized from his son in 1599 (cf. next entry).

John Whitmore (the younger), son of John Whitmore of Thurstaston, gentleman, and his first wife, Elen (q.v.), lost by seizure goods worth £7 13s. 4d. and lands worth £22 13s. 4d. a year in November 1599, and was indicted for absence at the Assizes and assessed for a fine of £240 in the following September (R.R., 8, m. 10d). He was presented as a recusant and non-communicant at the Diocesan Visitation, 1601 (E.D.V., 1, 12a, f. 55).

Richard Whitmore, tailor and his wife *Katherine*, of Guilden Sutton, were presented as absentees and non-communicants at the Metropolitan Visitation, 1578 (York, R.VI, A 7, f. 19), indicted at Quarter Sessions for absence, May 1582, and May 1584 (C.S.F., 1582, F 1, D 26: 1584, F 1, D 22), imprisoned in Chester Castle, *c.* 1587 (Chester, 21, 1, 133v), after which Richard seems to have conformed to some extent, for while he was presented as a non-communicant at the Metropolitan Visitation, 1590, his wife was presented as a recusant (York, R.VI, A 12, f. 95v), and attended a mass in Christleton, 1591 (Q.S.E., 4, f. 3; C.S.F., 1592, F 2, D 4).

Ann Wilbraham, daughter of Owen and Joan Wilbraham (q.v.) of Malpas, was presented as a recusant at the Diocesan Visitations, 1598 and 1601 (E.D.V., 1, 12, f. 41: 12a, f. 45v), and indicted at the Assizes and assessed for a fine of £240, September 1600 (R.R., 8, m. 10d).

Hugh or *Hugo Wilbraham*, smith, of Malpas, was indicted for hearing a mass and for absence, May 1582, at Quarter Sessions, and for absence, May 1584 (C.S.F., 1582, F 1, D 14 & 27; 1584, F 1, D 21), imprisoned in Chester Castle, c. 1587 (Chester, 21, 1, 133v), and indicted for absence at the Assizes, 1587 (ibid., 29, 325, m. 16d). Cf. also, Margaret Wilbraham, his wife, and Joan Wilbraham, probably his daughter-in-law. He was said to be old in 1582.

Joan or *Jane Wilbraham*, wife of Owen Wilbraham, smith, of Malpas, and probably daughter-in-law of Hugh Wilbraham (q.v.), was presented as a recusant at the Metropolitan Visitation, 1590 (York, R.VI, A 12, f. 85v), and as an absentee at the Diocesan Visitation, 1592 (E.D.V., 1, 10, f. 55v). She was indicted for absence and assessed for a fine of £720 at the Assizes, April 1593, and September 1600 (Chester, 29, 334, m. 17; R.R., 1, m. 6: 8, m. 10d), presented as a recusant at the Metropolitan Visitation, 1595 (York, R.VI, A 14, f. 8), and the Diocesan Visitations, 1598 and 1601 (E.D.V., 1, 12, f. 41: 12a, f. 45v), and for absence, November 1604, April and December 1605, and September 1606, at Quarter Sessions (Harl. MSS., 2095, 7, f. 10).

Margaret Wilbraham, wife of Hugh Wilbraham of Malpas (q.v.). The same as Ann Wilbraham.

Elen Wilden of St. Oswald's parish, Chester, maid to Margaret Massey (q.v.), was presented at Quarter Sessions for absence, 1588 (Q.S.F., 37, 53), and was a prisoner for recusancy in the Northgate, *c.* 1592–8, 'well known to your worshipes' when the Chester High Commission sat, 1592 (Q.S.E., 4, ff. 1, 10 & 19). She was presented as a recusant prisoner at the Metropolitan Visitation, 1595 (York, R.VI, A 15, f. 33v), and the Diocesan Visitation, 1598 (E.D.V., 1, 12, f. 17), fined 12d. at Quarter Sessions for absence, January 1597, and November 1598, and when presented again for absence was referred for punishment by the justices to the High Commission, May 1599 (M.B., 1596–9, 21 January, 39 Eliz.: 7 November, 40 Eliz.: 4 May, 41 Eliz.).

Thomas Williamson, yeoman, of Edge, Malpas, was indicted for absence at the Assizes, September 1587 (Chester, 29, 325, m. 16d).

John Wilson, yeoman, of Wardle, Bunbury, was imprisoned in Chester Castle, 1592 (Chester, 21, 1, 159 & 162), presented as a recusant at the Diocesan Visitation, 1592 (E.D.V., 1, 10, f. 93), indicted for absence at the Assizes and assessed for a fine of £240, April 1593 (Chester, 29, 334, m. 17; R.R., 1, m. 6). Goods worth 16s. 8d. and lands worth 24s. a year were seized from him, April 1594, and a further 6s. 8d. worth of goods, May 1598 (R.R., 2, m. 6: 6, m. 12). He was buried 5 November 1597 (Bunbury Parish Register, 1559–1653, f. 140).

John Wilson of Wardle, Bunbury, probably the son of John Wilson (q.v.), was presented as an obstinate recusant at the Diocesan Visitation, 1598, and, along with his wife, *Joan*, as an absentee and non-communicant, 1601 (E.D.V., 1, 12, f. 64v: 12a, f. 64v).

Randle Wilson, yeoman, of Ridley, Bunbury, was presented as a recusant at the Diocesan Visitation, 1592 (E.D.V., 1, 10, f. 93), and indicted for absence at the Assizes, April 1591, April 1592, and April 1593, when he was assessed for a fine of £240 (Chester, 21, 1, 156v: 29, 333, m. 11: 334, m. 17; R.R., 1, m. 6).

Randolph Wilson, gentleman, and his wife, *Katherine*, of Tattenhall, were presented as absentees at the Diocesan Visitation, 1598, and as recusants, 1604 (E.D.V., 1, 12, f. 43v: 13, f. 13).

William Woodhall, tailor, of St. Bridget's parish, Chester, was presented as an absentee and non-communicant at the Metropolitan Visitation, 1595 (York, R.VI, A 14, f. 2v), and as an absentee at the Diocesan Visitation, 1598 (E.D.V., 1, 12, f. 13).

Eve Woodward, wife of Richard Woodward of Agden, Malpas, was fined 40s. by the High Commission, February 1581, for her failure to answer an unstated charge, and 20s. in June for 'irreverent and prophane behaviour at the tyme of holye communion . . .', though each of these fines was remitted on her conformity (Ex. Dep., m. 3 & 12). Eve Woodward of Haughton, Bunbury, was presented as a recusant at the Metropolitan Visitation, 1590 (York, R.VI, A 12, f. 109), and was buried on 12 December 1596 (Bunbury Parish Register, 1559–1653, f. 138).

Thomas Woodward, yeoman or husbandman, of Haughton, Bunbury, was indicted for absence at the Assizes, September 1587 (Chester, 29, 325, m. 17), and again in April 1593, when he was assessed for a fine of £240 (ibid., 334, m. 17; R.R., 1, m. 6). He was presented as negligent in church attendance at the Metropolitan Visitation, 1590 (York, R.VI, A 12, f. 108v), as a recusant at the Diocesan Visitations, 1592 and 1598, and as an absentee and non-communicant, 1601 (E.D.V., 1, 10, f. 93: 12, f. 64v: 12a, f. 64v). He was again indicted and assessed for a fine of £240 at the Assizes, September 1600 (R.R., 8, m. 10d).

Elen Wooley or *Walley*, wife of Randle Wooley, husbandman, of Bunbury, was indicted at Quarter Sessions for absence, May 1582, and May 1584 (C.S.F., 1582, F 1, D 5: 1584, F 1, D 19). She was probably the Elen Owley of Bunbury who was presented as a recusant at the Metropolitan Visitation. 1590 (York, R.VI, A 12, f. 109). She was presented as a recusant at the Diocesan Visitation, 1592

(E.D.V., 1, 10, f. 92v), indicted at the Assizes for absence and assessed for a fine of £240, April 1593, and also, September 1600 (Chester, 29, 334, m. 17; R.R., 1, m. 6: 8, m. 10d). As a widow, she was presented as an obstinate recusant at the Diocesan Visitation, 1598, and as an absentee and non-communicant, 1601 (E.D.V., 1, 12, f. 64v: 12a, f. 64v), and was indicted at the Assizes for absence September 1610 (Chester, 29, 370, m. 9). She was probably the 'widow Walley', who, dying excommunicate, was buried without church rites, 11 December 1617 (Bunbury Parish Register, 1559–1653, f. 158).

Henry Wooley or *Walley* of Bunbury, husbandman, was indicted for absence at the Assizes, April 1591 (Chester, 21, 1, 156v).

Mrs. Richard Wooley of Marbury was presented as a recusant at the Diocesan Visitation, 1598 (E.D.V., 1, 12, f. 68v).

William Wooley or *Walley*, husbandman, of Bunbury, was indicted for absence at the Assizes, April 1591 (Chester, 21, 1, 156v), and September 1600, when he was assessed for a fine of £240 (R.R., 8, m. 10d). He was presented for having a child christened 'not knowne where or bye whom' at the Diocesan Visitation, 1592, and as an obstinate recusant, 1598 (E.D.V., 1, 10, f. 94: 12, f. 64v).

Alice Worsley, wife of Ralph Worsley, of Chester (q.v.), was indicted at the Quarter Sessions for absence, May 1582, and fined 12d. for absence by the justices, January and November 1584 (S.P., 12, 153, 65; M.B., 1582–4, 21 January, 26 Eliz.: 1585–9, 6 November, 26 Eliz.).

Ralph Worsley, lawyer, of St. Oswald's parish, Chester, was probably the son of Ralph Worsley, a Lancashire man who had settled in Chester and acquired most of the property of Birkenhead Priory at the Dissolution; the elder Ralph died, aged 80, in 1573 (W.N. & Q., II, 69). Ralph the lawyer may well have been the Ralph Worsley who absented himself when due for questioning at an inquiry of 1569 about the religious practices of the members of the Inns of Court, and who was expelled from Gray's Inn in 1577 for religious reasons (Trimble, op. cit., 58–60). He was listed as being worth £40 in goods in the diocesan return of recusants, 1577 (S.P., 12, 118, 49), and presented as an absentee and non-communicant at the Metropolitan Visitation, 1578 (York, R.VI, A 7, f. 18v). He was fined 12d. for absence, September 1579, at Quarter Sessions (M.B. 1578–81, 22 September, 21 Eliz.). He began an imprisonment as a recusant that lasted from 1581 to *c.* 1590 when he was imprisoned in Chester Castle by the High Commission, June 1581: when he was indicted for absence, October 1581, at Quarter Sessions, he fruitlessly raised a legal objection, was assessed for a fine of £120 and returned to prison (C.S.F., 1581, F 3, D 15 & 61–2). At the turn of 1581–2 he was transferred to the New Fleet, Salford, as one of several prominent recusants (A.P.C., 1581–2, 279; Peck, I, 112). He remained there until 1585, co-operating a little more readily with his gaoler than did his intransigent fellow-prisoners (S.P., 12, 152, 48: 153, 6 & 45: 155, 73). In 1585 he returned to Chester Castle, where he remained until at least 1590 (Chester, 21, 1, 134Av ff.: 29, 323, m. 11: 324, m. 14), when he probably died or was released, though he was indicted for absence as a prisoner in Chester Castle and assessed for a fine of £240 at the Assizes as late as April 1593 (ibid., 29, 334, m. 17; R.R., 1, m. 6). His wife, Alice, and servant, William Whitehead, were also recusants (q.v.).

Alice Yardley, wife of Randolph Yardley, yeoman, of Shocklach, was presented as a recusant at the Metropolitan Visitation, 1595, when her wish to conform was reported (York, R.VI, A 14, f. 8), though she was still presented as an absentee at the Diocesan Visitations, 1598 and 1601 (E.D.V., 1, 12, f. 43v: 12a, f. 43v).

Roger Yardley, husbandman, and his wife, *Margaret*, of Agden, Malpas, were indicted for hearing a mass, which took place at their home, and for absence, May 1582, at Quarter Sessions (C.S.F., 1582, F 1, D 18 & 27). Margaret was presented as an absentee and non-communicant at the Diocesan Visitation, 1592 (E.D.V., 1, 10, f. 56), and was indicted for absence and assessed for a fine of £60 at the Assizes, April 1593 (Chester, 29, 334, m. 17; R.R., 1, m. 6).

APPENDIX II

A list, in alphabetical order, of recusant priests who were born or active in Cheshire during this period, with a brief summary of what is known of each, where this seems useful.

Ralph Antrobus, born 1576, son of Ralph Antrobus of Peover, Cheshire. Entered Brasenose College, Oxford, 1596, became a Protestant cleric, but was converted to Catholicism, and went to Rome in 1603. He died in 1626. (H.N. Birt, *Obit Book of the English Benedictines*, 10).

Richard Bannister, an old priest, was reported to be in Runcorn, 1586 (E. Baines, *History of the County of Lancaster*, I, 241).

Benet: a Welsh priest, assisted in celebrating a mass at Agden, Malpas, April 1582 (C.S.F., 1582, F 1, D 1). He may have been the John Bennett of Bryn Canellan, Flintshire, listed in Anstruther. Could he have been the 'Baret' whom John Whitmore was said to have been sheltering at about this time?

Hugh Bentley, a Cheshire man, in England as a priest from 1595 (Anstruther).

Brereton (Brewerton), a Jesuit who was reported as in Scotland, 1582, was said to be from Cheshire (*Cal. Border Papers*, I, 85, cited A. L. Rowse, *The expansion of Elizabethan England*, 36). He may have been related to the recusant William Brereton of Shocklach or to another branch of the Brereton family. Edward Barlow, a priest of Lancashire birth who trained at Douai and Valladolid in the early seventeenth century, was the fourth son of Sir Alexander Barlow and Mary, daughter of Sir Urian Brereton of Handforth, Cheshire, and evidently used his mother's maiden name as an alias.

John Bushell, a former chantry priest of Bunbury Collegiate Church, was reported as being in Bunbury parish, 1577 (S.P., 12, 118, 49).

John Butler, alias *Banister*, sent to England, 1589, was to be indicted at Chester Assizes, May 1591 (Anstruther).

Edmund Campion may have visited Hatton, near Warrington, February 1581 (S.P., 12, 148, 11).

Cowper. A priest named Cowper was said to have been in Chester, *c.* 1588 (Q.S.E., 4, f. 18).

Ralph Crocket, who was arrested at sea while on his way to England, 1586, and executed at Chichester, 1588, was born, 1552, at Barton-on-the-Hill, Cheshire, and had spent two years in Cheshire as a schoolmaster before becoming a priest (Anstruther). Was he perhaps related to either of the Katherine Crockets who were recusants? (Cf. Appendix I.)

John Culpage or *Coppage*, an old priest. T. G. Law pieced together an outline of his life in his introduction to Vaux's Catechism (*Chetham Society*, N.S., IV), and to this a little more information can be added. Culpage was a priest of the Collegiate Church in Manchester at its dissolution, 1547. He had held a vicarage worth £4 a year, 1535, and received a pension of £6 13s. 4d. after the dissolution of the college. When it was refounded, 1557, he was appointed Fellow-chaplain, along with Laurence Vaux. When John Bradford, the Lancashire Protestant martyr, was a prisoner in the Poultry prison he was appointed to reason with him, from which it may be inferred that Culpage was a man of some ability. He did not appear before the High Commission, 1559, when it dealt with the college, but was eventually imprisoned, possibly by 1571, if his inclusion in the list of Nicholas Sanders in *De Visibile Monarchia* is reliable; this is open to question, as he was receiving his pension from the college as late as 1574 (op. cit., 9–11, & 75–6). He was, however, a prisoner in Chester Castle by 1577 (S.P., 12, 118, 49), where he remained (Lansd. MSS., 28, 97, f. 213; C.S.F., 1581, F 3, D 37 & 62) until transferred to the new Fleet, Salford, at the turn of 1581–2, along with other recusant prisoners (A.P.C., 1581–2, 279; Peck, I, 112). When his former colleague, Laurence Vaux, was in the Gatehouse Prison, 1583, he and Culpage wrote to each other (Law, op. cit., 78–9; S.P., 12, 162, 14). This is almost the last occasion on which Culpage appears in extant documents. After 27 Eliz., c. 2, which made the entry or presence in England of Catholic priests an act of treason, about 70 were banished within a year, including about 20 from the northern prisons: they were mainly elderly. Culpage might have been one of them, as he disappears after the opening of 1584 from among the recusants named in extant correspondence between the Council and the Keeper of Salford Fleet. On the other hand, he may have died in the Salford Fleet or been transferred elsewhere. By 1585 he would have been 86 years old, if still alive.

John Damford, born 1576 in Cheshire, died in Valladolid not long after being ordained there (Anstruther). May he have been John Davenport, brother of Peter (infra)?

Peter Davenport, probably son of William and Margaret Davenport of Bramhall, was admitted to the English College, Valladolid, 1600, joined the Society of Jesus, 1603, and died, 1607 (C.R.S., XXX, 62).

Davies, a seminary, said a mass in Christleton, October 1591 (Q.S.E., 4, ff. 3 & 26; C.S.F., 1592, F 2, D 4). He could be either Roger Davies or William Davies (of Denbighshire birth), who are listed in Anstruther.

Thomas Egerton, of Chester diocese by birth, was probably from a branch of the Cheshire Egertons. He was admitted to the English College, Valladolid, 1591, but died, 1592, c. 21 years old, and thus was not actually ordained priest (C.R.S., XXX, 15).

Francis Fitton, son of Sir Edward Fitton of Gawsworth, was ordained priest at Douai (Gillow, op. cit., II, 345).

Humphrey Hanmer, son of Mr. Hanmer of Levadon Heath, was suspected to be a priest, 1592 (Q.S.E., 4, f. 15). Born, 1546, possibly in Flintshire, he was ordained priest, 1584, and sent to England in the following year (Anstruther).

Richard Hatton, born at Stockton-yate, the second son of William Hatton (a Thomas Hatton of Stockton, near Malpas, was a recusant: cf. Appendix I), was a Marian priest who was deprived under Elizabeth. He was arrested in Lancashire, 1583, and though condemned to death received forfeiture and life imprisonment instead (Gillow, op. cit., 165–6).

Thomas Holford, alias *Acton*, a seminary, born, 1541, at Aston, Cheshire. A schoolmaster in Hereford, he was ordained abroad and returned to England, 1583, and was arrested at Nantwich in spring, 1585. He escaped in London, was re-arrested there and executed as a priest, 1588 (cf. supra, 60–2, and Anstruther).

Thomas Houghton, an old priest, was indicted as a gentleman of Wrenbury at

Quarter Sessions, January 1578 (C.S.B., Indictments, 1565–92, f. 112), and presented, as an old priest from Wrenbury, at the Metropolitan Visitation, 1578, as an absentee and non-communicant (York, R.VI, A 7, f. 10). By mid-1581 he was a prisoner in Chester Castle (C.S.F., 1581, F 3, D 38 & 62), and was transferred to the New Fleet, Salford, at the turn of 1581–2 (A.P.C., 1581–2, 279; Peck, I, 112). In connection with the New Fleet he is last mentioned, October 1582 (S.P., 12, 155, 73), whereas other priests who were there with him are mentioned in later correspondence, so that he probably died, c. 1582–3, unless he was transferred elsewhere.

Edward Hughes, who celebrated a mass at Wichaugh, Malpas, 1586 (C.S.F., 1586, F 1, D 9–10) was active in the nearby parts of north-east Wales (E. Gwynne-Jones, op. cit., 116–17).

Thurstan Hunt, a Yorkshireman who was executed as a priest at Lancaster, 1601, worked in Lancashire, Yorkshire and Cheshire during his 15 years as a priest in England (H.M.C., *Salis MSS.*, XI, 109 & 167). Cf. also, Anstruther.

George Huxley, son of Thomas and Elizabeth Huxley (q.v., Appendix I) of Alpraham, Bunbury, was arrested when trying to escape overseas, 1595 (cf. supra, 112–4), but escaped to Ireland about two years later, to be admitted to the English College, Valladolid, 1599. He died shortly after returning to England as a priest, 1607 (C.R.S., XXX, 54). His sister, Margery, was also a recusant (cf. Appendix I).

Thomas Leake, alias *Stamford*, a seminary, was captured, August 1601, in Nantwich, and sent to appear before the Council, subsequently spending many years in the Clink and Gatehouse prisons (Anstruther). Cf. supra, 124–7.

Edward Leigh, possibly son of Sir Piers Leigh of Lyme, left England in the early 1590's to train as a priest (Anstruther).

John Maddocks, an old priest, probably a schoolmaster in the early years of Elizabeth's reign (E.D.V., 1, 3, f. 23), was described as 'an old poore fellow and malicious, but no Seminarye' (S.P., 12, 195, 72). He helped to prepare for a mass celebrated at Agden, Malpas, April 1582 (C.S.F., 1582, F 1, D 1), and was reported to be at Hugh Bromley's home at Hampton Post, March 1584, but was a prisoner in the Counter by October–November, 1585. He seems to have been transferred to Wisbech, December 1586, though he was still listed as being in the Counter, July 1587 (S.P., 12, 169, 27: 190, 42: 195, 51 & 73–4: 202, 61), and in that year was listed as still at liberty in Cheshire (Lansd. MSS., 55, 58, f. 169).

John Maddocks, almost certainly son of John and Matilda Maddocks (cf. Appendix I) of Agden, Malpas, entered the English College, Valladolid, 1608; then aged 18, he had been imprisoned when he had made an earlier attempt to leave England (C.R.S., XXX, 99).

Thomas Minshull, probably son of Edward Minshull of Church Minshull and his wife, Margaret, daughter of Hugh Mainwaring of Nantwich. He entered the English College, Douai, 1605, and died, 1617 (H. N. Birt, op. cit., 5).

John Morwen or *Murren*. D.N.B., XIII, 1067, outlines his life to 1561, when he issued a tract, 'An Addicion, with an Apologie, etc.', in Chester, after which it concludes, 'from this time he disappeared', while A. C. Southern dates his death as possibly in 1568 (*Elizabethan Recusant Prose*, 1559–82, 57). In fact he led the life of a fugitive recusant priest for many years. Thus, the authorities were on the watch for him, 1568, when both the bishop and the Sheriff of Lancaster were ordered to seize certain deprived ministers, including Morwen (S.P., 12, 46, 32–3). He was active in Lancashire, 1570, when several Lancashire recusants were ordered by the Diocesan High Commission not to harbour various priests, including Morwen (E.D.A., 12, 2, 126v–30; S.P., 12, 48, 36 & 38). Still later, c. 1583, Lady Egerton of Ridley was said to have harboured 'for the mooste parte of hir Majestie's reigne . . . Chapleins late Bishop Boners (i.e., Morwen) and suche like' (S.P., 15, 27, 94). He thus seems to have ministered in Lancashire and Cheshire, evading arrest until he was aged, for not until 1582–3 do the authorities appear to have laid hands on him; by the opening of 1583 he was a prisoner in the New Fleet, Salford, for he was indicted as a prisoner there for absence, in January 1584, and he would have been a prisoner during the 12 months for which he was indicted (S.P., 12, 167, 40–1). Like John Culpage he may have ended his life there or have been one of the old priests deported, 1585–6, or have been transferred elsewhere.

John and *Thomas Price* were born in Cheshire and left England to train as priests in the early 1590's (Anstruther). There were several recusants bearing their surname in Cheshire at this time.

John Shert, alias *Stalie*, who was executed at Tyburn, 1582, was of Cheshire birth. Captured in July 1581, he was condemned with Campion, November 1581, and executed at Tyburn, 28 May 1582 (Anstruther).

Edward Stanley, son of Sir Rowland Stanley of Hooton and brother of Sir William Stanley; he served with his brother in the Spanish army for 23 years, then became a priest, working in England for seven years from 1612, after which he became a Jesuit (A. J. Loomie, *The Spanish Elizabethans*, 180).

John Stanley, son of Sir Rowland Stanley of Hooton, and brother of Sir William and Edward Stanley, became a Jesuit (D.N.B., XVIII, 969).

John Starkey, alias *Amians*, third son of John and Alice Starkey (née Dutton) of Oulton (for Alice Starkey, cf. Appendix I). Born 1570, he left England c. 1601 to train as a priest after being educated at Knutsford (Anstruther; Ormerod, II, 192).

Stone, a priest or seminary, said a mass at Christleton, 1591 (Q.S.E., 4, ff. 3 & 26). He may have been William Coxie, alias Stone, who was born in Cheshire (listed in Anstruther).

Richard Sutton, an old priest, was a prisoner in Chester Castle, 1577 (S.P., 12, 118, 49) and 1579 (Lansd. MSS., 28, 97, f. 213). As John Culpage (q.v.), a prisoner with him, and Thomas Houghton (q.v.), both priests, were among a group indicted for absence, October 1581, and were later imprisoned in Chester Castle and the New Fleet, Salford, and Sutton does not appear to have been with them, Sutton probably died in prison between 1579 and 1581, unless he was transferred elsewhere.

Christopher Thules or *Ashton*, born in Whalley, Lancashire, 1560, was arrested in Cheshire along with two other priests who are known only by their surnames, Jones and Salisbury, probably in the first half of 1587 (Harl. MSS., 6998, f. 235v). He spent many of the subsequent years in prison (Anstruther).

Robert Wilcocks, seminary, who was executed, 1588, was born in Chester, 1558 (Anstruther).

William Worthington, an old priest, is said, c. 1584, to have been sheltered by

Lady Warburton of Congleton, to whom he acted as butler under the name of Watkins (S.P., 12, 175, 110).

Note. Several other priests are listed as from Cheshire in the Diary of the English College, Rome, and the entry books of the English College, Valladolid, but the word Cheshire is used loosely, often referring to the diocese, and the priests in question cannot clearly be identified as being of the county of Cheshire.

APPENDIX III

Information throwing light on the family background and religious loyalties of the gentlemen suspected of popery in the document of *c.* 1583 (S.P., 15, 27, 94) which is discussed in Chapter V.

Part I. 'The names of the gentlemen whose houses are greatlie infected with popery and not loked unto'.

Sir Randle Brereton of Malpas. In spite of his later elevation to the office of Sergeant-at-Law in 37 Eliz. (Ormerod, I, 69) and the vast estates that he held at his death in 1611 (ibid., II, 687), suspicion of Catholic sympathies had dogged Brereton in the 1570's and 1580's. He was cited before the High Commission in York in October 1571, though the charge is unknown; below his name is scrawled 'Nil erat actum', a remark which typifies the attitude of the authorities if he was merely sympathetic to Catholicism without being recusant (York, H.C., Box 25, 1571–2, A.B., 16, f. 79v). In 1574 he was listed as a supporter of Mary Stuart, though the list, regarded by H. N. Birt (*The Elizabethan Religious Settlement*, 546) as compiled by a Catholic, is quite unreliable (S.P., 12, 99, 55). Indeed, he was knighted in 1577. He is accused of being a papist in the 1583 list, though in the 'Note of the disposition, etc', he is said to be 'an obedient subject' (S.P., 12, 165, 23). About 1587 he was apparently left off the Commission of the Peace because of the recusancy of his wife, Frances, daughter of Sir Robert Throgmorton of Coghton (S.P., 12, 206, 85); for his wife, Lady Frances, cf. Appendix I.

Hugh Bromley of Hampton Post: cf. Appendix I.

William Davenport of Bramhall Hall, Bramhall, was the son of Sir William Davenport of Bramhall, who died in 1576, and father of Sir William Davenport of Bramhall, who died *c.* 1640, and he died himself in 1585 (Ormerod, III, 827). His wife, Margaret, was a recusant (cf. Appendix I), while it was almost certainly his son, Peter, who became a priest (cf. Appendix II): when he entered the English seminary at Valladolid the authorities there recorded his mother as a Catholic, but his father as schismatic, i.e., Anglican (C.R.S., XXX, 62). Another of his sons, John, may have become a priest (cf. John Damford in Appendix II), but the main line of the family remained Protestant.

John Dutton of Dutton, the son of Hugh Dutton of Dutton, married Eleanor, daughter of Hugh Calveley of Lea, and died in 1608, aged 70 (Ormerod, I, 651). His eldest son, Peter, married Elizabeth, daughter of the recusant, Richard Massey of Waverton, and was in turn recusant for some time (cf. Appendix I). Though regarded as 'not favourable' to the Elizabethan religious settlement in the diocesan return on the loyalty of the justices, 1564 (*Camden Misc.*, IX, 75), he was still a J.P. in 1569, when he declared his loyalty to the Crown (S.P., 12, 60, 30) and he contributed £25 to the national defence, 1588 (*Cheshire Sheaf*, First Series, III, 157). He remained prosperous enough, petitioning for a licence to impark 200 acres of his demesne, 1591 (H.M.C., *Salis. MSS.*, IV, 159).

Roland Dutton of Hatton, son of Ralph Dutton of Hatton, on whom suspicion of recusancy had fallen, 1581 (cf. supra, 23). His mother, Ann, came from a Catholic

family, the Townshends, and his sister, Alice, was a recusant (cf. Alice Starkey
in Appendix I). He married Eleanor, daughter of Thomas Scriven of Frodesley,
Salop (Ormerod, II, 796). He contributed £25 to the defence of the realm, 1588
(*Cheshire Sheaf*, loc. cit.), and was a J.P. in later years. He died in February 1605.

Lady Egerton of Ridley: cf. Appendix I.

Sir Piers Leigh of Lyme, son of Piers Leigh of Lyme and Margaret, daughter of
Nicholas Tildesley of Tildesley, Lancashire. He married Margaret daughter of
Sir Thomas Gerard of Brynn. He built the sixteenth-century wing of Lyme Hall,
was Sheriff of Lancashire (1551) and Cheshire (1554), Provost Marshal of
Lancashire and Cheshire (1585), Deputy Steward of Macclesfield Hundred, and
Commissioner of the Court of Survey (1587). He died on 6 December, 1589
(Ormerod, I, 651). In 1564 he was noted as 'not favourable' to the religious
settlement (*Camden. Misc.*, IX, 75), though he was named as a heretic in the
list of supposed adherents of Mary Stuart (S.P., 12, 99, 55). He was marked
as 'neutral' in the 'Note of the Disposition, etc', 1583 (S.P., 12, 165, 23), and in
the list of J.P.s drawn up in 1587 for government use he was singled out neither
for zeal, indifference or unsoundness in religion (Lansd. MSS., 53, 86, f. 180).
It was probably his son, Edward, who left England early in the 1590's to train for
the priesthood (cf. Appendix II), and another of his sons, Henry, who then
travelled to Rome as a Catholic (H. Foley, *Records of the English Province, S.J.*,
VI, 565). His fourth son, Thomas Leigh of Alkrington Hall, Middleton, near
Manchester, was a recusant suspect whom Burghley marked on his well-known
map of Lancashire, 1590 (C.R.S. *Misc.*, IV, 221-2).

John Manley of Poulton was probably the 'Manley of Poulton', and nothing of
any significance has been found about him. Details of his family are given in
Ormerod, II, 861.

George Massey of Puddington was the son of William Massey of Puddington,
who died in 1579, and Anne, daughter of George Booth of Dunham. Aged 48 in
23 Eliz., he married Dorothy, the daughter of Thomas Pigot of Chetwynd
(Ormerod, II, 561). In the 'Note of the disposition, etc', 1583, he is stated to be
'could' (S.P., 12, 165, 23), but he was still a J.P. in 1587, when, in the list of
J.P.s drawn up for government use he was not singled out in any way (Lansd.
MSS., loc. cit.). In the following year he contributed £25 to the national defence
(*Cheshire Sheaf*, loc. cit.). In the seventeenth century Puddington Hall seems to
have been a Catholic refuge: one priest died and another was arrested there.
The Hall contained a secret room and the family had a reputation as Catholics
from early in the century. A hunting song of 1615 describes the travels of an
adventurous hare and includes the following:

> Ore Burton Hill to Puddington Halle
> There she would be bold to calle,
> And she hoped that she might pass
> For he was at service and she was at mass.

> (W. N. & Q., II, 19–20)

These lines seem to indicate the not uncommon recusancy of the wife along with
the husband's conformity, but this indicates nothing of the situation while George
and his wife were still alive. Then, in 1598, his brother, John, and his wife were
presented at the Diocesan Visitation as non-communicants at their parish church

of Backford; they had, however, 'received' at Puddington Hall (E.D.V., 1, 12, f. 29v).

John Massey of Coddington, who died 14 October 1591 (Ormerod, II, 732), was said to be 'cold' in the 'Note of the disposition etc', 1583 (S.P., 12, loc. cit.). His fourth wife, Mary, was a recusant (cf. Appendix I).

Richard Massey of Aldford: cf. Appendix I, as also for his wife, Margaret, his eldest son, Richard, and his wife, Jane.

William Massey of Sale was presumably the 'Massey of Sale'. Nothing of any significance has been found about him.

William Tatton of Wythenshawe was the son of Robert Tatton of Wythenshawe, who died in 1579, and Dorothy, fourth daughter of George Booth of Dunham, who died in 1600. William died in 1611 (Ormerod, III, 609). In the 'Note of the disposition, etc', 1583, he was labelled as 'cold' (S.P., 12, loc. cit.), while his second wife, Mary, daughter of Thomas Tildesley of Wardley, Lancashire, was a recusant (cf. Appendix I).

Part II. 'Justices of the Peace not knowen to be of any religion, and therefore suspected to be Papistes'.

Sir Richard Buckley does not feature in Ormerod's pedigree of the main branch of the Buckley family. He was regarded as sound in the 1587 list of justices (Lansd. MSS., loc. cit.) and was still a justice, 1605 (*Cheshire Sheaf*, Second Series, I, 147).

William Glasier of Lea, Vice-Chamberlain of Chester, who died in 1619 (Ormerod, II, 386), sat on the Ecclesiastical Commission at this very time (Ex. Dep., passim), though his wife or daughter-in-law fell under suspicion of recusancy: cf. Mrs. Glasier in Appendix I.

Thomas Leigh of Adlington was son of Thomas Lea of Adlington (1527–48) and Mary, daughter of Richard Grosvenor of Eaton, who, as Lady Mary Egerton, was a prominent recusant (cf. Appendix I). Born, 1547, he married Sybel, daughter of Sir Urian Brereton of Handford. He enlarged Adlington Hall, was Sheriff of Cheshire, 1588, and died in 1601 (Ormerod, III, 662). When Sheriff in the Armada year he contributed £25 to the national defence (*Cheshire Sheaf*, First Series, III, 157) and was regarded as sound in religion in the 1587 list of J.P.s (Lansd. MSS., loc. cit.). The 'Note of the disposition, etc', listed him as 'neutral' in religion (S.P., 12, loc. cit.).

Thomas Leigh of High Leigh was son of Robert Leigh of High Leigh, and Alice, daughter of Hugh Starkey of Oulton. He rebuilt the hall and chapel of East Hall, High Leigh, 1581, married Isabel, daughter of George de Trafford of Garret Hall, near Manchester, and died in December 1590 (Ormerod, I, 462). The diocesan list of J.P.s, 1564 (*Camden Misc.*, IX, 75), the 1587 list of J.P.s (Lansd. MSS., loc. cit.), and a list of those who contributed to the defence of the realm, 1588 (*Cheshire Sheaf*, loc. cit.) all show him as loyal and sound in religion, though his lack of zeal for Anglicanism is confirmed by the description of him as a 'worldlinge' in the 'Note of the disposition, etc' (S.P., 12, loc. cit.).

John Poole of Poole, in the Wirral, married Susanna, daughter of Sir Edward Fitton of Gawsworth. He died, 1613, aged 82 (Ormerod, II, 423–4). He was named as worthy to be a justice in the 1564 diocesan list (*Camden Misc.*, loc. cit.), and if in contrast he was judged to be 'simple' in the 'Note of the disposition, etc'

(S.P., 12, loc. cit.), he was still a justice, 1603 (*Cheshire Sheaf*, Second Series, I, 147). In the list of justices of 1587 he was recorded without comment (Lansd. MSS., loc. cit.), and he contributed £25 to the national defence, 1588 (*Cheshire Sheaf*, First Series, loc. cit.).

Sir Rowland Stanley was second son and eventually heir to William Stanley and Grace Griffith of Hooton. He married, first, Margaret, daughter of Hugh Aldersey of Chester, and secondly, Ursula, daughter of Sir Thomas Smith (Ormerod, II, 416). Although he fell under such suspicion of pro-Catholic sympathies that some writers (e.g. P. Sulley, *The Hundred of Wirral*) assume that he was an ardent Catholic, he was Sheriff of Chester, 1576, a special commissioner for musters, 1579, and remained a J.P. until at least 1603 (*Cheshire Sheaf*, Second Series, loc. cit.), though this was an undistinguished public career for one from so prominent a Cheshire family. On at least one occasion, when the recusant, John Hocknell, confided to him his tactless prophecies in 1589, he was careful to dissociate himself from disloyalty (Chester, 29, 328, m. 18d), though the assertion that he was in some degree responsible for the death of the seminary, Thomas Holford (C.R.S., *Misc.*, VIII, 93), seems to be based only on the fact that he was a J.P. at the time of Holford's arrest at Nantwich in 1585. The careers of his three sons doubtless cast a good deal of suspicion on him; the eldest, Sir William, betrayed Deventer in 1587; Edward served with him in the Spanish cause and eventually became a Jesuit, as, long before, had a third son, John. However, to the end of his long life in 1612, aged 96 (D.D.B., XVIII, 969) there is no evidence that Sir Rowland shared their beliefs.

Thomas Vernon of Haslington, son of Robert Vernon of Haslington, was probably the 'Vernon of Haslington, esquire' named in the list. In the 'Note of the disposition, etc', 1583, his name stands without comment (S.P., 12, loc. cit.), and he was listed as a sound J.P. in the 1587 list of J.P.s (Lansd. MSS., loc. cit.).

BIBLIOGRAPHY

MANUSCRIPT SOURCES

Borthwick Institute of Historical Research, York:
Act Books of the Ecclesiastical Commission, York, Nos. 25–6, 50–1.
Visitation Books, Metropolitan Visitations, Chester Diocese, 1578, 1590 and 1595.[1]

British Museum:
Cotton Manuscripts, Titus B. III, No. 20.
Harleian Manuscripts, 286, No. 19: 360, No. 39: 594, No. 11: 2095, No. 7: 6998: 7042.
Lansdowne Manuscripts, 28, No. 97: 53, Nos. 69 and 86: 55, No. 58: 64, No. 8.
Stowe Manuscripts, 160.

Chester City:
Assembly Books, 1559–1603.
Assembly Petitions (Assembly Files).
Mayors' Letters, 1541–1603.
Mayors' Books, 1558–1606.
Quarter Sessions: Depositions and Examinations, 1558–1600, Files, 1561–1603.
    Process Rolls: Estreats of Fines, 1561–1634.

Cheshire Record Office:
(a) *Secular records:*
Quarter Sessions: Estreats, 1560–1601: 1561–75: 1576–99.
Sessions' Books: Indictments, 1565–92, Indictments and presentments, 1592–1617.
    Recognisances, 1559–71: 1576–92: 1593–1608.
Sessions' Files, 1571–1600.
(b) *Ecclesiastical records:*
Bishops' Transcripts of Parish Registers.
Parish Registers deposited.
Proceedings of the Commissioners in Ecclesiastical Causes, Chester Diocese, 1562–73.
Visitation Books for the Diocese of Chester, 1561–1604.

Manchester Central Reference Library:
Plan of the Towns of Manchester and Salford, 1741, by R. Casson and I. Berry.

Public Record Office:
Chester Crown Books: Chester 21.
Chester Gaol Files, Writs, etc.: Chester 24.
Chester Plea Rolls: Chester 29.
Exchequer Depositions, E 134, 25, Trinity, No. 5, Lanc. & Dio. Chester.
Exchequer L.T.R., 22 A, 377, Pipe Roll Series, 1–12.
State Papers Domestic, Elizabeth I.

PRINTED SOURCES

Acts of the Privy Council, New Series, ed. J. R. Dasent, London, 1880–1907.

[1] Available on microfilm at Cheshire Record Office.

Birt, H. N., *Obit Book of the English Benedictines from 1600 to 1912*, London, 1913.

Calendar of State Papers, Domestic, London, 1856–72.

Camden Society, *Miscellany IX*, for *A collection of Original Letters from the Bishops to the Privy Council, 1564*, ed. M. Bateson, London, 1893.

Caraman, P. (ed.), John Gerard, *The Autobiography of an Elizabethan*, 2nd edn, London, 1957.—*The Other Face: Catholic Life under Elizabeth I*, London, 1960.

Catholic Record Society: *Miscellanea I and II*, for *Official Lists of Catholic Prisoners during the reign of Queen Elizabeth* [I], ed. J. H. Pollen, 1904–5.—*Miscellanea VIII*, for *Two Lists of Supposed Adherents of Mary, Queen of Scots, 1574 and 1582*, ed. J. B. Wainewright, London, 1913.—*Miscellanea XII*, for *Diocesan Returns of Recusants for England and Wales*, 1577, ed. P. Ryan, and, *Recusants and Priests*, March 1588, ed. J. H. Pollen, London, 1921.—Vol. X, *The Douay College Diaries, 1598–1654*, ed. E. H. Burton and T. L. Williams, London, 1911.—Vol. XVIII, *Recusant Roll, 1592–3*, ed. M. M. C. Calthrop, London, 1916.–Vol. XXX, *Registers of the English College at Valladolid, 1589–1862*, ed. E. Henson, London, 1930.—Vol. LVII, *Recusant Roll No. 2 (1593–4)*, ed. H. Bowler, C.R.S., 1965.

Chetham Society: O.S.: XLIX–L, The *Lancashire Lieutenancy under the Tudors and Stuarts*, ed. J. Harland, Manchester, 1859.—LIX–LX, *The Lancashire Chantries*, ed. F. R. Raines, Manchester, 1862.—N.S.: IV, *Vaux's Catechism*, ed. T. G. Law, Manchester, 1885.—LXXVII, *Lancashire Quarter Sessions' Records, 1590–1606*, ed. J. Tait, Manchester, 1917.

Historical Manuscripts Commission, *Salisbury Papers*, 15 vols, 1883 onwards.—Eighth Report, XV, 355 ff., *The City of Chester 1881*.

Hooker, R., *The Laws of Ecclesiastical Polity*, Everyman Edn., 2 vols, London, 1925.

Leigh, E., *Ballads and Legends of Cheshire*, London, 1867.

[Parker, M.]. *The Correspondence of M. Parker, 1535–75*, ed. J. Bruce and T. T. Perowne, Cambridge, for the Parker Society, 1853.

Peck, F., *Desiderata Curiosa*, 1779 edn., London.

[Pilkington, J.]. *The Works of J. Pilkington*, ed. J. Scholefield, Cambridge, for the Parker Society, 1842.

Purvis, J. S., (ed.), *Tudor Parish Documents in the Diocese of York*, Cambridge, 1948.

Record Society of Lancashire and Cheshire: LXXXIX, *Prescot Court Leet and other records*, ed. F. A. Bailey, 1936.—XCIV, *Cheshire Quarter Sessions' Records, 1559–1760*, ed. J. H. E. Bennett and J. C. Dewhurst, 1940.

Statutes of the Realm, Record Commission, London, 1810–22.

Strype, J., *Annals of the Reformation*, 4 vols, Oxford, 1820–40.

SECONDARY SOURCES

Anstruther, G., *Elizabethan Seminary Priests, 1558–1603*, 3 vols, Leicester, 1966.

Aveling, H., *Post-Reformation Catholicism in East Yorkshire*, East Yorkshire Local History Society, 1960.—*The Catholic Recusants of the West Riding of Yorkshire, 1558–1790*, Leeds Philosophical and Literary Society, 1963.—*The Catholic Recusants of the North Riding of Yorkshire, 1558–1790*, 1966.

Baines, E., *The History of the County Palatine and Duchy of Lancaster*, revised and enlarged edn, ed. J. Croston, Manchester, 1888–93.

Baskerville, G., *The English Monks and the Suppression of the Monasteries*, London, 1937.

Beales, H. C. F., *Education under Penalty: English Catholic Education from the Reformation to the fall of James II, 1547–1689*, London, 1963.

Beamont, W., *The History of the Castle of Halton and the Priory or Abbey of Norton*, Warrington, 1873.

Beck, J., *Tudor Cheshire*, Chester, 1969.

Biographical Studies, 1534–1829, ed. A. F. Allison and D. M. Rogers, Bognor, 1951–3.

Birt, H. N., *The Elizabethan Religious Settlement*, London, 1907.

Black, J. B., *The Reign of Elizabeth*, 2nd edn, Oxford, 1959.

Brooks, E. St. J., *Sir Christopher Hatton*, London, 1946.

Burne, R. V. H., *Chester Cathedral from its founding by Henry VIII to the accession of Queen Victoria*, London, 1958.

Caraman, P., and Walsh, J., *Martyrs of England and Wales, 1535–1680, a chronological list*, London, 1960.

Chadwick, O., *The Pelican History of the Church*, III, *The Reformation*, Harmondsworth, 1964.

Challoner, R., *Memoirs of Missionary Priests and other Catholics of both sexes that suffered death in England on religious accounts from 1577–1684*, 1874 edn, Edinburgh.

Cheshire Index, A, issued by the Cheshire County Health Department, 2nd edn, Chester, 1955.

Cheshire Notes and Queries, ed. W. Astle: First Series, 1881–5, Stockport and London, Second (New) Series, 1886–9, Stockport and London, Third Series, 1896–1911, Stockport and London.

Cheshire Sheaf, First Series, ed. T. Hughes, Chester, 1880–91, Second (New) Series, ed. J. P. Earwaker, Chester, 1891, Third Series, ed. W. F. Irvine, F. Sanders, J. Brownbill, F. C. Beazley and J. H. E. Bennett, Chester, 1896–1951.

Collinson, P., *The Elizabethan Puritan Movement*, London, 1967.

Crossley, F. H., *Cheshire*, in the County Book Series, Hale, 1951.

Croston, J., *County Families of Lancashire and Cheshire*, London, 1887.

Davies, C. S., *A History of Macclesfield*, Manchester, 1961.

Dickens, A. G., *The English Reformation*, London, 1964.

Dictionary of National Biography, ed. Sir Leslie Stephen and Sir Sidney Lee, reprinted, Oxford, 1949–50.

Dore, R. N., *The Civil Wars in Cheshire*, Chester, 1966.

Earwaker, J. P., *The History of the Church and Parish of St. Mary on the Hill, Chester*, London, 1898.

Ellison, N., *The Wirral Peninsula*, London, 1955.

Falls, C., *Elizabeth's Irish Wars*, London, 1950.

Foley, H., *Records of the English Province, S. J.*, 7 vols, London, 1877–83.

Frere, W. H., *History of the English Church in the reigns of Elizabeth and James I, 1558–1625*, London, 1904.

Frere, W. H., and W. M. Kennedy, *Visitation Articles and Injunctions of the Period of the Reformation*, 3 vols, Alcuin Club Collections, XIV–XVI, London, 1910.

Gee, H., *The Elizabethan Clergy and the Settlement of Religion, 1558–64*, Oxford, 1898.

Gillow, J., *A literary and biographical history, or bibliographical dictionary, of the English Catholics*, 5 vols, London, 1885–1903.

Hamilton, A. H. A., *Quarter Sessions from Queen Elizabeth to Queen Anne*, London, 1878.

Hill, C., *Economic Problems of the Church from Archbishop Whitgift to the Long Parliament*, Oxford, 1956.—*Society and Puritanism in Pre-Revolutionary England*, London, 1964.

Hughes, P., *The Reformation in England*, 3 vols, London, 1954.—*Rome and the Counter-Reformation in England*, London, 1942.

Hurstfield, J., *The Queen's Wards: Wardship and Marriage under Elizabeth I*, London, 1958.

Kennedy, W. P. M., *Elizabethan Episcopal Administration*, 3 vols, Alcuin Club Collections, London, 1924.

Knowles, D., *The Religious Orders in England*, 3 vols, Cambridge, 1948–59.

Laslett, P., *The World we have lost*, London, 1965.

Leatherbarrow, J. S., *The Lancashire Elizabethan Recusants*, Chetham Society, New Series, CX, Manchester, 1947.

Leys, M. D. R., *Catholics in England, 1559–1829, A Social History*, London, 1961.

Local Gleanings relating to Lancashire and Cheshire, ed. J. P. Earwaker, Manchester, 1875–8.

Local Gleanings, an archaeological and historical Magazine, ed. J. P. Earwaker, Manchester, 1879–80.

Loomie, A. J., *The Spanish Elizabethans: the English Exiles at the Court of Philip II*, London, 1963.

Magee, B., *The English Recusants*, London, 1938.

Manning, R. B., *Religion and Society in Elizabethan Sussex*, Leicester, 1969.

Mathew, D., *Catholicism in England*, London, 1936.

McGrath, P., *Papists and Puritans under Elizabeth I*, London, 1967.

Meyer, A. O., *England and the Catholic Church under Queen Elizabeth*, English translation by J. R. McKie, London, 1915.

Morris, R. H., *Chester, A Diocesan History*, London, 1895.—*Chester in the Plantagenet and Tudor reigns*, Chester, 1893.

Neale, J. E., *Queen Elizabeth*, London, 1933.—*Elizabeth I and her Parliaments*, 2 vols, London, 1953–7.—*The Elizabethan House of Commons*, London, 1949.

Ormerod, G., *History of the County Palatine and City of Chester*, 2nd edn, revised and enlarged by T. Helsby, 3 vols, London, 1882.

Recusant History, A Journal of Research in Post-Reformation Catholic History in the British Isles, Bognor, 1953 onwards.

Rowse, A. L., *The England of Elizabeth*, London, 1950.—*The Expansion of Elizabethan England*, London, 1955.

Southern, A. C., *Elizabethan Recusant Prose, 1559–1582*, London, 1950.

Sulley, P., *The Hundred of Wirral*, Birkenhead, 1889.

Trimble, W. R., *The Catholic Laity in Elizabethan England, 1558–1603*, Oxford, 1964.

Usher, R. G., *The Rise and Fall of the High Commission*, Oxford, 1913.

Victoria County History, Lancaster, ed. W. Farrer and J. Brownbill, 8 vols, London, 1906–14.

Watkins, E. I., *Roman Catholicism in England from the Reformation to 1950*, Oxford, 1957.

Waugh, E., *Edmund Campion*, 3rd edn, London, 1937.

Webb, S. & B., *English Prisons under Local Government*, London, 1922.

Wirral Notes and Queries, ed. F. Sanders & W. F. Irvine, 2 vols, Birkenhead, Chester and Liverpool, 1892–3.

Thesis

Cosgrove, J., 'The Position of the Recusant Gentry in the Social Setting of Lancashire, 1570–1642', Manchester M.A. Thesis, September 1964.

Articles

Axon, W. E. A., 'Chronological Notes on the Visitation of Plague in Lancashire and Cheshire', in *Transactions of the Lancashire and Cheshire Antiquarian Society*, XII, Manchester, 1895.

Bossy, J., 'The Character of Elizabethan Catholicism', in *Past and Present*, No. 21, 1962.

Coward, B., 'The Lieutenancy of Lancashire and Cheshire in the sixteenth and early seventeenth centuries', in *Transactions of the Historical Society of Lancashire and Cheshire*, Vol. 119, Liverpool, 1968.

Dickens, A. G., 'The First Stages of Romanist Recusancy in Yorkshire, 1560–90', in *Yorkshire Archaeological Journal*, XXXV, Keighley, 1943.—'The extent and character of recusancy in Yorkshire, 1604', in *Yorkshire Archaeological Journal*, XXXVII, Wakefield, 1951.

Dickens, A. G., and Newton, J., 'Further Light on the scope of Yorkshire recusancy in 1604 ', in *Yorkshire Archaeological Journal*, XXXVIII, Wakefield, 1955.

Gwynne-Jones, E., 'Catholic Recusancy in the Counties of Denbigh, Flint and Montgomery, 1581–1625', in *Transactions of the Society of Cymmrodorion* (1945), London, 1946.

O'Dwyer, M., 'Recusant Fines in Essex, 1583–93', in *The Month*, July, 1958, London.

Owen, D. M., 'Short Guide to Records, 8, Episcopal Visitation Books', in *History*, XLIX, London, 1964.

Peel, R., 'Notes on Wilmslow Parish Registers', in *Transactions of the Lancashire and Cheshire Antiquarian Society*, LVII, Manchester, 1944.

Price, F. D., 'The Abuses of Excommunication and the Decline of Ecclesiastical Discipline under Queen Elizabeth', in *English Historical Review*, LVII, London, 1942.

Tyler, P., 'The Significance of the Ecclesiastical Commission at York', in *Northern History*, II, Leeds, 1967.

Williams, J. A., 'Short Guide to Records, 11, Recusant Rolls', in *History*, L, London, 1965.

INDEX OF PERSONS

From the appendices only main names are included

INDEX OF PLACES

From the appendices only main places are included

GENERAL INDEX

Acts of Parliament: 1 Eliz., c. 2, Act of Uniformity (1559), 1, 8, 79: 5 Eliz., c. 15, Act against the dissemination of false prophecies (1563), 72: 14 Eliz., c. 5, Act for the punishment of vagabonds and the relief of the poor and impotent (1572), 39 f.: 23 Eliz., c. 1, Act to retain the Queen's Majesties subjects in their due obedience (1581), 24, 28, 30, 45, 79, 136: 28 & 29 Eliz., c. 6, Act for the more speedy execution of certain branches of 23 Eliz., c. 1 (1587), 68, 87 f., 106n, 115: 35 Eliz., c. 2, Act against popish recusants (1593), 121

Addicion, with an Apologie, etc., 2 ff., 176
Annals of the Reformation, 130
Assizes, 32, 37 f., 44n, 46, 56 f., 64, 66 ff., 70, 72 f., 75 f., 77n, 79, 82, 85, 86n, 88, 92 f., 99, 105 f., 114 ff., 126, 131
Attorney-General, 119

Bishops of Chester: cf. Scot, Downham, Chadderton, Bellot and Vaughan
Bishops' Transcripts, 129
'Bloody Questions', 89
Bond of Association, 54

Catholic Association, 23
Chancellor, diocesan, 81n, 96
'Cheshire elite', the, 135
Churchwardens, 28, 54, 78, 80, 93, 116
Communion bread, 17 f.
Community of priests, a, 39
Conformity, 27, 33, 35, 41, 44, 56, 86, 99, 116, 122 f.
Council of the North, 78 ff., 88, 106: of Wales, 4
Crown Books, 82n, 129
Custos rotulorum, 107

Declaration of Sports, 78
De Persecutione Anglicana Epistola, 90
Deputy lieutenant of the county, 73 f.
Desiderata Curiosa, 129 f.
De Visibile Monarchia, 175
Distribution of recusancy in Cheshire, 20, 31, 45, 85, 118, 132 f.

Ecclesiastical or High Commission, 6 f., 9 f., 12, 19, 21n, 22 ff., 36, 47 ff., 57 f., 61 f., 78 f., 80n, 82 f., 85, 86n, 88 ff., 105, 107 f., 116, 118, 123n, 128 f., 131, 135 f.
Exchequer, 27, 40, 48, 70, 86, 129
Excommunication, 18, 85, 128
'Exercises', 28, 59

Fines: 12d. for absence from church, 16, 56, 98, 129: £20 for absence from church, 24, 28, 32, 40, 47 f., 56 f., 61n, 62 ff., 68 f., 77, 87 f., 115, 119, 122, 129, 136: for non-appearance, 24 ff., 30 f.: for other reasons, 81n

Harleian MSS, 130
High Commission: cf. Ecclesiastical Commission
House of Commons, 53
House of Correction, 40

Imprisonment for recusancy, 87, 136: and cf. Chester Castle and Northgate, Halton Castle, and Clink, Counter, Gatehouse, Fleet, Marshalsea, New Fleet, and Poultry prisons
Inns of Court, 172

Jesuits, 21, 29, 42, 49, 52 f., 72, 88 f., 91 ff., 100 ff., 105, 109, 114, 123, 175, 177
.P.s, 8, 17, 28, 45, 51 f., 60, 63, 65n, 73, 76, 78, 103n, 104 f., 107, 115, 130, 135

King's Bench, court of, 40, 115

Lansdowne MSS, 130
Lords Lieutenant, 107 f.

Mass, 41 ff., 61, 65 f., 71, 73, 93, 98, 101, 106, 126
Mayors' Books, 11n, 129
Military levy, 58 f., 63, 69

Non-communicants, 19, 26, 37, 70n, 75, 81, 91, 94, 117 f., 123
Northern rebellion (1569), 8, 10, 12
Number of Cheshire recusants, 19, 45, 75, 81 f., 102, 118 f., 130 ff.

THE FOLLOWING REPORT WAS SUBMITTED TO THE ANNUAL GENERAL MEETING OF THE CHETHAM SOCIETY, 28 MAY 1970

During the past ten years the Society has issued the following volumes in its Third Series, 11–18:

W. K. Jordan, *The Social Institutions of Lancashire 1480–1660* (1962)

Frances Collier, *The Family Economy of the Working Classes in the Cotton Industry, 1784–1833*, ed. R. S. Fitton (1965)

Derek Robson, *Some Aspects of Education in Cheshire in the Eighteenth Century* (1966)

J. D. Marshall (ed.), *The Autobiography of William Stout of Lancaster 1665–1752* (1967)

Robert Craig and R. C. Jarvis (eds), *Liverpool Registry of Merchant Ships* (1967)

W. Brockbank and F. Kenworthy (eds), *The Diary of Richard Kay, 1716–51, of Baldingstone, near Bury, a Lancashire doctor* (1968)

Christopher Haigh, *The Last Days of the Lancashire Monasteries and the Pilgrimage of Grace* (1969)

A. N. Webb (ed.), *An Edition of the Cartulary of Burscough Priory* (1970)

The Society suffered a heavy loss in the death in December 1962 of Dr. G. H. Tupling, who for many years had acted as its Editor, and this was in part responsible for the slow rate of publication during 1961–4. Since 1964, however, the aim of the Council to bring out at least one volume a year has been more than fulfilled, and, taking the decade as a whole, eight volumes have been published.